THE REVELS PLAYS

Founder Editor
Clifford Leech 1958–71

General Editors
F. David Hoeniger, E. A. J. Honigmann and J. R. Mulryne

THE FAWN

TO MY MOTHER
AND TO THE MEMORY
OF MY FATHER

THE REVELS PLAYS

PARASITASTER

or

THE FAWN

JOHN MARSTON

Edited by

David A. Blostein

MANCHESTER
UNIVERSITY PRESS

THE JOHNS HOPKINS
UNIVERSITY PRESS

© David A. Blostein 1978

First published 1978
by Manchester University Press
Oxford Road, Manchester M13 9PL
ISBN 0 7190 1508 1

Published in the United States of America, 1978, by
The Johns Hopkins University Press
Baltimore, Maryland 21218

ISBN 0 8018 2164 4
Library of Congress Catalogue Card Number 78–60170

British Library Cataloguing in Publication Data

Marston, John
    Parasitaster, or, The Fawn.—(The Revels plays).
    1. Blostein, David A
    I. Title
    822'.3   PR2694.P/

    UK ISBN 0–7190–1508–1
    US ISBN 0–8018–2164–4

Printed in Great Britain
by W & J Mackay Limited, Chatham

Contents

General Editors' Preface

The series known as the Revels Plays was conceived by Professor Clifford Leech. The idea emerged in his mind, as he tells us in the General Editor's Preface to the first of the Revels Plays, published in 1958, from the success of the New Arden Shakespeare. The aim of the series was, in his words, 'to apply to Shakespeare's predecessors, contemporaries, and successors the methods that are now used in Shakespeare editing'. We owe it to Clifford Leech that the idea has become reality. He planned the series, set the high standards for it, and for many years selected and supervised the editors. He aimed at editions of lasting merit and usefulness, that would appeal to scholars and students, but not to them alone; producers and actors were also much in his mind. 'The plays included should be such as to deserve and indeed demand performance.' And thus the texts should be presented in a form that is attractive and clear to the actor, with some space of the introduction devoted to records of productions, and some of the notes to comments on stage business.

The text of each Revels Play is edited afresh from the original text (in a few instances, texts) of best authority, but spelling and punctuation are modernised, and speech-headings silently normalised. The text is accompanied by collations and commentary, and in each volume the editor devotes one section of his introduction to a discussion of the provenance and trustworthiness of the 'copytext', the original on which he has based his edition, and to a brief description of particular aspects of his editorial method. Other sections of the introduction deal with the play's date and sources, its place in the work of the author, its significance as a dramatic work of literature in the context of its time and designed for a certain theatre, actors, and audience, its reputation, and its stagehistory. In editions of a play by an author not previously represented in the series, it has been customary also to include a brief account of the author's life and career. Some emphasis is laid on providing available records of performances, early and modern.

vi

Modernisation has its problems, and has to be practised with care and some flexibility if the substance of the original is not to be distorted. The editor emends, as distinct from modernising, the original text only in instances where error is patent or at least very probable, and correction persuasive. Archaic forms need sometimes to be retained when rhyme or metre demands them or when a modernised form would alter the required sense or obscure a play on words. The extent to which an editor feels free to adapt the punctuation will largely depend on the degree of authority he attributes to the punctuation of his copy. It is his task to follow the original closely in any dramatic or rhetorical pointing that can be trusted for good reason. Punctuation should do justice to a character's way of speaking, and to the interplay of dialogue.

In general, the manner of modernisation is similar to that in the Arden Shakespeare. Yet in the volumes since 1968, the '-ed' form is used for non-syllabic terminations in past tenses and past participles ('-'d' in Arden and earlier Revels volumes), and '-èd' for syllabic ('-ed' earlier). Act divisions are given only if they appear in the original text or if the structure of the play clearly points to them. Those act and scene divisions not found in the original are provided unobtrusively in small type and in square brackets. Square brackets are also used for any other additions to or changes in the stage directions of the original. But in no instances are directions referring to locale added to scene headings; for the plays (at least those before the Restoration) were designed for stages whose acting area was most of the time neutral and where each scene flowed into the next without interruption; and producers in our time would probably be well advised to attempt to convey this characteristic fluidity of scene on whatever stage they may have at their disposal.

A mixture of principles and common sense also governs the collations accompanying the text. Revels plays do not provide a variorum collation; only those variants which require the critical attention of serious textual students. All departures of substance from 'copy-text' are listed, including any relineation and those changes in punctuation which involve to any degree a decision between alternative interpretations; but not such accidentals as turned letters, nor necessarily additions to stage directions whose editorial nature is already made clear by the use of brackets. Press corrections in the 'copy-texts' are likewise included. Of later emendations of the text (or errors) found in seventeenth-century reprints of no authority or editions from the eighteenth century to modern times, in general only those are given which as alternative readings still deserve serious attention. Readings of a later text of special historical interest or influence are, in some instances, more fully collated.

One of the hallmarks of the Revels Plays is the thoroughness of their annotations. Besides explicating the meaning of difficult words and passages and alerting the reader to special implications, the editor provides comments on customs or usage, text or stage business—indeed on anything he judges pertinent and helpful. Glosses are not provided for words that are satisfactorily explained in simple dictionaries like the *Concise Oxford*. Each volume contains an Index to the Annotations, in which particular attention is drawn to meanings for words not listed in *O.E.D.*

The series began with some of the best-known plays of the Elizabethan and Jacobean era, but has expanded to include also some early Tudor and some Restoration plays. It is moreover not our object to concentrate solely on well-known plays but also to make available some of the lesser known of whose merit as literature and as drama we are convinced.

Early 1976 saw a change in the publisher of the Revels Plays, from Methuen & Co. Ltd to Manchester University Press. Since then the supervision and guidance of the Series have become the joint responsibility of three general editors. Several plays are being published this year and, under the new arrangements, the Series should continue to expand.

F. DAVID HOENIGER

E. A. J. HONIGMANN

J. R. MULRYNE

1977

Preface

The day has not yet arrived when editions of this kind are produced in committee as a matter of course, but even now an editor is often spared an extra hour or week of tedium or error through a word dropped by a friendly colleague. I was fortunate to begin work on *The Fawn* at the Folger Shakespeare Library, where such instances abound; I am particularly indebted to hints received there from John Russell Brown and the late John Crowe. At a later stage, I benefited from valuable comments by Roy Battenhouse, Robert Ornstein, Brian Parker, Peter Davison, Ronald Huebert, James Carscallen, and C. Anderson Silber. Others to whom I happily give thanks are John Peter, for his early assistance and encouragement, Philip London and Joel Kaplan, for their generosity in lending theses, and above all David Hoeniger, one of the General Editors of the Revels Plays, who has seen this edition develop slowly (very slowly) from graduate paper onwards under his patient, helpful guidance.

I acknowledge with pleasure the co-operation given me by the librarians of the numerous institutions and collections listed in the section on Text, and I should like to thank specially the librarians of Huron College, London, Ontario. Finally, I am grateful to the Canada Council for the Fellowship which enabled me to complete my research on this edition during a sabbatical year.

DAVID A. BLOSTEIN

Toronto
June 1977

Abbreviations

Brome, *Works*	*The Dramatic Works of Richard Brome*, ed. R. H. Shepherd (1873), 3 vols.
Chambers	E. K. Chambers, *The Elizabethan Stage* (1923), 4 vols.
Chapman, *Comedies*	G. Chapman, *Comedies*, ed. T. M. Parrott (1914).
Cooper	Thomas Cooper, *Thesaurus* (1584).
Crawford	Charles Crawford, *Collectanea*, new series (1907).
Cross	Gustav Cross, 'Some notes on the vocabulary of John Marston', *N&Q*, CXCIX (1954), 425–7; CC (1955), 20–1, 57–8, 186–7, 335–6, 427–8, 480–2; CCI (1956), 331–2, 470–1; CCII (1957), 65–6, 221–3, 283–5, 524–6; CCIII (1958), 5–6, 103–4; CCIV (1959), 100–2, 137–9, 254–5, 355–6; CCV (1960), 135–6; CCVI (1961), 123–6, 298–300, 388–9; CCVIII (1963), 308–12.
ELH	*Journal of English Literary History*.
Florio (1598)	John Florio, *A World of Words* (1598).
Florio (1611)	John Florio, *Queen Annas New World of Words* (1611). An enlarged version of the earlier work; where the two editions are substantially the same no date is given.
H.&S.	B. Jonson, *Works*, ed. C. H. Herford and P. and Evelyn Simpson (1925–52), 11 vols.
J.E.G.P.	*Journal of English and Germanic Philology*.
Linthicum	M. C. Linthicum, *Costume in the Drama of Shakespeare and his Contemporaries* (1936).
Middleton, *Works*	T. Middleton, *Works*, ed. A. H. Bullen (1885–6), 8 vols.

M.L.R.	*Modern Language Review.*
Montaigne	*Essays*, transl. Florio (1603), ed. Thomas Seccombe (1908), 3 vols.
Montaigne (Crawford)	(Indicates that the connection between Marston's passage and Montaigne's was first pointed out in Crawford's *Collectanea*.)
N&Q	*Notes and Queries.*
Nashe, *Works*	T. Nashe, *Works*, ed. R. B. McKerrow (1904–10), 5 vols.
O.E.D.	*Oxford English Dictionary.*
Partridge	Eric Partridge, *Shakespeare's Bawdy*, rev. ed. (1955).
P.Q.	*Philological Quarterly.*
Prince d'Amour	*Le Prince d'Amour, or, the Prince of Love, with a collection of several ingenious poems and songs; by the wits of the age* (1660).
Puttenham	G. Puttenham, *The Arte of English Poesie* (1589), ed. G. D. Willcock and A. Walker (1936).
R.E.S.	*The Review of English Studies.*
S.E.L.	*Studies in English Literature.*
S.O.D.	*Shorter Oxford Dictionary*, 3rd edition.
S.P.	*Studies in Philology.*
Sugden	E. G. Sugden, *A Topographical Dictionary to the Works of Shakespeare and His Fellow Dramatists* (1925).
Taylor	A. Taylor, 'Proverbs and proverbial phrases in the plays of John Marston', *Southern Folklore Quarterly*, XXIV (1960), 193–216.
Tilley	M. P. Tilley, *A Dictionary of Proverbs in England in the Sixteenth and Seventeenth Centuries* (1950).
Wilson	T. Wilson, *The Arte of Rhetorique* (1560), ed. G. H. Mair (1909).

John Marston's works are referred to as follows:

AM.	*Antonio and Mellida.*
AR.	*Antonio's Revenge.*
CS.	*The Metamorphosis of Pygmalion's Image, and Certain Satires.*
DC.	*The Dutch Courtesan.*
Fawn	*The Fawn.*
Hist.	*Histriomastix.*
Insatiate C.	*The Insatiate Countess.*
JDE.	*Jack Drum's Entertainment.*
Malc.	*The Malcontent.*
Soph.	*Sophonisba.*
SV.	*The Scourge of Villainy.*
WYW.	*What You Will.*

In addition to these, 'Halliwell' and 'Bullen' refer in the annotations to those editors' explanatory notes (keyed to their act, scene and line divisions) and 'Wood' to the annotations in Harvey Wood's edition of *The Plays of John Marston* (1934–9), keyed to volume number and page. Quotations from Marston's plays are from Bullen's edition of the *Works* (1887) unless otherwise noted. *Poems* refers to *The Poems of John Marston*, ed. Arnold Davenport (1961). Abbreviations used in collating textual readings for *The Fawn* are listed at the end of the Introduction.

All quotations from Shakespeare are from the Tudor Shakespeare, ed. P. Alexander (1951), unless otherwise stated, and lineation is that of the Globe Shakespeare. Abbreviations of Shakespeare's titles are those of C. T. Onions in his *A Shakespeare Glossary* (ed. 1941). References to Webster's *The White Devil* and *The Duchess of Malfi* are to John Russell Brown's editions in this series.

Introduction

I. JOHN MARSTON: THE CONTEXT OF COMEDY

We know more about John Marston than about most of his contemporaries.[1] His baptism was registered 7 October 1576 in Wardington, Oxfordshire, where a little more than a year earlier his parents had been married. His father, a prominent citizen of Coventry and equally prominent member of the Middle Temple, was descended from an old Shropshire family of considerable social standing. His mother's family was also prosperous; she was the daughter of an Italian surgeon who had married an English-woman and settled in London. With the death of John Marston senior in 1599, his son came into his inheritance almost at the very beginning of his career as wit and poet. Virtually alone amongst his literary and theatrical colleagues, therefore, he was a man of independent means—cause enough for resentment from the 'envious few' to whom he frequently refers. When his mother died in 1621, Marston acquired a further estate in Coventry, but by this time he had long been through with the London stage; he had been ordained in 1609, and after that date the only indication that he ever again showed interest in his former pursuit is that he evidently had his name removed from the title-page of William Sheares's edition of his *Works* in 1633, a year before he died.

It would only be speculation, of course, to connect Marston's 'wel beloved wiefe Marie' to the image of the witty, warm-blooded young woman who appears so often in his plays. As daughter of a court chaplain she would have had ample opportunity to be 'well exercised in discourse of the best men' (*The Fawn*, III.i.217), and certainly Marston trusted her intelligence enough to make her his sole executrix. But Dulcimel of *The Fawn* (*c.* 1604) and Crispinella of *The Dutch Courtesan* (*c.* 1605) are already anticipated in Rossa-line of *Antonio and Mellida* (*c.* 1600), 'the first representative of a dramatic type which was to prove indispensable to writers of comedy for the next hundred years . . . the woman whose wit depends on her frank and flippant attitude toward sex'.[2] Whatever the source for this figure, it is a pivotal one for the direction of Marston's career. A morose satirist might be expected to condemn such women; here they are presented as both admirable and charming in their honesty. As such, the outspoken Crispinella and Dulcimel, who figure so strongly in the plays Marston was writing about the time of his courting and marriage (probably in 1605), serve as signposts of his transition from satirist to humorist. If in his formal satires of 1598 and 1599 he concentrated his exaspera-tion with human weakness on sexual lust (as most satirists did), a new understanding and acceptance of the passions—probably connected with his reading of Montaigne—made it possible for him eventually to achieve something like a comic vision. In *The Dutch Courtesan*, he was to work out 'the difference betwixt the love of a courtesan and a wife', but already in *The Fawn* he could take the normality of sexual passion more or less for granted: in the comic intrigue *all* are involved in either negotiating, pursuing, advertising, rejecting, or thwarting love. Yet there is no whipping satirist to lash the abusers of passion. Instead, a disguised ruler, himself dominated by a passion for which he cannot account, simply encourages fools and apparent villains to indulge their vices and follies, confident that they will eventually 'fall most lame' when their faults turn into blatant, self-proclaimed, and therefore (according to the common theory) self-correcting folly.

   It is true that for most Renaissance writers comic theory over-laps with satiric theory, and in large part theirs was a satiric theory of comedy. Yet there are distinctions to be made, and O. J. Campbell argues that it is precisely such a distinction that Marston establishes in *What You Will* (*c.* 1601). Though Quadratus dispenses ridicule throughout the play,

> . . . the spirit which animates the ridicule is neither severe nor strident; consequently, the mirth of comedy and the impulse toward deflation of the fools harmonize. . . . [T]he drama acquires

some historical importance because of the author's partially
successful effort to domicile in English comical satire a spirit like
that of Aretino, who . . . had first effected a successful union of
the apparently incompatible genres of satire and comedy.[3]

As far back as the eleventh Satire of *The Scourge of Villainy* (1599),
Marston had observed that 'Cheeke dimpling laughter', while it
has no place in dealing with vice, is permissible when handling
mere 'humours' or social affectations.[4] And even in *The Malcontent*
(1602–4), Malevole recognises that if he is to have moral efficacy
as satirist, his victims must first find him amusing—'for he that
laughs and strikes / Is lightly felt, or seldom struck again'. But
Malevole remains more a satirist than humorist, and the direction
Marston was taking in *The Fawn* involved a growing ascendance
of the comic spirit over the satiric. This development implies the
kind of 'amused tolerance' and optimism that Alvin Kernan sees
as the dividing line between satire and comedy proper: 'Fools in
comedy only need to be given enough rope and they will hang
themselves, for Nature operates to restore the balance.'[5] To
understand how such confidence in natural processes could be
acceptable to a writer so generally categorised as a sharp-tongued
satirist, it is necessary to turn to the philosophical and psychological context in which the change of direction took place.

Though Renaissance thought was undeniably influenced by
classical philosophies, these philosophies were not always fully
understood by the Renaissance poets and playwrights who put
them to work—nor even, in some cases, clearly distinguished. A
person educated in English schools at the end of the sixteenth
century, reading texts almost totally drawn from the pagan classics
and admonished to be a good Christian, might be forgiven for
becoming philosophically eclectic and at times self-contradictory.[6]
Where precisely did one draw the line between Christianity and
the several brands of neo-classical piety which were already mixed
with it in popular theology? A catch-all term like Neo-Stoicism
proves, once one has modified it sufficiently to cover the particular
case at hand, less useful than one might hope.[7] Stoic characters
and themes do occur in John Marston's works, and he is pleased,
on occasion, to declare himself a friend of Epictetus. But it is

questionable to approach him as a firm adherent of a philosophy which much of his work is aimed at refuting. Better to pursue T. S. Eliot's observation that the popularity of Stoicism amongst the Jacobean playwrights was founded less on any philosophical consistency it might provide for their plays than on the stance or stances which bolstered the integrity of individuals in conflict.[8] Stance, rather than philosophy, is the stuff of dramatic characterisation, particularly in this period. It has the added convenience for the dramatist that it can be shifted more rapidly than doctrine.

Through the works of Seneca, Epictetus and Cicero, early modern Europe received a tradition of two such stances which both were called Stoic. They are what Michael Higgins has shrewdly called 'harsh' and 'soft' Stoicism: the 'soft' stance shrugs the shoulder; the 'harsh' stance puts a chip on it.[9] To resist the onslaught of evil circumstances by gritting the teeth and even taking arms against a sea of troubles is a recognisable Stoic stance; but so is 'divine apathy', a readiness to acquiesce to the fates or (and here is where a natural affinity with one strand of Christian tradition is apparent) to accept the will of a blind or inscrutable god or God. Of the first category are the heroes of Chapman's tragedies, as well as those of Webster, Tourneur, and (in the *Antonio* plays but not so noticeably in *Sophonisba*) Marston. The 'soft' stance is more appropriate to pathos (one thinks of the repentant usurper Pietro in *The Malcontent*) and to a comic, as distinct from a satiric, view of human weakness—a view that sees happy endings possible even in a very imperfect world. This requires a capacity for ethical toleration decidedly lacking in Marston's early work, and present, but too often ignored by critics, in his later. The softening process was made easier for Marston by the fact that Stoicism itself, while perhaps the most universally respected philosophical stance available to him, was by no means the only one, nor one which he (or his contemporaries for that matter) maintained wholeheartedly. Indeed, a groundswell of *anti*-Stoic sentiment, though not so vocal as it was to be a little later in the seventeenth century, had already made inroads into the thought of a European Christianity that had long made an all too comfortable liaison with pagan ethics. As Henry W. Sams points out, anti-Stoicism was derived from even less study of the classical Stoic texts than Neo-Stoicism itself:

> In fact, the usual conceptions were based on three rather casually arrived at points. . . . (1) The Stoics advocated the complete suppression of passion, (2) they were pagan, (3) they put overweening trust in the efficacy of human reason. So far as it concerned the generality of English writers, Stoicism may be sufficiently characterized in these points. . . .[10]

Marston may be trusted to have done more homework than the 'generality of English writers', but his objections are basically the same as theirs: '(1) the passions are good, (2) Christian sanctions are the only sound basis for ethics, (3) human reason is untrustworthy.'[11] The formulas of anti-Stoicism became increasingly convincing for Marston in his later work, but already in *Certain Satires* and *The Scourge of Villainy*, despite their load of philosophical jargon, Marston's interest in Stoic thought was tempered by suspicion of it. Aware that Stoicism sits uneasily at best with satiric writing, he associates his abandonment of satire (at the end of *CS.*, v) with the name of Epictetus. Then when he returns to satire, he pointedly rejects that stance: 'Preach not the Stoickes patience to me . . .' (*SV.*, II, 5). The whole of Satire IV of *The Scourge of Villainy* attacks the Stoic doctrine which reconciles happiness with destiny, on the grounds that the concept of destiny denies that of free will. And in the collapse of Pandulpho's Stoic fortitude in *Antonio's Revenge*, Marston replaces an old stance by one that is newer but nevertheless recognisable and acceptable to his contemporaries. As Robert Ornstein suggests, 'Marston's "unconventional" rejection of Stoic rationality is quite conventional; he is the first Jacobean to exploit dramatically the skepticism about Stoic self-sufficiency expressed by Erasmus and Montaigne and implicit in the moral philosophy of the Elizabethan Age.'[12]

Yet some Stoic ideas did find a secure home in Marston's spirit. The Stoic admonition *nosce teipsum* might stand as a motto for this peculiarly self-conscious writer, a fulfilment, perhaps, of his father's dying wish that God should give the young poet 'trewe knowledge of hymself'. What Marston senior evidently saw as a block to such self-knowledge was young Marston's 'delight in

playes vayne studdyes and fooleryes'.[13] Throughout the Satires the
poet gives evidence of an inner debate involving the act of writing
poetry itself. There is certainly an element of gentlemanly *sprez-
zatura* in much of what Marston says about his writing—and he
has much to say about it in his Satires, prefaces, prologues and
epilogues. The point is, he keeps saying it; and the formula reads
much like a perpetual Defence of Poesy. On the one hand, he
acknowledges that ordinary readers of poetry do resort to it for the
wrong reasons, as 'vayne studdyes and fooleryes', either for mere
fashionable pastime or to gain a reputation for wit by malicious
criticism; when he finds it too oppressive to prostitute his Muse
for the one kind, or to bear the envious detraction of the other, he
gives up the battle in a mood of Epictetan resignation. On the
other hand, his return more than once from 'retirement' is
explained by the genuineness of his poetic gift. He 'cannot hold'
(*SV.*, II, 1), he is 'seduced with this poesie' (*SV.*, x, 70). It is an
irresistible humour (*SV.*, x, 73), a 'sickness', 'vice', 'addiction'
(Preface to *The Fawn*, *passim*). His head becomes 'great with
child', and must give birth, no matter what. And there is always
the hope that there might 'iudiciall perusers' and 'diuiner wits'
with sufficient judgement and sensitivity to gain substantial
spiritual benefits from it (*Poems*, pp. 98, 100).[14] His defence
of poetry is thus twofold: (i) poetry ought not be called vain simply
because vain people read it; (ii) its source is a natural phenomenon,
not something idly chosen or affected by a Matthew or Crispinus,
and therefore the gift must be indulged not repressed, madness
though it may seem (*SV.*, VI, 111–12; x, 71).

When Marston attacks Hall for fouling the poets' nest (*SV.*, x),
he acknowledges in a coda entitled 'Medice cura teipsum' that the
love of poetry is a kind of illness, which he intends to cure by
vomiting it out in the form of hate. Besides anticipating Horace's
emetic in *Poetaster*, the statement provides a rationale for satire
itself.[15] The same motto explains both why Marston had to write
satire when he did and why satire would not eventually be the best
form for his poetic gift to take. For the physician who would heal
himself, the regimen is to probe till his worst proclivities and
weaknesses are known and by this knowledge to achieve their

purgation or sublimation into a higher substance. In short, a comic *anagnorisis* and *catharsis* are involved, which—as in Aristotle's view of tragedy—are most effective when they come close upon each other.[16] This process is manifestly foreign to Stoicism, which advocated suppressing, inhibiting or simply ignoring those internal commotions that buffeted the fortress of reason. In doing so, Stoicism was fundamentally at odds with Renaissance psychology, which had a strongly physiological basis. If psychological ailments are physically caused by in-dwelling poisons, they cannot simply be ignored: they must be got rid of, by one of the two methods universally employed for correction of the body's ills—the 'two sovereign remedies, letting blood or "lanching", and purging by tartar emetics and sharp cathartics'.[17] So it is not surprising that a Renaissance moralist should turn to satire to expose and correct what he believed vicious in the lives of men. The physician lanced or purged the body; the satirist did the same with the soul. And while satirists and Stoics disagreed as to methods, they agreed in the assumption that the passions were dangerous or even evil. In this assumption they were often joined by the preachers and the theologians. At least since St Paul, Christian thought has had to wrestle with the problem of the partnership of reason and passion in the soul—how to establish the hegemony of reason without denying the normality of the passions themselves. This characteristic Christian balance was frequently upset by tendencies within Christian thought itself, for instance the Augustinianism of protestant theology in the late sixteenth century, preoccupied as it was with lust rather than pride as the chief of spiritual offences.[18]

But a few independent thinkers opposed the unholy alliance of Stoic and Christian thought—an opposition best illustrated by the use of the term Opinion. In its original Stoic and Neo-Stoic settings, 'Opinion' is the word for popular, unthinking beliefs which in their very thoughtlessness present a threat to the rule of reason over the natural impulses. Reversing this definition, and opposing the equation of 'Nature' with 'natural reason', Donne and Daniel equated nature with the natural impulses and dismissed the arguments of a tyrannical reason as products of 'custom' and 'opinion'.[19] This is precisely what Marston does in Hercules' first

soliloquy in *The Fawn*. To oppose the 'stream of blood' and to
'beat down affection from desired rule' is only 'to keep the God /
Of fools and women—Nice Opinion' (1.i.52–9). Marston's more
liberal view was supported by contemporary psychology, whose
exponents, most of them divines, were among the leaders of the
anti-Stoic defence of the passions. As Paul M. Zall has shown,
Marston employs faculty psychology as an ethical foundation of
his dramaturgy by concentrating on 'the problem of the normality
of concupiscence', which was 'the precise point of inevitable
conflict between those who accepted faculty psychology as integral
to conventional Christian ethics and those who, like the Calvinists
or the amorphous Neo-Stoics, saw in the unruly passions sure
signs of the depravity of man or of his weakness. Love was the
highest Christian virtue; at what degree was it to be considered a
passion, and an abnormal passion ?'[20] Zall traces Marston's treatment of the question through a 'trichotomy' of love as virtue, love
as a 'natural affection', and love as lust. Marston differentiates
between a natural humour of hypersexuality and passions largely
shaped or misshaped by social pressures and restrictions; his
'norm' is found in those characters 'who accept love as the natural
passion it is, without compromising their virtue. . . . They
scorn . . . the exercise of reason alone without passion. . . . They
reject behaviour founded exclusively on passion.'[21]

Ironically, this essentially Christian balance finds its most
effective support in the sceptic Montaigne. At least since the turn
of this century we have been aware of 'borrowings' from Montaigne
in Marston's later plays, particularly *The Dutch Courtesan* and
The Fawn.[22] But he did not come to Montaigne unprepared. By the
time Florio's translations of the *Essays* appeared in 1603, Marston's
'Stoicism' had already undergone considerable 'softening'. The
first half of the pseudo-Epictetan slogan—$\alpha\nu\acute{\epsilon}\chi ov$, to 'bear', as it is
translated in *The Fawn*[23]—had already begun to make sense to the
rather harried playwright as he approached the middle of his short
writing career. The second half of the dictum—$\alpha\pi\acute{\epsilon}\chi ov$, to 'forbear'
—was less congenial, because unrealistic; Marston, the incessant
ironist, had a well-developed sense of the real. With Montaigne,
he saw that much of the burden he must bear was precisely what

Epictetus demanded he should *for*bear—the pull of the appetites and passions. Here is the source of that curious yet not altogether unsatisfactory blending of Montaigne and Epictetus in Marston's mature comedies, in which characters not only endure malicious attacks from without but accept the inevitable force of the passions within. It was a blending that included a new confidence in the corrigibility of overdeveloped appetite, not by violence or suppression, but by toleration and even encouragement.

His guide here may well have been Shakespeare. John Hollander argues persuasively that in *Twelfth Night* Shakespeare created a 'moral play' embodying a process of moral achievement through stages of indulgence of appetite, satiety and ultimate self-revelation, a process neatly summarised in Duke Orsino's well-known opening speech.[24] To kill appetite through accepting its existence and surfeiting it rather than ignoring it or abstaining involves a most unstoical confidence in the strength of the soul in the face of loosened passions. But after all, 'it is the Appetite, not the whole Self . . . which is surfeited: the Self will emerge at the conclusion of the action from where it has been hidden.'[25] Similarly, Alvin Kernan picks out as 'the concluding moral' of *Volpone* the lines: 'Mischiefes feed / Like beasts, till they be fat, and then they bleed.' But he points out that in that play viciousness and idiocy are considered incorrigible and are therefore chained up.[26] Marston's mature comedies share with *Twelfth Night* a more optimistic view of the moral efficacy of indulgence. This applies not only to the correction of such obvious 'villains' as Pietro and Aurelia (*The Malcontent*) or Zuccone (*The Fawn*) but also to more central and sympathetic characters like Malheureux in *The Dutch Courtesan* and even to Hercules, the protagonist of *The Fawn*. Malheureux becomes truly virtuous only after his latent humour of carnality swells to bursting; but there is no question of his being punished simply for possessing that humour (as might happen in Jonson) or for being tempted to exercise it. *The Fawn* goes a step further: the heat which fills the veins of the ageing Hercules as the play begins is directed into prompting others to mischief, a process which eventually effects both their purification and his own.

There are several metaphors, common in the literature of the day, which describe the process fairly adequately. The first, as in *Twelfth Night*, is overeating, with consequent sickening and even vomiting. Another is impostumed sores, which go through stages of swelling, bursting and subsequent relief. The effect is similar to lancing and purging—balance is restored through riddance of excess—but without the need of the physician's or surgeon's drastic methods. In *The Malcontent*, Malevole had already seen that an uncontrolled humour can bring about its own correction:

> Envious ambition never sates his thirst,
> Till sucking all, he swells and swells, and bursts.   (I.iv.79–80)[27]

'Swell, you impostumed members, till you burst,' cries Hercules, as he decides to reform Urbin's court by flattery rather than by invective (*The Fawn*, II.i.588). And Freevill advises Malheureux in *The Dutch Courtesan*:

> take this as firmest sense:-
> Incontinence will force a continence;
> Heat wasteth heat, light defaceth light,
> Nothing is spoiled but by his proper might.   (II.i.125–8)[28]

The metaphor is apparently alchemical; it is manifestly so in *The Fawn*, in the same passage in which Hercules refers to impostuming: 'Without immoderate heat, no virtues shine' (II.i.596). Through the extremity of fire, the chaotic element can be transmuted into gold, into something 'mere divine'. Clearly, in this image of hermetic sublimation, Marston is not condoning uncontrolled passion, but arguing for its purification. To accept that the passions exist is not to accept them untransmuted or permanently out of balance with reason. But to indulge them is a kind of partly-controlled experiment which, however it turns out, cannot help but provide the involved person with self-knowledge and personal freedom. In a sense, self-knowledge brings about a freeing of and from the self; freedom of spirit results from liberating the natural impulses to the degree that they may be recognised, acknowledged, and examined in the light of reason.[29] Hence we are dealing with a concept which combines aspects of such ostensibly incompatible views as the Stoic and the Libertine.

Such a mixture can readily be found in Montaigne:

We ought somewhat to yeeld unto the simple auctoritie of Nature: but not suffer her tyrannically to carry us away: only reason ought to have the conduct of our inclinations.[30]

And, as Robert Ornstein suggests, it can be found in Donne. Both Donne and Montaigne, 'like the Renaissance Libertines ... denied that nature establishes immutable and categorical imperatives. But unlike the Libertines, they reaffirm in unmistakeable terms, the rule of reason in human life.'[31] Independently of Donne, but certainly under the influence of Montaigne, Marston felt his way towards the solution of the dilemma of body-*versus*-soul and passion-*versus*-reason that brought both English poets to the same end, the church, but in very different states of mind: Donne abandons the career of practical libertine for a most stringent and almost Calvinistic raising of the mind above the body; Marston moves from a contempt of the body's weaknesses to an increased sympathy for them. As a result, Marston eventually comes to a point—perhaps best indicated by his unwillingness to punish harshly, in *The Malcontent*, *The Dutch Courtesan*, and especially *The Fawn*—when he has too much tolerance for fools and too little dread of the wicked to be a dramatist, let alone a satirist. His acceptance of the body's appetite is in the last analysis an orthodox Christian one; sin is recognised as the perversion of an otherwise good gift of God. But after acceptance came withdrawal. As Theodore Spencer put it,

From the very beginning his writings are full of a very high, and exalted, opinion of the possibilities of the human soul . . . and this opinion could only be justified . . . by a religious way of life. Shakespeare apparently achieved equanimity without feeling the necessity of religion; men with a less capacious understanding, though with equal sensitiveness, like Marston and Donne, needed the authority of a revealed sense of values, if they were not to be driven to madness or suicide.[32]

Marston seems finally to have acknowledged that the imaginative depiction of such a moral viewpoint was in its deeper expression beyond his poetic capacities. There is considerable evidence to suggest that *Sophonisba*, his last full essay in dramatic form, was to be a final masterwork. Yet in the patent artificiality of subject and moral assumptions (Roman thoughts for Roman characters), it was as much a moral capitulation as a manifest attempt to prove his worth as a poet in the generally accepted philosophical and dramatic modes for masterworks.[33] So he withdraws from literary life. The pattern is similar to one observed by José Axelrad:

> L'observation de l'homme et de la société inspire à John Marston trois mouvements que nous retrouvons dans la plus grande partie de son théâtre: dégout, puis révolte; lassitude enfin et renoncement à la lutte.[34]

'Giving up the battle' need not in this case be regarded as tragic or cowardly. With what we know of Marston's developing thought, we may assume fairly confidently that his departure from the stage to the pulpit was—so far as his restless nature could allow—a voluntary and fundamentally happy decision, rather than a forced-march to a *pis-aller*.

2. THE COMEDY

a. 'The Manacles of Form'

At first glance the framework of *The Fawn* seems loose and spindly. Duke Hercules of Ferrara sends his son Tiberio as his matrimonial ambassador to the court of Urbin, follows him in disguise, and watches as the ingenious Princess Dulcimel draws the young man into loving her himself. As 'Faunus', the old but energetic Hercules discovers that many in the court, including the Duke of Urbin himself, are dominated to an alarming degree by ruling passions. He decides to encourage them to pursue these weaknesses, and rises swiftly through his flattery. At the end all are invited to an entertainment which he has supervised, a Parliament of Cupid, during which the follies of the court of Urbin are exposed as such and punished by forced passage on the Ship of Fools. Finally, Hercules reveals his true identity, and Gonzago, the now chastened and enlightened Duke of Urbin, is reconciled with his daughter and Hercules' son, who have meanwhile been secretly married.

The framework turns out to be both sturdy and adaptable. It would have to be, to come near to fulfilling Marston's promise, borrowed from Juvenal, that his piece deals with all the doings of mankind. The result may fall short of a complete view of life, but it does contain all Marston's major preoccupations—the court, sex, language—in a remarkably well-integrated network of thematic and poetic relationships. Throughout Marston's works, courtly society provides models for human behaviour on both social and individual levels: it is a pattern of how people ought or ought not to live with each other, and an emblem of the twin pulls of government and liberty within the human soul. The court is also a natural context for Marston's study of the relationship between the sexes, for the courtier's life affords both the temptation and the leisure for the expense of spirit in a waste of shame. As for his well-known obsession with language, his linguistic audacity is accompanied by a consciousness of the uses and abuses of words for intellectual and moral ends. Nowhere amongst his works do these three preoccupations receive richer or more direct treatment than in *The Fawn*, and the play shows how closely they were affiliated in his mind. Up to this stage of his career, court, sex and language were seen largely through the eyes of the moralist and satirist; in *The Fawn*, moral philosophy and satire are themselves implicitly the subject for treatment, examined from the fresh perspective of the comic dramatist or the humorist (in the modern sense). It is clear from Hercules' back-to-back soliloquies at the end of Act IV and the beginning of Act V that Marston's purpose is still to 'correct' as well as please, to provide moral learning, which for Marston is interchangeable with self-knowledge. *The Fawn* shows that such knowledge may come, not directly through the mind, but indirectly through the heart or even the loins.

Comparison with Marston's own *The Malcontent* (1602–4) is inevitable and instructive. In both plays, the disguised ruler story, so appealing to Englishmen during the years of Elisabeth's decline and James's early reign, is adapted to show a disguised duke discovering and exposing wrongs in society.[35] In the earlier play, there is more urgency to the proceedings because the society in question is the duke's own; power has been wrested from him by force. In *The Fawn*, Hercules' departure is voluntary and temporary. Though he learns much about himself and his own society while in Urbin, his very foreignness lends detachment and lightness to his criticisms. More important, the corrective methods of the two dukes are diametrically opposed. Early in *The Malcontent* there is a character sketch of Malevole, the deposed Duke Altofronto in his malcontent disguise: '[H]is highest delight is to procure other's vexation, and therein he thinks he truly serves heaven; . . . therefore does he afflict all in that to which they are most affected' (I.i.21–6). But when Hercules finally decides what course he will pursue in his disguise as Faunus, he vows to expend his energy 'in flattering all / In all of their extremest viciousness . . .' (*The Fawn*, I.ii.347–8). Malevole openly derides and afflicts people for their special weaknesses; Faunus flatters and encourages them to indulge. The goal is the same—to correct by making truth known. But in *The Fawn*, Hercules turns a fairly conventional complaint of satirists—that 'the sharpness / Of reprehensive language is even blunted / To full contempt, since vice is now termed fashion, / And most are grown to ill even with defence' (I.ii.341–4)—into action by seeking an alternative that will work.

We have seen how in *The Malcontent* and *The Dutch Courtesan* Marston touched upon that alternative process, which takes as its base the psycho-physiological belief that a humour when indulged to its utmost reaches a bursting point of self-purgation. But it is only in *The Fawn*, as we shall see shortly, that Marston finds a metaphor for the process and a dramatic structure to embody the metaphor. As long as humours are vicious but not fully ripened they are tolerated by humorous and non-humorous characters alike; they are virtually invisible in a world where 'vice is now termed fashion'. Only when it is manifest that the fashion's a fool does putting out humours become a moral as well as comic event.

The key is to be found in the role of the moralist critic. It is never unambiguously clear in *The Malcontent* whether Malevole is a mere convenient role which the high-minded Altofronto plays on the way to his restoration, or whether he is a natural outgrowth of Altofronto's resentment at being deposed. As a result the moral reference point of the play wavers. In *The Fawn*, the complexity of Hercules' motivation and his relationship with his role as

'Faunus' are precisely what make the moral reference point clear. His declared intentions in the opening scene are vague and tentative; as a foreigner at the court of Urbin he lacks even the kind of knowledge a satirist needs to get on with the job. He is in complete control neither of events nor of himself. For Hercules, like those he hopes to cure, is dominated by a humour—the humour of blood. He is aware of this, but can account for his condition only as a 'most prodigious heat, / That falls into [his] age like scorching flames / In depth of numbed December' (I.ii.345–7). As the play develops we find ourselves watching the agent of correction gradually working out his own correction: in the hyper-energetic Hercules of the first two acts of *The Fawn* we have a very different man from the gentle, perhaps exhausted, Hercules who assures Gonzago at the play's end that 'all things sweetly fit' (v.i.476).

At the end of the play's first scene, Hercules has accepted his unaccountable energy as a madness that, despite its late advent, it would be perilous to resist. He further observes that the habit of dignified behaviour is not admirable when achieved at the cost of unnatural suppression of the passions that ought to come with youth. So while he acknowledges that his forthcoming May–December marriage is 'full of ridiculous expectation' he resolves to spend his delayed 'heat' in this way. It is only after he has seen Tiberio and Dulcimel together and has heard the courtiers' malicious yet justified comments on the match that he realises that his energy must be redirected: 'I never knew till now how old I was' (I.ii.318). Even before he arrives at Urbin, the Duke sees his former solemnity, so admired by the multitude, as servile, a kind of imprisonment or enslavement to what he calls 'the manacles of form'. As a servant, during the play's second scene, he watches those same manacles of form enfeeble the duties of the court, the bond between the sexes, the very function of language. Here Marston unites Renaissance political theory with the Stoic precept *nosce teipsum*. The greatest duty of the good magistrate, as of everyone else, is to know himself. The chief duty of the courtier is to aid the magistrate in this task. Where the magistrate is so sick of self-love that he shuns self-knowledge, the rightful relationship is weakened from the top down. Implicit is an assumption that the strongest friend of self-knowledge is language and the strongest enemy abuse of language—particularly the abuse that goes under the general heading of soothing or flattery, which confirms the willing victim in his ignorance. It thus corrupts 'form' while seemingly upholding it.

At Urbin Hercules soon learns from Gonzago's egregious example that 'a prince / Whose tender sufferance never felt a gust / Of bolder breathings, but still lived gently fanned / With the soft gales of his own flatterers' lips, / Shall never know his own complexion' (I.ii.319–23). His first reaction is to 'repent / Severe indictions to some sharp styles': the perfect kingdom is that in which men are free to 'Speak what [they] think, and write what [they] do speak, / Not bound to servile soothings' (I.ii.335–6). Clearly his argument supports the unreformed muse of the Satires and *The Malcontent*. Yet at the same moment that Hercules recognises the destructive power of flattery he is aware (evidently from his own past indictment of critics, since Marston gives us no other reason) that in a society deaf to plain talk, critical satire is self-defeating and harmful to the satirist alone. Acknowledging flattery's imperviousness to direct attack, he hits upon the 'revenge' of flattering the flatterers, confident that 'in their own loved race they [will] fall most lame, / And meet full butt the close of vice's shame' (I.ii.349–50). With his own manacles broken, he thus sets out to break more.

b. 'The A B C of Courtship'

It might seem paradoxical that the chief object of satiric attack in *The Fawn*, flattery, is also the basic *method* of that attack. But the word is being used in two senses: one is a mishandling of truth, the other a corrective procedure. Flattery as social and political abuse is basically, for Marston, a wilful breakdown of communication, an offence against truth. So not only the extravagant praise that Nymphadoro employs in courting women, but also Gonzago's self-praise and Granuffo's silent acquiescence in it, Herod's amorous boasting, his impotent brother's claim to fatherhood, even Zuccone's would-be cuckoldry—all these are flattery. All are offences against communication, basic to a healthy society, and against truth and self-knowledge, basic to the health of the soul. As Hercules 'reassures' Herod when he has been caught lying, the man who does not use his tongue to misrepresent himself to advantage 'has not learned the very rudiments or A B C of court-ship' (IV.i.178–9).[36] These rudiments the courtiers of Urbin have learned all too well.

But Hercules is not merely a hypocrite when he chooses flattery as a method of correcting flatterers; for in that choice he acknow-ledges that a defect can correct itself—with a little help from its enemies. This other sense of flattery amounts to an embodiment of a morality of indulgence, a faith that evil has a natural tendency to trip itself up. As Act II closes, Hercules sees himself, sur-rounded by the vice of Urbin,

> As on a rock, from whence I may discern
> The giddy sea of humour flow beneath,
> Upon whose back the vainer bubbles float
> And forthwith break.   [II.i.577–80]

The metaphor depicts a comic process: below its surface, out of reach, the sea of human behaviour contains masses of vicious habits, which through a natural tendency rise to the surface not in their original, poisonous form of vice but as a distinct though related kind of human misbehaviour—folly. Folly is less horrifying than vice because less deeply fixed in the soul: it is a bubble easily seen through in daylight and quickly burst in fresh air. Signifi-cantly, the term 'vice' appears several times in the first two acts of *The Fawn* but is virtually absent in the second half, when Faunus's strategy of flattery is in full swing, 'thrusting on' the natural transformation of vice into folly, like a doctor hastening the imposthuming of a boil:

> Swell, you imposthumed members, till you burst;
> Since 'tis in vain to hinder, on I'll thrust,
> And when in shame you fall, I'll laugh from hence,
> And cry, 'So end all desperate impudence.'   (II.i.588–91)

Marston was always adept at mock encomiums (see the dedications to *Certain Satires* and *The Scourge of Villainy*). In *The Fawn* he discovers a way of introducing his morality of indulgence through a character whose chief weapon is the praise of folly. Herod is praised by Faunus for his lying and boasting, Nymphadoro for his Ovidian philandering, Sir Amoroso for his impotence, his wife Garbetza for her unfaithfulness, Zuccone for his determination to divorce his innocent wife, Gonzago for the witless wit that blinds him to what is going on in his realm. Yet Faunus rarely tells people what to do; he merely encourages them to persist in their vices beyond self-protective limits, until their excess exposes them to shame. Significantly, vice does not trouble any of these characters (see especially ii.i.195–8), but having to recognise publicly that they have acted like fools becomes for them the painful first step towards self-understanding and improvement. As Zuccone says at his moment of recognition, ''Twas thou flatteredst me to this, and now thou laughest at me, dost? Though indeed I had a certain proclivity, but thou madest me resolute' (iv.i.545–7).

That Hercules makes Zuccone and the other gulls resolute in their ostensibly mediocre faults has bothered some readers.[37] But not all knaves, as Dulcimel observes (iii.i.196–7), are patently fools, and vice may have to be made more serious before the vicious can be shamed out of it. The formula is put most succinctly when Hercules pronounces on Herod's case during the Court of Cupid in Act v. Herod has been committing incest with his impotent brother's wife, as a result of which she has become pregnant, thereby preventing Herod from inheriting his brother's estate. 'Thy vice,' says Hercules, 'from apparent heir, has made thee an apparent beggar, and now of a false knave hath made thee a true fool' (v.i.302–4). Far from producing 'a black sea of suspicion and misanthropy' (Allen, p. 153), the pattern is basically as genial as it is just.

The risk of nastiness is further allayed by two activities that round out Hercules' function in the plot—his series of exchanges with Tiberio and his soliloquies. With Tiberio, his secret benevolence is presented regularly and, as is to be expected, ironically. The young man is as susceptible to flattery as the rest of the court; when at the end of Act II he confides in his father without recognising him ('Fawn, thou dost love me . . .' ii.i.564) it is only by luck that he happens to be correct.[38] Such ironic confidence is repeated at the end of Acts III and IV, with Hercules continuing to benefit his son and the royal line of Ferrara by manipulations appropriate only to Faunus. The continual switching back from cogging Faunus to soliloquising Hercules also helps to keep the benevolence of the old duke's role uppermost in our minds (rather than the trickery or malice). As Joel Kaplan puts it, 'We are most likely to refer to "Malevole" as the central character of *The Malcontent* but think of Hercules, not "Faunus", as the dominant figure in *The Fawn*.'[39] In any case, it is always clear when the old duke is speaking as Faunus, when as Hercules, and when as Hercules *and* the author's mouthpiece. The character has some seven soliloquies in the play, including the Epilogue (and excluding the Prologue, which may or may not be his). Of these the most interesting is a sort of progress report at the end of Act IV. Hercules speaks here as a self-aware character with dramatic individuality, but also as an authorial creation conscious of being located in a play—and a play in the process of being written or performed:

> Where are we now ? Cyllenian Mercury,
> And thou quick issue of Jove's broken pate,
> Aid and direct us. You better stars to knowledge,
> Sweet constellations, that affect pure oil
> And holy vigil of the pale-cheeked muses,
> Give your best influence, that with able spright
> We may correct and please, giving full light
> To every angle of this various sense:
> Works of strong birth end better than commence.
>
> (IV.i.694–702)

The passage is thoroughly Marstonian in its mixture of self-confidence and humility. The mixture is especially apt here, since it would hardly do, in a comedy dealing with flattery's obstruction of self-knowledge, not to recognise one's limitations as protagonist, actor or poet.

Gonzago, whom Marston sets up as a foil to Hercules, has his formulas of humility too, but he uses them consciously to demonstrate his supposed brilliance:

> 'Tis wisdom to acknowledge ignorance
> Of what we know not; we would not now prove foolish.
>
> (V.i.140–1)

For Gonzago, wisdom consists of 'policy'—shrewd calculation in
language and action. Fittingly, he reduces love, as he does eloquence, to 'tricks' (v.i.410 and i.ii.187). His speeches are encrusted
with parenthetical asides evaluating his own felicitous phrases,
glossing the rhetorical figures he has just employed, confessing
second thoughts on word choice (see especially iii.i.443–54). Even
his appeals to nature are artificial: in the same breath he can
whisper to Granuffo to note one of his 'figures' and announce
aloud, 'We use no rhetoric' (i.i.188). When a favourite naturalistic
technique of Marston's, the self-interruption, appears in one of
Gonzago's speeches, it is followed immediately by its rhetorical
label, *aposeopesis*. Nature itself is subject to his conscious control:

> Does not my colour rise ?
> It shall rise, for I can force my blood
> To come and go, as men of wit and state
> Must sometimes feign their love, sometimes their hate:
> That's policy, now.   (ii.i.510–14)

Hercules has surrendered 'the secret arts of rule' in order to seek
wisdom in natural impulse. Gonzago's view is quite the opposite:
'. . . for as we be flesh and blood, alas, we are fools, but as we are
princes, scholars, and have read Cicero *de Oratore*, I must confess
there is another matter in't' (iv.i.612–15). Though he is self-
conscious, he is not, like Hercules, self-aware. And since the only
communication he solicits from his courtiers is approbation (his
favourite courtier is a fake mute), Gonzago is himself the source
of the flattery which corrupts his court.

c. Courtship and Concupiscence

The central action of *The Fawn* is bound up with Tiberio's
matrimonial mission. When Dulcimel successfully recasts ambassador as bridegroom she encapsulates what the play has to say
about the proper relationship between the sexes. In this double
courtship, desire is displayed in its proper form, strong and un-
suppressed but obedient to the principle of proportion; for a
match between Hercules and Dulcimel does not offend reason: it
offends proportion.[40] Gonzago's calculated speech and 'policy'
derive from over-confidence in the power of reason over natural

inclinations, sexual or otherwise. But to claim a wisdom above nature is, as Lampatho in *What You Will* and Malheureux in *The Dutch Courtesan* learn too well, both unnatural and unwise.

In the long dialogue between Dulcimel and Philocalia, strategically placed at the middle of Act III, the claims of flesh and blood against rational wisdom are skilfully presented. In several ways, Philocalia would seem to be the spokesman for Marston. Her name means love of beauty, and the play specifically sets up a connection between beauty as the perfection of all proportion and woman as the living manifestation of that perfection (III.i.514–15). Above all, women are seen as naturally compassionate; pity leads to love and love to pity; one of the prime attributes of Philocalia is her capacity for pity (III.i.162–5). Besides, Philocalia combines the two warring principles upon which the play is polarised—nature and art. She is 'most modestly artful, though naturally modest' (III.i.168). We may well feel at first that her Neo-Stoical arguments for the precedence of reason are therefore authoritative. Yet we have here a shifting scale of value. Philocalia *is* the norm long enough to establish that she is the fitting, natural match for Hercules once he has indulged his 'madness' of belated youth and returned to his proper dignity. But the debate between her and Dulcimel chiefly serves to reaffirm the value of heroic risk, which is essential to Hercules' adventure as well as to Dulcimel's. It also signals a return to heavy borrowing from Montaigne. Dulcimel repeatedly rejects the modest artfulness of Philocalia's talk:

> Fie on these philosophical discoursing women! Prithee confer with me like a creature made of flesh and blood, and tell me if it be not a scandal to the soul of all being, proportion, that I, a female of fifteen, of a lightsome and civil discretion, healthy, lusty, vigorous, full, and idle, should forever be shackled to the crampy shins of a wayward, dull, sour, austere, rough, rheumy, threescore and four. (III.i.187–94)

So it is Dulcimel, rather than Philocalia, who establishes that the soul of all being is proportion—the proportion, for instance, that makes Philocalia a suitable match for Hercules and Dulcimel for Tiberio. In her rough simplification of the amount of intelligence necessary (and unnecessary) for women, Dulcimel directly

rejects Philocalia's 'understanding' and, more important, her un-
spoken claim to 'wisdom'; and the princess eventually makes good
her claim that a natural, witty, well bred girl 'shall make fools of
a thousand of these book-thinking creatures' (III.i.218–19), though
the bookish fools turn out to be not women but her husband-to-be
and father. (In so doing, she helps her father learn his cardinal
lesson—the folly of pursuing wisdom and the wisdom of pursuing
nature.) There is good sense in Philocalia's attempts to restrain the
young Princess, and much that is immature (though charmingly
so) in the fifteen-year-old girl; yet Marston arranges that Dulcimel
(or Montaigne) always has the last word. Dulcimel is one of the
fortunate whose madness falls in youth, and though she has no
exchanges with Hercules, he more than anyone else in the play
shares common cause with her, even a common state of mind. In
following nature, they are luckier than the rest, in that they do no
harm by neglecting duties, and positive good by helping to correct
others. Their careers show that wisdom finds its true, unfettering
form through nature's need for proportion.

Placing the exchange between Dulcimel and Philocalia at this
central juncture thus fulfils several purposes. The passage deals
with artifice and nature at their best. Philocalia is a thoughtful
woman of the most admirable kind, one whom control, artifice and
form have matured; and Dulcimel, with her wit and burgeoning
wisdom, is herself an example of nature taking its course, a sort of
Shavian embodiment of the Life Force. Moreover, the debate's
location fixes the centrality of women and marriage in the play's
values. We have seen how important one sense of courtship—
court-craft—is to the satiric subject matter of *The Fawn*; the
other sense—amorous courting—is at least as important, and the
rest of the play, particularly after this scene, leads to the amalgamation of these two subjects in the Court of Cupid. The courtier
Nymphadoro quite frankly admits that all his professions of love
are made 'in the trade of marriage' (III.i.71). Dulcimel's friskiness,
though far less calculated in its honest sexuality, is no less aimed
at the goal of institutional marriage. For all its audacious argument
for the naturalness of concupiscence, the play does not challenge
that institution. Dulcimel, for instance, never for a moment speaks

of 'enjoying' Tiberio in any but wedded circumstances. (The *fabulae argumentum* of *The Dutch Courtesan* naturally comes to mind, with its stress upon 'the difference betwixt the love of a courtesan and a wife.') It is clear, too, that the abuses to be judged in the Court of Cupid are against not only love but marriage and (even more) women.

At this point, two observations ought to be made about Marston's use of the Parliament or Court of Cupid. In each arraignment, whatever the wording of the indictment, the manner of offence of which the defendant is accused is wilful misrepresentation; in other words, they are all accused of being the flatterers, the alphabeticians of courtship, that they are. But the *substance* of offence is the abuse of courtship in its other sense— the process of obtaining a woman's acquiescence to marriage (or something like it) through solicitous behaviour and the language of compliment. The behaviour and language of Nymphadoro, Herod and his brother Amoroso, Zuccone and even the silent Granuffo is offensive to women, and even when Amoroso's wife Garbetza is mentioned as an offender she is exonerated because of her husband's prior offence. Clearly this is one of the most noteworthy differences between *The Fawn* and court satires such as Jonson's, in which the age-old Complaint theme of voracious, vain women is used intact.[41] In *Cynthia's Revels*, for instance, there are about as many female gulls as male. But in *The Fawn*, though Garbetza and Puttota are certainly comic objects, they are also comic victims, and their stupidity is more than balanced by the wittiness and attractiveness of Zoya and Dulcimel and the dignity and good humour of Philocalia.

The women in *The Fawn* are numerous, remarkably well delineated, and even when presented comically, generally treated sympathetically. We are reminded again of Montaigne, who ends 'Upon some verses of Virgil', dedicated to a discussion of love, with a vindication of women and a rejection of the double standard.[42] We are reminded as well of Juvenal, from whom Marston gets the play's motto—*Dat veniam corvis, vexat censura columbas*. Marston used part of it previously as the motto for *The Malcontent*, to make the point that big offenders usually get off scot-free. But when he uses the complete phrase for *The Fawn* he calls up the original context in Juvenal, which, as Richard C. Harrier remarks, is an apology for women, whose offences are nothing compared to those of men.[43] This favourable attitude towards women is worked into the very structure of *The Fawn* through two key reversals of opinion. Zuccone abuses his wife and women in general throughout the first three and a half acts of the play. When he finally recognises the terrible consequences of his actions, he apostrophises women as 'comforters of life, helps in sickness, joys in death, and preservers of us in our children after death' (IV.i.548–50). And after his wife and 'Parliament' have forgiven him, he adds more quietly:

> Until they lose, men know not what's a wife.
> We slight and dully view the lamp of heaven,
> Because we daily see't, which but bereaved
> And held one little week from darkened eyes,
> With greedy wonder we should all admire. (v.i.365–9)

But fully as important is the warming of Tiberio's 'cooler blood'. To take the stance that Tiberio does early in the play is to share the same narrow (and ultimately vicious) view of women that Zuccone, Herod and Nymphadoro espouse and that Faunus pretends to agree with: that women are weak, treacherous, and useful solely as a higher type of entertainment or chattel. But Tiberio is not required to undergo the corrective humiliation of the others; he is saved fairly early by Dulcimel's love and his father's ironic prompting, and Marston gives him the happy task of establishing, with youthful charm, the play's evaluation of women:

> Thou last and only rareness of heaven's works,
> From best of man made model of the gods—
> Divinest Woman: thou perfection
> Of all proportions, Beauty—made when Jove was blithe,
> Well filled with nectar, and full friends with man:
> Thou dear as air, necessary as sleep
> To careful man—Woman! (III.i.512–18)

Clearly Dulcimel and Philocalia are not opposites but complementaries. The true courtier loves beauty because he loves proportion, and proportion entails an equal acceptance of body and mind.

d. Court, Ship, and Comedy

To summarise: If the play's basic value is proportion, its implicit argument is that proportion may be achieved by unorthodox means, and that at times natural impulse must dominate rational control to achieve a lasting, healthy balance. The play is a comedy because it has the traditional purpose to 'correct and please'; its chief comic agent is one who hopes that 'Another's court shall show . . . how / Vice may be cured' (II.i.592–3); and his and the play's dominant comic technique is the practice of 'Ironia' in a systematic praise of folly that exploits human weakness but only in order to modify it. The comedy's moral message is related to that of *The Dutch Courtesan*: 'incontinence will force a continence', in some cases by exhausting the uncontrollable impulse, in others (such as Dulcimel's) by setting it in its proper context, and in more vicious cases, by suppling it to the bursting point where it dissipates in folly, shame, self-knowledge, and (theoretically) automatic correction. An opposition is set up between nature and artifice through the figures of two dukes, one of them seeking wisdom by giving up claims to control nature and the other dead set in ignorance because of his belief that he has already achieved wisdom *by* control over nature. Gonzago must be faced with his folly, must acknowledge that he is the compendious fool, reserved for place of honour at the end of a series of judgements on folly, because 'protested wit', the *claim* to wisdom, is the greatest folly of all.

The dramaturgy follows this pattern in both characterisation and structure. Each of the first four acts is constructed to demonstrate the two main senses of 'courtship'. In the middle of each act, Gonzago gives an example to his court of the wilful blindness of self-admiring wisdom through his equation of rhetorical virtuosity with philosophical depth; the nominal subject of these speeches is Tiberio's courtship of Dulcimel for his father, but increasingly it becomes Tiberio's supposed courtship of her for himself. Before the Gonzago scene in each act, the various courtiers demonstrate their own respective blindnesses, invariably involving abuse of the conventions of 'courtship' in relation to women, and demonstrating at least in part the parallel abuse of 'courtship' in relation to their duties as courtiers, in which (as Hercules says of Tiberio) they follow courses that support only appetite and not their honour or duty (ii.i.560–2). During these scenes, Faunus flatters one after the other of the courtiers towards a point in the future—the Court of Cupid in the last act—at which their vices may have ripened to harvesting and (to labour the conceit) been ground into the flour of folly, nutritious when baked in the bread of self-knowledge. And in the short scene that follows these first two parts of each act, we find Tiberio gradually succumbing to the double and doubly devious blandishments of Dulcimel and Faunus. Finally, the temporarily unmasked Hercules is left on stage to report, indirectly or directly, on what he has himself learned from his actions and others'.

Yet despite the elements of symmetry in *The Fawn* there is substantial dramatic flow. Except for the short scene that starts Act I, each act forms one continuous scene, with the stage vaguely representing somewhere in the palace—possibly the presence chamber, but more likely an open courtyard (the tree leading to Dulcimel's chamber is pointed at near the end of Act IV and used at the beginning of Act V). Indeed, the 'presence' seems to be wherever Gonzago is, for Gonzago's court is remarkably peripatetic, with the Duke huffing and puffing on and off, trailing his courtiers behind him. A certain sinuosity of relationships between characters also ties the scenes together, through what might be called a shifting hierarchy of acumen. For instance, that egregious duo Herod and Nymphadoro are genuinely witty and frequently perceptive; their intelligence is ultimately their saving grace and the measure of their offence. They see that the Dulcimel–Hercules match is wrong; they know what Tiberio should have said but did not (i.ii.193–9); they look down on Sir Amoroso and Zuccone for the right reasons; they can see the good qualities of Zoya and Philocalia; and they take their public humiliation and punishment well and understand the point of it. Though Nymphadoro lightly accounts for his universal amorousness as a 'humour' he is nonetheless corrigible because of his intelligence. So is Zuccone for that matter. Only Amoroso, perhaps because 'his brain's perished' from sexual abuse (II.i.187–8), seems to lack the capacity for self-understanding. In this way, Marston arranges his shifting hierarchy of wit and even morality, through which something like a Middletonian œconomy of vice[44] is at work, not through having the big fish eat the little fish (socially it is the reverse), but through a sleight of hand by which the audience can, for instance, accept the views of Nymphadoro and Herod as a standard when they criticise Zuccone and Amoroso yet watch them in turn put down frequently by Dulcimel and occasionally by Dondolo.

In short, just as Gonzago—with his self-indulgence, abuse of language, claims to wit and wisdom, and attempts to thwart nature—is a compendium of the follies in the court of Urbin, so each of the characters is in a sense a compendium of the same weaknesses as the others. Whatever the relative weights of individual faults, all the courtiers must contend with an inner lust for something, if only for words; all of them indulge their lusts and (again with the exception of Amoroso, whose incontinence has forced a rather drastic continence) all are the better for their indulgence. As we have seen, indulgence in this comedy is both a method of characterisation and a dramatic strategy. Constant references to festivity in the background, though they add up to something less than Saturnalian release, contribute to the atmosphere of indulgence.[45]

This ambiance of festivity is crucial, since it constantly draws us back from satiric detail to comic context. At the very outset, Urbin is 'afire' with celebrations of Princess Dulcimel's birthday, which continue till the end of the last act. Music and pageantry accompany the entrance of the ambassador, Prince Tiberio, and the first act ends with a reference to a 'feastful entertainment' to follow. Act II, filled with references to food and feasting, begins with a couple of courtiers sitting down to eat the remnants of the feast at which they had acted as 'court servitors', and in Act III Gonzago invites Tiberio to yet another 'feastful waking'. In Act IV, new entertainment is announced to celebrate the birthday and an added

cause of rejoicing is later announced by Gonzago (IV.i.664 ff.), the
supposed thwarting of Tiberio's attempts on Dulcimel's honour.
Act V begins with a prothalamium for the newly-wed couple,
continues with dancing (V.i.122.1), is given over to a masque
(V.i.139.1–3) and to a mock parliament, and ends with the pre-
sentation of the married couple to the now chastened and enlightened Gonzago. In Gonzago's reformation all the indulgence
of the festivity and of Faunus's flattery has its accumulated moral
effect. 'By the Lord, I am ashamed of myself . . .' Gonzago says,
'But I know wherefore this parliament was' (V.i.473–4). It was for
the brain-proud duke who tried to thwart nature.

The Parliament, Court of Cupid, or General Council of Love,
as it is diversely called, is apparently the invention of Hercules and
Dondolo.[46] Its efficacy with Gonzago and his court, however, is the
result of its amalgamation with a device, the Ship of Fools, of
which Gonzago is himself the author (IV.i.233–4). From its first
mention (I.ii.33) the Ship is known to be in Dondolo's charge
(Dulcimel says he is the captain, III.i.141–2), and the device affords
sufficient opportunity for general satire on philosophers, critics,
naive citizens, and so on, to be useful simply as a figure of speech.
Only in the fourth act, with Gonzago's reported wish to ship all
fools out of his dominions (IV.i.233–4), does the reality of the Ship
become certain. Shortly after, the Court of Cupid is first announced
(IV.i.255–62), but we must wait until the last act before the connection between the two devices is made. The two organisers—
disguised duke Hercules and professional fool Dondolo—carefully
hide it from the victims-to-be till the right moment: they 'will not
unshale the jest before it be ripe' (IV.i.274–5).[47] And though there
are hints before that right moment comes, the jest becomes ripe
only with the arraignment of Nymphadoro. Moments before,
Faunus, as court officer, proclaims a law against the plurality of
mistresses; the punishment—to 'be arrested by folly's mace, and
instantly committed to the ship of fools, without either bail or
mainprize . . .' (V.i.239–41). Nymphadoro is shocked, especially
when he sees his supposed friend Faunus bring witnesses to his
philandering. But the exposure of his folly brings self-understanding; Nymphadoro acknowledges the justice of his fate:

> Thus he that loveth many, if once known,
> Is justly plagued to be beloved of none.   (v.i.259–60)

And so for the rest of the offenders. In turn, Amoroso, Herod, Zuccone and Granuffo are shown to be fools in their double offences against love (particularly through the exploitation of women) and truth (the 'laws' they have transgressed are related respectively to counterfeiting, forging and uttering, slandering, and mumming).

At this point there arises a problem involving staging. If the Ship of Fools is located off-stage, the starkness of the playing area as it becomes gradually bereft of actors would be striking; furthermore, the political implications of a duke on the point of being arrested by his own guards and being led into exile would be lost neither on Marston nor on James's intelligencers in the audience, and the atmosphere would be unnecessarily tense. Since the stage directions indicate only two exits by prisoners, quite possibly they do not actually leave the stage. The space where Cupid's Court is located suggests a solution. The fifth act, we remember, begins with Hercules standing beneath Dulcimel's window; his 'squirrel' son has just climbed a tree to get to her. We are, one gathers, in an open courtyard, which may as easily give on to an inlet in which bobs the visible part of a ship as it can support a prop tree big enough to support the weight of a boy actor climbing on to a chamber 'above'. The benefits of the physical presence of a small, moveable mansion are several, though there are difficulties as well. Since the unpurged passengers have receded, ship and all, at the start of the act (v.i.46–9), the ship will have to heave into sight in motion—not too difficult to do with wheels, even in a Jacobean private theatre, and a great *coup de théâtre* to boot.[48] Cupid and his party probably descend from the ship and the allegorical characters are played by the same 'fools that were appointed to wait on Don Cupid' (v.i.46–7). Best of all, this means that when in turn Nymphadoro, Sir Amoroso, Herod, and Granuffo are arrested, they board and then remain in view, embarrassed but also ready to join in the laughter at each other's follies, and to approve of the ultimate comic resolutions—the proportionate marriage of Dulcimel and Tiberio and the coming to wisdom of the would-be wizard

Gonzago. The opportunity for universal concord (including even Amoroso, once he has had time to cool off and apply his perished brain to the proceedings) makes the comic ending of the play rather more convincing than the alternative of an off-stage ship. It makes the exile, even when 'real', part of a festive event, in which our interest in love and folly are kept in balance.

When finally Gonzago's turn arrives in the Court of Cupid, he erupts in a last, glorious cascade of verbosity. What stands out in the passage (v.i.397–416) is the combination of Marston's deadly aural accuracy and a resumé of abuses, ironically boasted by the foremost in this company of fools: lust of speech, self-conscious wit in discourse, abuse of women, crass *machismo*, wilful frustration of love, and self-glorification. After all the rhetoric in which Gonzago has indulged and all the use of artifice in his attempts to frustrate nature, Hercules can nevertheless say that Urbin's duke has done all these foolish things not out of policy but inadvertently, as a 'plain natural'. The phrase is entirely felicitous. And when Dulcimel, mimicking her father's Ciceronian style, addresses him as 'royally wise and wisely royal father', Dondolo's comment brings out of hiding the rhetorical figure which has been lurking at the heart of the comedy: 'A figure called in art *Ironia*'. All has proceeded through irony. Through it, the pretended parasite has been the agent for restoring proportion to the Court of Urbin and to his own soul.

Two important interpretations of *The Fawn* deserve separate discussion, for though they do not mix well with the present one, they offer alternatives worthy of consideration. Of these studies, Joel Kaplan's does agree basically with the approach taken in this introduction: that the play traces a process of social correction not by castigation or suppression but by 'curative exuberance', and that Hercules, the agent of this process, himself develops through the span of action. But Kaplan centres his argument on symbolic values in the protagonist's names:

> For Marston . . . the figure of Hercules, first at the Augean stalls and then in the bedrooms of Beotia, was associated with both the carting of filth and the creation of progeny. Appropriately these

acts are, in the broadest sense of the terms, the respective domains of renaissance satire and comedy; the realms of the satirist and what we may call the saturnalian character.

    Marston's Duke Hercules fulfills both functions. He is at the same time a satiric and saturnalian figure, cleansing Gonzago's polluted court at Urbin while perpetuating his own house at Ferrara.[49]

Kaplan also sees the name 'Fawn' or 'Faunus' as suggesting 'not only "flatterer" but both a variety of the savage man and Faunus (Pan) himself, god of fertility and abundance' (p. 337).

The problem with such an approach is that while it provides a useful critical terminology for describing the play's intellectual pattern, it cannot stand up as an accurate account of how the play's imagery actually functions dramatically. The only definition of 'Fawn' that the text hints at (Prologue, 34–5; II.i.84–5) is simply 'flatterer'; the spirit of Pan may hover nigh, but the play never says so. There is no reference to the Augean stables and the dominant imagery of moral process is curing sickness, not cleansing filth. Of references to the mythological Hercules, one (V.i.146) uses an alternative name, Alcides, and tells of his subservience to Cupid's power, and the other (II.i.237–9) uses the fight with Antaeus (whom Marston mistakenly calls 'Achelous') for a libel of women. As for the apocryphal thirteenth labour of Hercules (the deflowering of fifty virgins), to which Kaplan gives great importance as an image of fertility, in none of the frequent applications of the story in Marston's writings is a happy construction put upon it. Indeed, in Marston's fullest account (*CS.*, v, 47–58) he comments on Hercules' deification for his 'lewd act' in virtually a paraphrase of the motto he was to use for *The Fawn*: 'Thus little scapes are deepely punished, / But mighty villanes are for Gods adored' (*Poems*, p. 88). With such reservations as these, Kaplan's essay is a stimulating and generally valid introduction to the pattern of satiric and comic development in *The Fawn*.

    Philip J. Finkelpearl's valuable research into the Christmas Revels of the Inns of Court (referred to in Sources and in the explanatory notes) firmly establishes Marston's debt to the conventions of those entertainments and also indicates a lightness of tone in *The Fawn* which might otherwise be overlooked.[50] But in his full-length study of Marston,[51] he argues further that these correspondences, when combined with others, are evidence of parochialism. In his chapter on *The Fawn* Finkelpearl revives Albert W. Upton's theory that Gonzago is meant to be a comic portrait of the 'wisest fool in Christendom', King James. However manifest the connection may be (the evidence is by no means as overwhelming as the two writers maintain though not easily dismissed), Finkelpearl's point is important: the validity of Upton's theory

> radically affects the aesthetic experience of this play, as the discovery that Shakespeare modeled Hamlet on Prince Henry would not. *The Fawne* is not simply a topical satire, but it is very strongly tied to a certain time and place. . . . Marston's basic artistic task in *The Fawne* was fairly simple. He had to find a plot that would permit him to display Duke Gonzago at length, and he had to place him in an atmosphere that would reflect the Duke's character.[52]

Finkelpearl thus starts from the direction opposite to that of Kaplan, who places Hercules at the play's thematic centre. It leads him to regard the Gonzago set-pieces as the 'main plot' and the rest of the activities (involving over seventy-five per cent of the text), in which Hercules/Faunus usually takes direct part, as 'subplot'. I suggest that this involves a drastic dislocation of the emphasis the text actually gives to the function of the two dukes, and underestimates the degree to which Marston has integrated them into a single moral allegory. It would be naive to claim for *The Fawn* that it is for all time, but it is rather more than merely of an age. *The Fawn* is a minor gem, but a gem, in which diverse facets sparkle within a single comic design.

3. DATE

In the Stationers' Register for 12 March 1606, we find: 'William Cotton Entred for his copie vnder the handes of the wardens A Playe called the *ffaune* PROVIDED that he shall not put the same in prynte before he gette alowed lawfull aucthoritie'.[53] This establishes the latest date for the play, although Marston was still adding and revising slightly while printing proceeded on the quartos (both dated 1606). Extensive borrowings from Montaigne fix the earlier limit as 1603, when Florio's translation of the *Essays* appeared in England. Since the title-pages of both quartos state that the play had been presented at Blackfriars 'by the Children of the Queenes Maiesties Reuels', it is unlikely that it was produced before 4 February 1604, when the Queen's patronage was officially bestowed upon the company. Moreover, because of the plague of 1603 the theatres were shut down until 9 April 1604, which establishes that as the earliest possible date of performance. Marston's *Sophonisba* was registered 17 March 1606, hard upon the registration of *The Fawn* (which has a reference in the second quarto to the imminent publication of *Sophonisba*). This means that Marston courted and married Mary Wilkes and had a hand in at least four plays (*The Fawn, The Dutch Courtesan, Eastward Ho*, and *Sophonisba*) in the space of only two years. *Sophonisba* evidently came last, since there is no reference in the title-page to the Queen's patronage, lost early in 1606, though it was a Blackfriars play. Anthony Caputi argues strongly on a number of grounds for the composition of *Eastward Ho* and *The Dutch Courtesan* in early to middle 1605,[54] which leaves the most likely room for *The Fawn* in 1604. There is more persuasive evidence than mere calendar arithmetic for this date, however. The title-pages of the quartos show that the play had been around a good while. Both state that it had been 'divers times presented at Blackfriars', and that of the second quarto adds 'and since at Powles'. The Paul's boys probably got hold of a script when Edward Kirkham transferred his allegiance (and evidently a few prompt books as well) some time in 1605[–1606], but it seems unlikely that Paul's would produce it very shortly after the Blackfriars production.[55] Otherwise, '[t]he only additional evidence that we have supporting 1604 is the play's obvious kinship to *The Malcontent. The Fawn* is not only a disguise-plot play, like *The Malcontent*, but it also uses the same motto used for *The Malcontent*.'[56]

In 1888, Wilhelm Creizenach argued that *The Fawn* was either the source of a play or the identical play that was performed

by a group of English actors touring Germany in 1604.[57] One
W. Eichelin (perhaps their German impresario) applied for
permission that year to perform the story 'von Annabella eines
hertzogen tochter vonn Ferrara' in Nördlingen (near Nürnberg)
and one 'vonn Annabella, eines Margraffen tochter von Mont-
ferrar', apparently the same play as the other, at Rothenburg ob
der Tauber (about forty miles from Nördlingen). Creizenach, and
Johannes Bolte after him, identified this play with a German one
in a manuscript in the Danzig Stadbibliothek, part of the literary
remains of Georg Schröder, which Bolte published in 1895.[58] Bolte
named the untitled play *Tiberius von Ferrara und Anabella von
Mömpelgard* after its principal characters.

The similarities are striking though few. A duke of Ferrara
sends his son Tiberius to negotiate a marriage with Anabella,
daughter of the Margrave of Mömpelgard, but disguised as
Bartholomaeus, an old soldier, he goes along to see how his son
conducts himself. Like Tiberio in *The Fawn*, Tiberius appears
first as a cold youth, impervious to women, but unlike Marston's
prince, he falls head over heels as soon as he meets the princess.
Alternating with a farcical plot involving Hans, a buffoon, we have
scenes verging on tragicomedy as opposition to the young couple's
love increases till they are supposedly drowned while trying to
escape on a ship. A sudden announcement that they were not
drowned after all brings the proper comic conclusion. Most of the
resemblances to *The Fawn* are in the first two acts of *Tiberius*. One
exchange in particular is very close to *The Fawn* I.ii.108–10, 136–9,
and 141–3:

> *Tiberius.* Frewlein, ich verhoffe nicht, das mein vngestümes
> Anhalten E. Gnaden in Betrubnuss bringe.
> *Anabella.* Gantz nicht, gnediger Herr, sondern ich beschawe
> E. Gn. Herrn Vatern Contrafactur. Ist es ihm auch ehnlich.
> *Tiberius.* Ja, gnediges Frewlein, alss wen Ihr ihn selber zugegen
> sehet.
> *Anabella.* Ist es muglich, ein so durrer Baum vndt so schöner
> Zweich! Wie aldt ist er woll ?
> *Tiberius.* Irgend vierzig Jahr.
> *Anabella.* Ja, da diess gemahlt ist; dan die Hende scheinen gahr
> zu durre. Ich muss bekennen, gnediger Herr, E. Gn. Herr

Vater hette keinen bessern Agenten finden konnen, der so fleisich sollicitiret hette, vndt mochte wunschen, das E. Gn. diese Muhe nach meinem Begehren belohnet wurde, vndt soldt ich gleich selbst die Besoldung sein.[59]

Yet it would be dangerous to rely too much on the play produced by Eichelin's company in 1604 for dating Marston's, for there is no clear evidence that *The Fawn* was based on Eichelin's play, or indeed that Eichelin's play was based on *The Fawn*, and the two may well derive from a common original. As Bolte points out,[60] Anabella was evidently the name of the heroine in the English original of *Tiberius*, since there is an exchange in iv.iv. involving an obvious English pun on 'bell':

Dux. Wo ist das Frewlein Anabella ?
Hagewoll. Die Klocke gesch[l]agen ?

And since the name 'Anabella' appears in both titles referred to in 1604 (rather than 'Dulcimel'), the differences between the German play and Marston's must have already existed then. On the other hand, some of the similarities may have been added much later, including the dialogue between the prince and princess. Schröder was born in 1635, and since there is apparently no evidence to establish when the translation was made, it may well have been his own, which would place it in the mid to late seventeenth century. Creizenach and Bolte assumed that the 1604 play was the same as one performed in Dresden by John Green's travelling English company on 11 June and 24 September 1616, with the title 'Comoedia vom Hertzog von Ferrara'. But Green's play may as easily have been *The Fawn* itself, since the title refers, as Marston's does, to the duke as central character. The German version, therefore, may be the result of a conflation of two descendants of the same, now lost, play.

Internal evidence for dating is always a tenuous matter. I find none of it convincing in the case of *The Fawn*. References to public executions (iv.i.297–301) could allude, as Caputi points out, to any number of similar ones between 1603 and 1606, and indeed *any* topical references, given the leisurely and gossipy format of the play, could simply have been inserted during various revivals during the same period. P. J. Finkelpearl prefers 1606 on two grounds: that, as E. K. Chambers argues (III, 432), the execution of Sir Everard Digby on 30 January 1606 is the most likely execution to be alluded to; and that there are possible references in the play to King James and the Gunpowder Plot.[61] The evidence in both cases is extremely doubtful, however. Chambers offers 1606 only for a hypothetical 'written up' version, acknowledging that the play must originally date 'from 1604 or 1605' (III, 432); Finkelpearl, too, must be satisfied only with a conjectured 'augmented form' of the play that might date from 1606. The most likely date remains 1604.

I have been unable to find any evidence of the play's production since Marston's time.

4. SOURCES

If Marston was influenced by an old play about a disguised Duke of Ferrara and his son Tiberius or (more probably) by a story on the subject going the rounds of London, it cannot be established at present. But there is more certainty about other sources. It was Langbaine who first pointed out that 'The Plot of *Dulcimel* her cozening the Duke by a pretended Discovery of *Tiberio*'s Love to her, is borrow'd from *Boccace*'s Novels, Day 3. Nov. 3'.[62] In *The Decameron*, Filomena tells this story as a put-down to the pretentions of friars. It concerns a young woman who grows restless and falls in love with a man of higher social standing than her husband. The man keeps company with a pious but rather dull friar, and it is through the unwitting intercession of the friar that she conducts her courtship. First, she complains to the friar that his friend has been talking to her of love and asks him to convey her disapproval. In doing so, the friar of course opens the man's eyes, and (unlike Tiberio) he is immediately enthusiastic. As in *The Fawn*, the second deception involves the 'returning' of a gift, in this case a girdle and a purse; again the messenger is the friar, who rebukes his friend angrily. The third trick is once again similar to the corresponding one in *The Fawn*. The lady goes to the friar and tells him that her husband has left for Genoa, and that the young man, taking advantage of this fact, climbed a tree which happens to reach the window of her bedchamber, but that luckily she was able to rush to the window and shut it in time, naked as she was. All of this the friar angrily tells his friend, who takes his indirect instructions well, to the ensuing (and frequent) satisfaction of both himself and the lady.

Though he retains the three-staged format of the device, Marston makes it thoroughly his own. We should note particularly that though Dulcimel takes the initiative in the actual courtship, it is Gonzago himself who unwittingly first recommends Tiberio's suitability to her and hers to Tiberio. Before Tiberio even arrives, Gonzago warns Dulcimel against the young prince's 'life-full eyes and well-filled veins, complexion firm, and hairs that curls with strength of lusty moisture', since he comes to court her for his father who is 'well in years' (I.ii.89–94). Shortly after, Gonzago just as wisely warns Tiberio not to be provoked by Dulcimel's youthful loveliness (I.ii.161–82).

The word 'parasitaster' can be found in Terence's *Adelphi* (v.ii.779) as a diminutive of contempt for a hanger-on. Marston's usage probably owes more to Jonson than to Terence (see commentary for Prologus, 35), and similarities between the two plays are few apart from the common New Comedy pattern of trickery between the old and young generations.[63] But there are more certain resemblances between *The Fawn* and George Chapman's *All Fools* (1599) which is itself partly based on *Adelphi*. In *All Fools* Rinaldo, a sort of Chapmanesque Brainworm, sets out to gull Gostanzo, the pompous father of his neighbour and friend, Valerio, and eventually to reconcile Gonstanzo to Valerio's 'stolen' or secret marriage. Meanwhile, in the sub-plot, the young men persecute Cornelio, a 'start-up Gentleman', for his relentless and causeless jealousy of his wife. The two old gulls in *All Fools* have their counterparts in *The Fawn*. Like Zuccone, Cornelio is tricked into divorcing his wife, then led into a reconciliation. Like Gonzago, Gostanzo is an old man who prides himself in being able to thwart the love-tricks of the young, contrasting the weakness of silly youth nowadays to his own prowess in the old days.[64] There is also a possible foreshadowing of Herod (and perhaps Nymphadoro as well) in the young courtier Dariotto, who has the humour of pursuing women till they give consent—which is apparently all he is after—and who is lectured by Valerio for boasting about the favours he has obtained from women (III.i.361 ff.). But the correspondences are not exact. For example, though Gonzago and Gostanzo share a pretension to 'politicness' and Zuccone has the same wretched ambition as Cornelio to be known as a cuckold, it is to Gonzago that Marston gives Cornelio's claim of prescience.

Marston may have picked up from Chapman a delight in the ironic praise of folly which runs through *All Fools*. The page's witty defence of women's rights (*All Fools*, III.i.182–257) is paralleled by Hercules' mock argument in favour of feminine promiscuity (*The Fawn*, II.i.362–86); and Valerio's *tour de force* oration in praise of 'the horn' (*All Fools*, v.i.230–326) has its counterpart in Hercules' paean to drunkenness (*The Fawn*, v.i.163–74). As we have noted, Marston had always had a predilection for mock encomium, and in *What You Will* Quadratus had already employed mock praise as part of his arsenal of harangue. But in *The Fawn*, Marston seems to have returned to the gentler irony of the sunny though slightly old-fashioned style of Chapman's humours play; and the 'stratagem' of indulgent flattery, which Chapman's Rinaldo used to trap Gostanzo and Cornelio (and eventually himself), becomes the central principle of both the comedy and the morality of *The Fawn*.

There are indications that Marston knew *The Merry Wives of Windsor* (these consist chiefly of parallels between Master Ford and Zuccone), but not enough to warrant its being designated a source.[65] More important is the relationship amongst *The Fawn*, *Measure for Measure* and Middleton's *The Phoenix*, all of which have for their central character a disguised duke or prince who deals with folly and wickedness, though they share little else. That *The Fawn* is indebted to either of the other plays cannot be proven with the help of dating. J. W. Lever argues that *Measure for Measure* was written and performed between May and August 1604 (Arden edition, xxxv), which would make it almost exactly contemporaneous with *The Fawn*, and the plays differ greatly in plot, characterisation and spirit. There are more similarities between *The Fawn* and *The Phoenix*, which is usually dated between 1602 (R. C. Bald) and 1604, though it was published only in 1607.[66] As in *The Fawn*, a father and son are involved, though it is the son who lurks *incognito* in Middleton's play. And while Tiberio warms to the beauty of Woman, Middleton shifts the love interest away from Phoenix (who inexplicably uses the same name while disguised as when at court). Indeed, if *The Phoenix* was a source for Marston, it may have been as something to react against, for though the one value most advertised in the play is patience, it has an irascible tone and atmosphere: the plots of Proditor are more vicious and practicable than those of Herod and Nymphadoro; the Captain is incorrigibly cruel; the satire on lawyers is less fully integrated into the total scheme; women are more grimly dealt with (Marston's Garbetza and the Jeweller's Wife commit virtually the same offence and with the same mitigating factors: Marston's character is pardoned, Middleton's punished). The disposal of the Captain—he is 'condemned' to go back to sea, which is where he wants to go anyway—could have contributed to Marston's introduction of the Ship of Fools. But it is the prince, not an obvious fool like Gonzago, who thinks he can get rid of vice and folly simply by shipping the vicious and foolish out of his realm. The task is made easier for him by the fact that Middleton neatly relates all the characters by family or other ties; eradication of the symptoms thus constitutes eradication of the total disease. It is a simple-minded solution by a rather simple-minded, and priggish, young prince. Other similarities are striking, though they can probably be accounted for by shared convention: e.g., a speech by Falso recalling the adventures of youth (*The Phoenix*, III.i.58–75) resembles Gonzago's at v.i.397–416; and Phoenix's apostrophe to Law (*The Phoenix*, I.iv.197–227) is couched in the same style as Tiberio's to Woman at III.i.512–21.[67]

It would be gratifying to be able to establish that Marston was influenced by Erasmus's *Praise of Folly* but there is no evidence in *The Fawn* or elsewhere that he read anything by Erasmus besides, perhaps, the *Adagia*.[68] Similarly, though wise fools, jealous husbands, boasters and flatterers appear in the works of Brandt and Barclay, they show not the slightest kinship in tone or detail with this play: the device of the Ship of Fools, important as it is, must have originated in the phrase alone, or just possibly in the ship which figures in *Tiberius von Ferrara und Anabella von Mömpelgard* and which may have been in the source of that play and Marston's. The influence of Jonson's *Cynthia's Revels* (1600) can be sensed in the court scene that ends *The Fawn*. As in Jonson's play the scene consists of an entertainment, including a masque, which is advertised from early on in the play, and in both comedies the entertainment is presided over by Cupid. Marston's Court of Cupid is a far more rollicking affair, however, without Jonson's poetic pretensions; if there is indebtedness to Jonson on this account it would more likely be through the court scene at the end of *Poetaster* (1601), in which Marston himself (in the guise of 'Crispinus') was the victim of satiric justice.

The most important influence on the entertainments in the last Act of *The Fawn*, however, is undoubtedly the Christmas Revels of the Middle Temple, as Philip J. Finkelpearl has convincingly demonstrated.[69] Elaborate entertainments, lasting from three to five weeks, were regular occurrences in the Inns of Court at Christmas time, from the fifteenth century to the Restoration. The detailed account which survives of the Middle Temple's Christmas Revels of 1597/8[70] indicates a variety of activities including a mock trial. Arraignments 'pursued the fiction of a Kingdom of Love' (201) and the presiding figure was known as the 'Prince d'Amour'. Marston's purposes precluded duplicating the main 'trial' of a discontented lover and a jealous lover, but equivalents of most of the laws in his Court of Cupid can be found in the Revels, including those against plurality of mistresses, impotent lovers, braggarts, slanderers of women, even silent courters. There is no real precedent for Gonzago's offence, though Finkelpearl suggests one (204). The paradoxes which proliferate throughout *The Fawn* and the almanac 'prognostications' which precede the Court proper (v.i.51–89) also were conventions of the Christmas Revels. In 1898 William A. Neilson had suggested that Marston's Court had its source in the medieval courts of love,[71] but Finkelpearl is surely right when he says that 'it is very unlikely that Marston would reach back for material long unused in England when he saw such Courts held annually at the place in which he resided for many years' (205).

The pervasive influence of Montaigne on *The Fawn* may not seem at first sight to constitute a source, but since so many of the borrowings come from the same essay, we might well entertain the validity of the idea. 'Upon Some Verses of Virgil'[72] supplies Marston with passages to illustrate virtually every subject of his 'farrago'.[73] The 'verses of Virgil' in question are an erotic passage in the *Aeneid* (viii, 387–92 and 404–6); and Montaigne hangs the whole of his essay on the theme of love—its various definitions, its problems, its forms in various civilisations, what it tells us about men and women. He speaks of the trade of marriage in Italy (135), boasting (104), jealousy and cuckoldry (105 f.), the keeping of secrets (78 f.), the perversity of restraining healthy appetites in women (136 f.), the pitfalls of eloquence and rhetoric (119), and the beneficial effect of confession and public exposure of one's faults (77 f.). In doing so, he provides precedents and often the very words for Nymphadoro, Herod, Zuccone, Dulcimel and Gonzago, and a rationale for the mock trial at the end of the play.

More important, the impulse which spurs Hercules to put off the secret arts of rule in exchange for a fling at adventure is the same that Montaigne articulates at the beginning of his essay:

> When I was young, I had neede to be advertised, and sollicited to keepe my selfe in office: Mirth and health (saies one) sute not so well with these serious and grave discourses. I am now in another state. The conditions of age do but over-much admonish, instruct, and preach unto me. From the excesse of jollity, I am falne into the extreame of severity: more peevish and more untoward. Therefore, I do now of purpose somewhat give way unto licentious allurements; and now and then employ my minde in wanton and youthfull conceits, wherein she recreates hir selfe. . . . As I have heretofore defended my selfe from pleasure, so I now ward my self from temperance: it haleth me too far back, and even to stupidity. I will now every way be master of my selfe. *Wisdome hath hir excesses, and no less need of moderation,* then follie. (71–2)

Montaigne is not sure where his mental travelling will take him,

but he is determined to set off regardless. Hercules' first soliloquy
in *The Fawn* (I.i.37–62) is made in much the same state of mind,
and follows a very similar line of reasoning. And throughout the
rest of the comedy, Marston camouflages his shrewd dramaturgical
craftsmanship with a leisurely, discursive texture that imitates the
process of a mind like Montaigne's recreating itself in wanton and
youthful conceits. The line between 'debt' and 'source' can be thin
indeed.

5. THE TEXT

a. The early texts

There were three printings of *The Fawn* during Marston's lifetime.
The third, in William Sheares's collection of Marston's plays
(1633), is without authority; it was printed from the first quarto,
and Marston had no more to do with the entire book than to have
all traces of his authorship removed from the title-pages in the
later impressions. This leaves us with the two quartos, both
published in 1606, which are a familiar bibliographical curiosity.
The second quarto, as we now know, is only partly a new edition.
For almost half the book, the type set for Q1 was largely left
standing and re-employed for Q2. The rest of Q2 is newly set, but
in such a way as not to alter the collation: quarto, A1–I4*v*: A1,
title-page; A1*v*, blank; A2–A2*v*, Preface, 'To my equall Reader.';
A3, 'Prologus.'; A3*v*, 'Interlocutores.'; A4–I4*v*, text.[74] Besides the
same date, the two quartos even share the same title-page, though
the type is shifted to give space to two additions: that the play was
produced by the Paul's boys (its 'divers' productions at Blackfriars
had already been mentioned in Q1); that the new quarto is 'now
corrected of many faults, which by reason of the Au- / thors
absence, were let slip in the first edition'.

An addendum to the address to the reader in Q2 (on A2*v*) says
that the corrections were made by the author himself:

> Reader, know I haue perused this coppy, to make some satis-
> faction for the first faulty impression: yet so vrgent hath been my
> busines, that some errors haue styll passed, which thy discretion
> may amend . . .

This apparently gives weight to the authority of the second quarto. But what of the first? In a passage which appears in both quartos (on sig. A2), Marston says:

> *If any shall wonder why I print a Comedie, whose life rests much in the Actors voice: Let such know, that it cannot auoide publishing: let it therefore stand with good excuse, that I haue been my owne setter out.*

That Marston could be his 'owne setter out' while absent from the printing of 'the first faulty impression' may seem inconsistent; but essentially it means that he provided the manuscript to serve as copy, so that a different script would not be used for a rival edition. And though Marston may not have personally supervised its printing, Q1 derives considerable authority from his having supplied the printer's copy for it.

What does Marston mean in Q2 by the phrase 'I haue perused this coppy'? Literally 'this coppy' seems to refer to a completed Q2. But more probably it refers to a copy of Q1, bound or un-bound, which the printer used to prepare Q2. And 'perused' leaves the method of correction wide open: page-by-page, partial but thorough, hasty and sketchy—all these are possible. Finally, granting that 'the first faulty impression' is the same as 'the first edition', what were the 'many faults which were let slip' in Q1, and which the 'errors [that] haue styll passed' in Q2? An attempt will be made here to deal with these questions by reconstructing, as far as can be done, the story of the printing of the two quartos.

b. Copy for Q1

Some time in 1605–6 Edward Kirkham, a master of the Children of the Queen's Revels at Blackfriars, abandoned the company for its chief rival, and 'appeared triumphantly before the Treasurer of the Chamber's paymaster the following spring as "one of the Masters of the Children of Pawles"'.[75] Kirkham apparently had taken some Blackfriars play-books with him, including the prompt-book of *The Fawn*, and Marston, anticipating that his erstwhile partner might use it for publication, provided the printer with a copy of his own for an edition more lucrative to himself. This edition, the first quarto, betrays many characteristics of an author's

copy, better than foul papers sometimes were, but still containing
more inconsistencies of names and vagueness of punctuation than
one might expect in a fair copy prepared for press. To support this
view, W. L. Halstead has pointed to the 'literary style' of using
Latin phrases to indicate the ends of Acts III and IV, and to the
inclusion of stage directions in the body of the text even when
there is no evident shortage of space.[76] After observing the fairly
small number of variants and revisions between the two quartos,
Halstead concludes that 'Marston found no great fault with the
text of [Q]1';[77] and though a number of his other observations are
dubious, Halstead's opinion that 'the author approved the copy
used by the printer'[78] may be adopted with confidence.

c. Copy for Q2

For almost half of Q2, the question of 'copy' is irrelevant, since
essentially these pages are later states of Q1. For the rest, the
evidence strongly favours still-unbound sheets of Q1. Most of Q2
corresponds to Q1 line by line; and all pages in Q2 begin and end
with the same words as their Q1 counterparts except at A2–A2v
and C1–C1v–C2, where substantial authorial additions have made
adjustment necessary. Numerous substantive errors are repeated.[79]
Above all, the retention of several Q1 catchwords which do not
match the first word on the next page demonstrates both the close
(and frequently slavish) copying in Q2 and something of the
process of composing the new settings. The most striking instances
occur at A4v / B1 and E1v / E2; the bracketed word is the first one
on the succeeding page:

	Q1	Q2
A4v	Pag: [*Nimp*:]	*Pag*: [*Nym*:]
E1v	You [*Her.*]	You [*Herc.*]

There are similar indications at B3v/B4, E2/E2v, E4v/F1, F2v/F3,
and H1/H1v that the Q2 compositor has no idea what the catchword is supposed to catch. What is noteworthy is not that Q2
repeats inaccurate readings from Q1 but where these readings
occur. If the Q2 compositor were reading his copy out of a bound
quarto, it would be simple for him to find the error of the catchword by glancing at the top of the next page (or in E2/E2v,

flipping the page). But if he were setting from sheets rather than from a book, he might have to turn the fairly large sheet upside down (for E1*v*, B3*v*, F1*v*, and F3*v*), a procedure which seems to have taken place only once (for F3*v*); and for A4*v*, E2, and E4*v*, he would have to consult proof for the other forme, on the other side of the sheet, or a different sheet altogether. In the only places where text that would appear adjacent on a proofsheet produces a different reading (C2*v* and H2*v*), the Q2 reading corrects Q1.

The evidence suggests that copy for Q2 was not a corrected Q1 quarto but still unbound Q1 sheets, and in that case the inference is warranted that the printing of Q2 followed swiftly upon that of Q1 (even overlapping at points); more, that anyone intending to prepare copy for Q2 would have to work in rather hectic conditions, doing his best to proof-read sheets in time to hand them on to the compositors.[80]

d. Composing and printing the First Quarto

There are very few variants among extant copies of Q1, most of them simply press corrections. The errors are usually obvious, the correction of none of them required the supervising eye of the author, and it is fairly safe to assume that though Marston was his 'owne setter out', he was not this time his own proof-reader. In any case, we need not seek him in the style of the printing, which differs perceptibly between sheets A to D and E to I.[81] For example, in sheets A–D, there are signatures for each of the four recto pages; E–I signs the first three only. Almost all speech headings are followed by a colon in A–D, but by a full stop in E–I. Speech headings for Zuccone are in A–D consistently spelled *Zucc*; in E–I, *Zuc*. A–D speech headings for Hercules fluctuate between *Her* and *Herc*, causing an occasional ambiguity when Herod is also on stage, since Herod appears variously as *Her* and *Hero* in A–D. None occurs in E–I for though *Her* and *Herc* both continue to designate Hercules, Herod never appears as *Her*, only as *Hero* and *Herod*. The spelling of Fawn itself helps to distinguish the two parts. From A to D, both *Fawn* and *Faun* (and their variants *Fawnus/Faunus*) are used, with a slight preponderance of *Faun*. From E to I the 'w' spelling appears exclusively (though the 'u' crops up twice on E3v of Q2, just as the *Zuc* spelling appears in the re-set parts of Q2 A–D). In A–D the normal spelling of 'lady' is 'ladie'; the spelling with '-y' appears only once, on C2, where '-ie' also occurs. But in E–I the majority spelling is 'lady'. Also in E–I, participles ending '-ed' are very frequently spelled '-de' or '-'de'— which happens only once in A–D.

A–D seems to have been printed more carefully and accurately, with stage directions better separated from speeches and the type more regularly spaced. E–I is more careless or rushed. Even the width of the type measure differs between the two parts of Q1, with the sticks used for composing A–D on the average two millimetres wider than those for E–I. (In the reset parts of Q2, a narrower stick appears for B and C, a wider one for F outer.) Most significant perhaps is the fact that in each of sheets A–D and E–I, one can trace the running titles as they are re-used from forme to forme and even from Q1 to Q2—but never from one half of the book to the other. The evidence points to the use of two presses, and possibly two shops.

Sheets A–D of Q1 were composed seriatim, by two compositors. Compositor X set 1–2v of each sheet, and Compositor Y, 3–4v. Compositor Y was the more regular of the two workmen. His speech heads are invariably followed by a colon. From signature B onwards, he regularly uses *Her:* for Hercules, *Hero:* for Herod. He seldom runs out of italic caps. Compositor X is much less regular in speech heads; he uses both colons and full stops, though more often colons. Until C1v he uses *Her:*, *Hero:*, *Hero.*, for Herod; in the midst of this page he begins to avoid ambiguity by normalising to *Hero:* and *Herc:*. His italic caps are fouled with roman, and he runs out of *H*. Compositor Y prefers the spelling 'very' to X's 'verie', generally 'bloud' to X's 'blood', 'yeare' to X's 'yeere', and 'complection' to X's 'complexion'. All but one spelling of Fawn with a 'w' comes in X's part, though both X and Y are inconsistent with variants such as 'Fawnus' and 'Faunus'. The only spellings of 'eye' as 'eie' occur in X's part.

The same two sets of running titles were used for B and C, where the order of printing was probably B (i), B (o), C (i), C (o). Then the set for C (i) was used to impose D (o), and a new set prepared for D (i). Both these formes, with running titles intact, were retained to print sheet D of Q2.

The story of E–I of Q1 is much more complex. This part of the manuscript was almost certainly more rough and difficult to read, and whoever apportioned copy to the compositors was frequently misled into giving uneven assignments, causing procrustean stretching at some points and squeezing at others. That is one of the reasons why spelling variants are generally unreliable for compositorial analysis in E–I. However, the same kinds of evidence that show A–D was composed seriatim—crowding and stretching, type exhaustion, and so on—generally point in E–I to copy cast off for setting by formes.[82] They are supported by the pattern of running titles. We saw that A–D used the same two sets for each of signatures B, C and D, indicating a simple and efficient pattern of two skeletons and one press. But these running titles, though re-used in printing A–D of Q2, never appear in E–I. Instead, for signature E we discover a new set of running titles, which is used for both inner and outer formes. This would at first suggest the slower process of one skeleton and one press. But for signature F we find yet another new set of running titles, and again used for both formes; and for signature G a third set of running titles is used yet again in both formes! Then H uses the set from E and I uses that of F. (The next time the G set turns up it is in G inner of Q2.) But the single-skeleton pattern of imposition might be more apparent than real.

First, it should be clear that all work in E–I was connected with a press different from that used in A–D, and that the two sets of workmen were operating approximately simultaneously. Second, the three sets of running titles in E–I, set for the most part in formes, indicate the participation of at least three workmen. Signature G, as we shall see shortly, is anomalous; its workmen were probably not much involved, if at all, in the rest of E–I. But the repetition of the remaining two sets of running titles is entirely irregular for single-skeleton printing. Furthermore, it seems improbable that such a slow, time-wasting process would be used when so much else points to haste.[83] The solution evidently is that one forme of E and one of F were imposed together as if they were the two formes of a single signature; then the other formes of each were treated in the same way; and so on for H and I. (The incidence of variants for these sheets is consistent with this pattern.)

Signature G produces anomalies like a Chinese box. It uses a different set of running titles from the rest of Q1. The spellings 'woman' and cognates with 'wem-', 'weom-', and 'woem-', occur only here—in G3 (three times), G3*v*, G4 and G4*v* (where it is changed, probably by a different compositor, to 'wom-' in corrected Q1). Short speeches begun on the same line as the one on which a previous speech ends are set up so that they end flush to the right-hand margin on each page except G4 (unless unavoidable on this page owing to crowding).[84] G4 is in any case an anomaly within an anomaly. It is excessively crowded: fully a third of the lines contain speech from more than one character at least. Only five of its thirty-five separate speeches begin with a capital letter (though all speech heads are capitalised); undoubtedly this reflects a manuscript practice here (most of the speeches are part of a continuous, corporate roasting of Zuccone), but similar passages are normalised elsewhere. And it is the only page of the book in which the catchword shares a line with speech.[85]

The unusually consistent spelling of '*Herc.*' in speech heads throughout G (except on G4) again differentiates this signature from all others of E–I, where *Herc.* and *Her.* are continually mixed. In addition, the consistent method of justifying lines containing speech of more than one character; the reappearance of past participles with '-'d' and '-ed' without added '-e' (particularly on G4*v*); the division of copy in the middle of a word between G2*v*–G3 yet the continued exhaustion of capital W throughout G3, G3*v* and G4*v*, all point to most of G being the work of a single compositor.

e. The overlap
With one man composing almost a full signature, with only one skeleton used for imposing both formes, and with time taken to correct the outer forme, work on G would be slowed down considerably, but not sufficiently for the other workmen on E–I to finish their assignments before G was complete. At any rate, the

standing type of G appears to have been the first to be ready for re-use in Q2; the variants and paper of Q2 show this to be so. As a result, though G outer of Q2 was prepared from already corrected Q1, by the time Marston was ready to read proofs for G inner, the workmen had already half-corrected the standing type and run off the first sheets of the Q2 version. So for this one forme, 'this coppy' means Q2. Several (though not all) of the second platoon of variants for the inner forme of G in Q2 appear clearly authorial, which indicates that this part of Q2 was being printed just as production was switching over from Q1 to Q2, at the time that the standing type of H and I was being prepared for reincarnation as H and I of Q2.[86] Last to be set in Q2 were E and F, from type distributed after H and I had been run off. Such wheeling round and working backwards took place in both parts of Q2. The set of running titles for I appears once more, in E inner of Q2; the set for Q2 inner G sustained a slight accident, and when re-used in outer G received a new running title for G2v; in this condition the set was used once more, for outer E. But in the distribution of signature H its set of running titles disappeared, so that F inner and outer required a new one. In A–D, both sets of running titles for sheet D appear in identical order in Q1 and Q2, after which they are cannibalised indifferently for C and B of Q2.

f. The author and the Second Quarto

Even with the order of printing generally established it is difficult to determine when, during that period, Marston was present to prepare copy for Q2. If efficiency were the chief criterion, we should expect to find the most extensive revision on the pages reset for the second edition, since they would be left unprinted while the standing type was soon (or immediately) put into press for running off. But this is not generally the case. Evidently Marston was not available at the most opportune times. As a result, the location, and sometimes the nature, of his revisions appear more arbitrary than one might expect from a 'corrected' edition.

We can be most confident of the authority of the Q2 readings when they are added or relocated stage directions, like those at

B2*v* (I.ii.148.1), E1*v* (III.i.125.1, but see collation for III.i.97), F1*v* (III.i.454.2) and I4*v* (v.i.469.1); or where new lines are added, as on C1*v* (II.i.27–9); or, as at G3 (IV.i.388), where one reading is substituted for another, in this case probably to clean up a passage that might be taken as perverse.[87] At other places one can question Marston's decision for change but not the fact that he made it; e.g. at v.i.370 (I3) and v.i.283 (on the adjacent I2*v*), where jargon is juggled with plain statement: these demonstrate not so much conscientiousness as mere fussiness. Evidently such substantive additions were written either along the margins of the copy sheet or on a separate piece of paper keyed to the text. But probably a good many minor alterations were made by Marston's simply noting the appropriate place where the compositor ought to consult manuscript—and this might account for their often being worse than the original errors. One of the best examples occurs on I1*v* (v.i.207), where the standing type has been altered to change 'soule lou'de of *Her*' to 'soule lou'de of him'. The italicised *Her* (Q1) shows that in the manuscript there was a name set off which the Q1 compositor probably interpreted as an abbreviation of *Hercules*.[88] But the phrase was undoubtedly 'soule lorde of *Himen*' (see commentary). Marston, had he written the corrected version in the margin, would have made certain that 'lord' and 'Himen' were unambiguous; but lacking either sufficient time or patience, he merely indicated where a correction should be made. And the Q2 compositor, consulting the manuscript, recognised the first three letters of 'Himen' and concluded that he was to correct a personal pronoun—'her' to 'him'. Another instance of this short-cut method of 'making satisfaction' occurs on F1*v* (III.i.447), where both compositors had trouble with Marston's Greek. Marston evidently wrote the motto *Anechou e apechou* in the original Greek characters, and the Q1 compositor, who seems to have known some Greek, transliterated the final Greek *u* as English *n*, an easy error to make. In Q2 the passage becomes a weird hybrid, based on the same manuscript but part Greek, part transliteration, part misreading of the stroke over the π as a nasal sign over the adjoining *a*.

A similar delegated (and undermined) authority probably

accounts for a curious paradox regarding punctuation. That of Q2 seems on the whole superior in that the idiosyncrasies of theatrical speech are more regularly indicated, particularly through the use of dashes to signify interrupted speech. Yet many of these 'improvements' are incorrect, and can only have been made by someone eager to make corrections yet not always fully aware of the meaning of the phrases involved. The obviously erroneous and misleading change on E3v (at III.i.294), a page typical otherwise of Q2's apparent superiority in punctuation, might serve as a cautionary example, showing that a general normalisation, even with the author's blessing, is not the same as authorial correction.

g. Some conclusions

I suggest, then, that we should regard the two quartos of *The Fawn* as being closely related indeed, with Q2 providing some corrections of obvious errors, some new errors caused by speed and carelessness, some additions made specially for the second issue, a fair amount of finicky alteration of no great importance by an author whose reasons for changing things are less sure than his determination to do so, and some independent alteration done by one or more compositors probably under the general sanction of the author. The kinds of revision vary from page to page, depending upon where and when the author was available. Yet it would be wrong for a modern editor simply to throw up his hands, no matter how complicated the relationship between rival claimants for title of 'copy text'. The evidence and reasoning I have presented clearly indicate that the closest thing we have to a copy text for *The Fawn* is Q1, but that each variant from Q2 can be weighed for its authority, according to our knowledge of the procedures of authorial and compositorial alterations during the printing of the two quartos.

The question remains: why a second quarto of *The Fawn* so remarkably soon after the first? The corrected 'faults' are not extensive, especially compared to other play quartos of the time. There are as many bawdy additions as there are excisions, and the few examples of simpler or clearer diction seem hardly enough to warrant belief that a second edition was made for their sake.[89] Some

remarks by Fredson Bowers provide the most probable explanation. Bowers, following up W. W. Greg's studies of second editions
printed from standing type, includes *The Fawn* in a category with
two plays by Dekker and another, *The Malcontent*, by Marston:

> For reasons which have never been satisfactorily determined but
> which seem to be associated with an unlawful attempt to save
> money by the use of standing type in a second edition planned
> from the very start of printing the first, some few books deliber-
> ately keep standing the type-pages of whole formes or gatherings
> according to a staggered pattern throughout the entire length of
> the book.[90]

We are dealing, then, with what amounts to a conspiracy—
apparently a successful one—to get around the make-work laws.
In anticipation of an unusually good market for the play, Thomas
Purfoot junior and John Marston decided from the beginning to
bring out an extra-large edition of *The Fawn*. But as the Stationers'
Company rules had since 1587 limited the number of copies in an
edition to not more than '1250 or 1500', the workmen would have
to be paid to do the job twice: set and pull one edition, then
distribute the type and start all over again. Purfoot, with his
co-operative author, decided for a less costly procedure.[91] This
would not be the first nor the last time Marston's activities would
risk a clash with the law. It gives an added twist to this comedy
about the foolishness of vice.

h. Later editions

The version of *The Fawn* that appeared in the 1633 octavo
collection of Marston's plays was based on a first quarto. Whoever
prepared the text for printing was an intelligent reader, and some
of his guesses in obscure passages are helpful, though certainly not
authoritative. The next editor, Charles Dilke in 1814, also based
his text on a first quarto. He contributed a few good annotations
and rather too many emendations. Two more editions of the play
came out in the nineteenth century. Halliwell's is part of his 1856
reprint of the Sheares collection (1633); he makes a small number
of changes. A. H. Bullen evidently consulted both quartos for his
edition of the *Works* (1887). He changes several prose passages to

verse, and provides good annotations, normalised nineteenth-century spelling and punctuation, and occasionally, like Dilke, unnecessary emendations. In this century, Harvey Wood's old-spelling edition uses Q2 as copy text, has numerous bibliographical faults, but is provided with very useful critical apparatus. Another old-spelling edition using Q2 as copy text is Philip London's unpublished University of Michigan thesis of 1964. It was the first attempt to establish a text on modern bibliographical principles but is, as the editor admits, eclectic, and fails to provide adequate security for several of its readings. This applies likewise to the edition in the Regents Renaissance Drama Series, by Gerald A. Smith, which uses Q1 for copy text but generally accepts Q2 readings when they differ substantively from Q1. These last two editions offer intelligent solutions for difficult readings not clarified in earlier editions.

The present edition follows the current general format of the Revels series, including the spelling '-èd' for final accented syllable, '-ed' rather than '-'d' for unaccented, even when the latter is the quarto spelling. All of the eleven copies of Q1 now known, and the seventeen of Q2, have been collated, either in the original or in photocopy.[92] With the co-operation of the libraries involved, I have been able to gather information on paper quality and water-marks sufficient (along with other evidence) to determine the order of printing with some confidence. I take Q1 as my copy text and consider each differing Q2 reading according to the probable circumstances and method of alteration, as described above. Variations in punctuation are collated when their effect is substantive. All other substantive variants are of course listed, and when a relationship is unusually complex it is discussed in the explanatory notes (e.g., for IV.i.340). Some obsolete forms have been silently normalised, e.g. 'indeed', which sometimes appears as 'in deed' in the quartos, but generally I have tried to keep emendations to a minimum. Of those that do appear in this edition, a good number are taken from the previous editors and annotators in the list below:

Q1   *Parasitaster, or The Fawne, as it hath bene divers times presented at the blacke Friars, by the Children of the Queenes Maiesties Reuels. . . .* 1606.

Q2   *Parasitaster, or The Fawne, as it hath been divers times presented at the blacke Friars, by the Children of the Queenes Maiesties Reuels, and since at Powles. . . . And now corrected of many faults, which by reason of the Authors absence, were let slip in the first edition. . . .* 1606.

TC   *The workes of Mr. Iohn Marston, Being Tragedies and Comedies, Collected into one Volume. . . .* 1633.
[The same edition, re-issued with new title-pages omitting Marston's name:] *Tragedies and comedies collected into one volvme. . . .* 1633.

Dilke   *Old Plays; being a continuation of Dodsley's Collection,* ed. Charles W. Dilke, 1816 [reprint of the edition of 1814), Vol. II.

JOH   *The Works of John Marston,* ed. J. O. Halliwell, 1856, Vol. II.

AHB   *The Works of John Marston,* ed. Arthur H. Bullen, 1887, Vol. II.

Deighton   *The Old Dramatists, Conjectural Readings,* K. Deighton, 1896.

Brereton   *Elizabethan Drama,* J. le Gay Brereton, 1909.

HHW   *The Plays of John Marston,* ed. H. Harvey Wood, 1934–39, Vol. II.

London   *John Marston's* Parasitaster or The Fawne: *A Critical Edition,* ed. Philip Whitney London, 1964 [unpublished].

Smith   *The Fawn,* ed. Gerald A. Smith, 1965.

NOTES

1 For a more complete biography, see G. K. Hunter's introduction to *The Malcontent*, in this series.
2 O. J. Campbell, *Comicall Satyre and Shakespeare's Troilus and Cressida* (1938), p. 149.
3 Campbell, *ibid.*, p. 181.
4 *Ibid.*, p. 36.
5 *The Cankered Muse* (1959), p. 20.
6 See Hardin Craig, 'The shackling of accidents: a study of Elizabethan tragedy', *P.Q.*, XIX (1940), 1–19.
7 Throughout his *John Marston, Satirist* (1961), for instance, Anthony Caputi applies this term to the playwright, but by the time he has modified it sufficiently to encompass Marston's many divergences from classical Stoics like Seneca or Neo-Stoics like Lipsius and du Vair, the term is virtually meaningless. See especially Caputi, *ibid.*, p. 72.
8 'Seneca in Elizabethan translation', in *Selected Essays* (1958), p. 72. See also 'Shakespeare and the Stoicism of Seneca', *ibid.*, p. 129.
9 'The convention of the Stoic hero as handled by Marston', *M.L.R.*, XXXIX (1944), 338–46.
10 'Anti-Stoicism in seventeenth- and early eighteenth-century England', *S.P.*, XLI (1944), 66–7.
11 *Ibid.*, p. 77.
12 *The Moral Vision of Jacobean Tragedy* (1960), pp. 157–8.
13 The two phrases are from David G. O'Neill's transcription of three and a half cancelled lines in Marston's father's will, which follow the bequest of his law-books: '. . . to hym that des[er]veth them not that ys my willful disobedyent sonne whoe I think will sell them rather then use them although I took paynes and had delighte therein god blesse hym and giue hym trewe knowledge of hymself and to foregoe his delighte in playes vayne studdyes and fooleryes. . . .' 'The commencement of Marston's career as a dramatist', *R.E.S.*, n.s. XXII (1971), 442–5.
14 Cf. Martial, II.lxxxvi:
> turpe est difficiles habere nugas
> et stultas labor est ineptiarum.
> scribat carmina circulis Palaemon:
> me raris iuvat auribus placere.

'''Tis degrading to undertake difficult trifles; and foolish is the labour spent in puerilities. Let Palaemon write poems for the general throng; my delight is to please listeners few and choice' (Ker, Loeb Library). Marston knew the passage well: he used the first line as the epigraph to *The Dutch Courtesan*.
15 Cf. Arnold Stein: 'As a fever is the body's medicine to help fight off contagion, satire is the medicine of the mind; and it attempts to externalize, to bring dissatisfaction out of the unconscious, and so provide relief.' 'Donne and the satiric spirit', *ELH*, XI (1944), 282.

16 It is probable that Marston, like Jonson, was aware of correspondences between tragedy and Old Comedy. Certainly *The Fawn* owes a debt, direct or indirect, to Greek conventions of character. In the terminology of the *Tractatus Coislianus* (*c.* fourth to second centuries B.C., derived from Aristotle's *Poetics*, *Rhetoric*, and *Ethics*), Gonzago and his courtiers typify the *alazon* of Old Comedy, self-aggrandising and self-deceived; as disguised duke, Hercules is the *eiron*, pretending to be less than he is and acting as an agent of the resolution of the plot; and as ostensible parasite, he is both *eiron* and *bomolochos* or buffoon, who was either an old rustic or witty slave, often with the special function of acting as prologue. See A. W. Pickard-Cambridge, *Dithyramb, Tragedy and Comedy* (1927), p. 270 n. 2, and Northrop Frye, *Anatomy of Criticism* (1968), 166–76, especially p. 174.

17 Mary Claire Randolph, 'The medical concept in English Renaissance satiric theory: its possible relationships and implications', *S.P.*, XXXVIII (1941), 136.

18 Herschel Baker, *The Wars of Truth* (1952), p. 54; and Theodore Spencer, 'John Marston', *The Criterion*, XIII (1934), 588.

19 See Peter Ure, 'A note on "Opinion" in Daniel, Greville and Chapman', *M.L.R.*, XLVI (1951), 332 and n.; also L. I. Bredvold, 'The naturalism of Donne', *J.E.G.P.*, XXII (1923), 474–5, 500.

20 'John Marston, Moralist', *ELH*, XX (1953), 186–7.

21 *Ibid.*, 190.

22 Most of these were brought to light in a series of notes published in *N & Q* by Charles Crawford, in 1905 and 1906, and gathered together in his *Collectanea*, second series (1907). More have been found by A. J. Axelrad (*Un Malcontent Elizabéthain* [1955]), and various Marston editors; see especially M. L. Wine's Appendix A to his edition of *The Dutch Courtesan* in the Regents Renaissance Drama series (1965), 112–20.

23 See the note to III.i.447 in this edition.

24 '*Twelfth Night* and the morality of indulgence', *The Sewanee Review*, LXVII (1959), 220–38.

25 *Ibid.*, 228.

26 Kernan, *ibid.*, p. 191 n.

27 The reference is to the Revels edition; Bullen emends the Qq's 'burstes' to 'burst'.

28 Montaigne again: '*Belike we must be incontinent that we may be continent, burning is quenched by fire*' (*Essays*, III, v, 97). Curing like by like, rather than by opposites, was a known, though not universally accepted, medical principle by the sixteenth century. See Allen G. Debus, *The English Paracelsians* (1965), p. 95.

29 '*One must survay his faultes and study them, ere he be able to repeat them. Those which hide them from others, commonly conceal them also from themselves; and esteme them not sufficiently hidden, if themselves see them. They withdraw and disguise them from their owne consciences.*' Montaigne, *Essays*, III, v, 78.

30 *Ibid.*, II, viii, 68.

31 'Donne, Montaigne, and natural law', *J.E.G.P.*, LV (1956), 214. See also Ornstein's *The Moral Vision of Jacobean Tragedy*, p. 39, where he quotes the above passage.

32 Spencer, *ibid.*, 588–9.

33 The dramatists of the period are often more philosophically honest in their casually written comedies than in their tragedies, since tragedy expects certain duties of its soldiers. Yet it is tempting to see *The Insatiate Countess*, with its chronicle of indulgence gone berserk and an ending something like an apotheosis of passion through its very excess, as an aborted essay to provide *Sophonisba* with its dialectical counterpart, as Marston had complemented *The Malcontent* with *The Fawn*. Our inadequate knowledge about the dating of Marston's work on *The Insatiate Countess* and the relative proportions contributed by himself and Barksted make this difficult to pursue at present.

34 *Un Malcontent Elizabéthain* (1955), p. 296.

35 Besides Marston's two plays, Shakespeare's *Measure for Measure* and Middleton's *Phoenix* fit this pattern.

36 A similar sense of 'courtship' as flattery (in this case more strictly false compliment) can be found in Middleton's *The Family of Love* (1602), III.iii.14–15: 'Courtship? cartship! for the tongues of complimenters run on wheels....' Like *The Fawn*, this play also is concerned with the naturalness of sexual appetite and careerism at court, and there is a mock trial as well. But Middleton's piece is a far less intelligible mixture than Marston's.

37 See especially Morse S. Allen, *The Satire of John Marston* (1920), p. 153.

38 'The thought must strike Hercules,' says Brian Gibbons, 'that neither the courtiers ... nor his son are deceived by his disguise' (*Jacobean City Comedy* [1968], p. 94). The conjecture is unacceptable. If struck by the thought, Hercules keeps it well hidden; nor do Tiberio and the courtiers disclose their recognition. (The latter could hardly be expected to identify a disguised foreigner.)

39 'John Marston's *Fawn*: A saturnalian satire', *S.E.L.*, IX (1969), 335–50, p. 343. It cannot be denied, however, that typesetting plays its part in this: throughout old and new editions of *The Malcontent*, speech heads for Altofronto/Malevole appear as *Mal.*; in *The Fawn*, Hercules/Faunus is always *Her.* or a variant. If these reflect manuscript practice, they give a useful reflection of Marston's own attitude towards the two characters. (Also see collation for III.i.0.1.)

40 Though clear, the principle is not simple. For Hercules to satisfy his latent wildness late rather than never satisfies proportion, but to do so by matching December with May overrides and cancels this proportion. Hercules must therefore transfer his energies to another outlet.

41 See John Peter, *Complaint and Satire in Early English Literature* (1956), pp. 86–91, for Complaint conventions regarding women.

42 *Essays*, III, v, 154. See also Rosalie Colie, *Paradoxia Epidemica* (1966), pp. 102–3, on humanist defences of women.

43 Edition of *The Malcontent* in *Jacobean Drama I* (1968), p. 475 n.

44 As R. B. Parker puts it, '... in a world without virtuous characters, the

rogues have to be made to punish each other.' 'Middleton's experiments with comedy and judgement', in *Jacobean Theatre* (Stratford-upon-Avon Studies I) (1960), p. 185. Thus we are introduced to the Court of Urbin in I.ii. without Hercules being present. We are compelled to pick our way through moral and other judgements which range from astute to merely cynical; the beginning of Act II works the same way. With the ostensible norm-establishing character Hercules usually speaking as a flatterer, the courtiers must function doubly as fairly reliable critics and objects of criticism. In practice the shifting hierarchy creates little difficulty.

45 See Kaplan, *ibid.*, *passim.*

46 When Gonzago asks, 'Of whose invention is this parliament?' Hercules replies, 'Ours' (V.i.127–8). It is thus faintly possible that Gonzago himself is the co-inventor, in which case the quotation is egotistically rhetorical, and the effect of the Parliament all the more ironic.

47 Dondolo functions largely as a newsvendor and a harbinger of entertainment to come. Though much of his speech is professional chatter, at least twice his jokes make important points about the role of communication in this play. At one point he describes his leave-taking—'in most sweet terms without any sense, and with most fair looks without any good meaning'—as 'most courtlike' (IV.i.276–7). And he notes the irony of Dulcimel's praise of her father's wisdom at the end of his (and Hercules') Court of Cupid, which could have been called 'All Flatterers but the Flatterer', or 'All Fools but the Fool'.

48 We know too little about the stage at the second Blackfriars, let alone Paul's, to be certain, but movable ships did appear frequently in pageantry, at least as early as the fourteenth century, and as often on land as on water. It is not clear which it was in Anthony Munday's Lord Mayor's Show of 1602, but the wheeled ship he used in that of 1616 (for which we have an excellent drawing) would well suit the purposes of *The Fawn*. See Glynn Wickham, *Early English Stages 1300 to 1600*, Vol. II, part I (1963), 224, plate XXVIII No. 40, and also Vol. I (1959), plates XIII No. 18 and XIX No. 25. Trees made frequent emblematic appearances in pageantry, and occasional ones in the theatre proper. For example, one rises and sinks in *The Arraignment of Paris*, and in *Eastward Ho* (partly Marston's, roughly contemporaneous with *The Fawn*, and also staged at Blackfriars), Slitgut climbs a tree in IV.i. to report on the activities of a ship which is, however, almost certainly offstage. See Glynn Wickham, Vol. II part I, 216–17, and David Bergeron, *English Civic Pageantry 1558–1642* (1971), p. 268. If we follow Richard Hosley's reconstruction of the second Blackfriars theatre (*The Revels History of Drama in English*, III [1975], 197–226), the ship would probably enter from the centre door of the three in the tiring-house façade.

49 Kaplan, *ibid.*, 338. 'Saturnalia is here used to define what C. L. Barber describes as a process of "clarification through release" in *Shakespeare's Festive Comedy: A Study of Dramatic Form and its Relationship to Social Custom* (Princeton, 1959).' *Ibid.*, 337 n.

50 'The use of the Middle Temple's Christmas Revels in Marston's *The Fawne*', *S.P.*, LXIV (1967), 199–209.
51 *John Marston of the Middle Temple* (1969).
52 *Ibid.*, pp. 227–9.
53 Edward Arber, ed., *A Transcript of the Registers of the Company of Stationers of London, 1554–1640* (1875–1894), III, 316.
54 Caputi, *ibid.*, pp. 219–20.
55 *Ibid.*, p. 267.
56 *Ibid.*, p. 268.
57 *Die Schauspiele der englischen Komödianten* (*c.* 1888), p. 334.
58 *Das Danziger Theater im 16. und 17. Jahrhundert* (1895), pp. 171–218.
59 *Ibid.*, pp. 183–4.
60 *Ibid.*, pp. 174, 199.
61 Finkelpearl, *ibid.*, pp. 223–4.
62 Gerard Langbaine, *An Account of the English Dramatic Poets* (1691), p. 351.
63 But note the similarity between Hercules' first soliloquy (I.i.37–62) and old Demea's resolve to change his harsh ways to a manner of complaisance: 'nam ego vitam duram quam vixi usque adhuc / prope iam excurso spatio omitto' (*Adelphi*, v.iv.859–60). 'The hard life, which up to now I have lived, now that my race is almost run I renounce' (transl. John Sargeaunt in Loeb Library edition, 1925). The connection between the two plays was first suggested by Paul Becker, *Das Verhältnis von John Marstons 'What You Will' zu Plautus 'Amphitruo' und Sforza d'Oddis 'I Morti Vivi'* (1904), p. 11.
64 Compare especially *All Fools* II.i.147–78 with *The Fawn* V.i.397–416; also *The Fawn* III.i.334–5 with *All Fools* V.ii.205–6: 'Young men think old men fools; but old men know young men are fools.' Gostanzo and Gonzago also share an overweening pride in their own eloquence.
65 See Commentary for II.i.149, IV.i.90, IV.i.318–20, IV.i.338, v.i.19–20. A bad quarto of *Wiv.* was published in 1602.
66 See R. C. Bald, 'The chronology of Thomas Middleton's plays', *M.L.R.*, XXXII (1937), 33–43, and Anthony Covatta, *Thomas Middleton's City Comedies* (1973), which provides a comparative chart of dates given to seven Middleton plays (including *The Phoenix*) by several authorities (p. 171).
67 For the tradition of the disguised ruler, going back through Sir Thomas Elyot's *The Image of Governaunce* (1541) to the Roman Emperor Alexander Severus, see Mary Lascelles, 'Sir Thomas Elyot and the legend of Alexander Severus', *R.E.S.*, N.S. II (1951), 305–18, and J. W. Lever's useful section on the subject in his introduction to the Arden *Measure for Measure* (1965), xliv–li. The *Arabian Nights*, which provides us with the more familiar story of the Caliph of Baghdad, did not receive a European translation till the eighteenth century.
68 See *Poems*, pp. 282, 365.
69 Finkelpearl, 'The use of the Middle Temple's Christmas Revels in Marston's *The Fawne*'. The case is made again in chapter XIII of his *John Marston of the Middle Temple*.

70 *Le Prince d'Amour* (1660).

71 *The Origins and Sources of the 'Courts of Love'* (1898), p. 267.

72 *Essays*, III, v, 71–154.

73 *The Fawn*, 'To My Equal Reader', 26.

74 On A2, an ornamental border has been removed from the top of the page and the 'T' in the Preface title has been changed to italic.

   Substantially retained from Q1 are A1, A1v (blank), A2, A2v, A3v, C1; all of both inner and outer formes of D; the inner forme of G, and parts of G1 and G3 of the outer forme; the inner forme of H, the outer forme of I, and much of each page of the inner forme of I. Besides additions and corrections to the retained formes, the following are newly set: A3, A4, A4v, both formes of B; both formes of C except for C1, both formes of E, both formes of F; G2v much of G1 and G3, G4v; the outer forme of H, and parts of each page of the inner forme of I. Some pages, such as G3, I3v and I4, are nightmarish mixtures of standing type, re-setting, and extensive correction of standing type.

75 E. K. Chambers, *The Elizabethan Stage* (1923), III, p. 51.

76 'An explanation for the two editions of Marston's *The Fawn*', *S.P.*, XL (1943), 28.

77 *Ibid.*, p. 29.

78 *Loc. cit.* We should add, however, that the condition of the manuscript was not consistent throughout, and that the second half was in a rougher state than the first.

79 Specially worth noting are errors on C2, C2v, E3v, E4v, and F3, which involve names, most of them inaccurate ascriptions of speeches, caused by crowding in the author's manuscript. A second compositor would be less liable to challenge the placing or spelling of names in printed copy than punctuation or even phraseology.

80 In one instance, where Q1 exists in both corrected and uncorrected states, copy for Q2 was evidently the uncorrected state. See this edition's collation for IV.i.107 and 108, and commentary for 107–11.

81 There is a similar division in *The Dutch Courtesan*, produced the previous year by the same printer, Thomas Purfoot junior.

82 One spelling variation might support this and indicate that two compositors were involved. The spelling of 'beauty' with 'bew-' occurs only in the outer forme of F (F1 and F2v), and the normal spelling on F2: all three instances are in verse, and so uninfluenced by exigencies of space.

83 *The Dutch Courtesan* provides more parallels here. Again the bibliographical characteristics show that the operation is split between two parts, A–E and F–H, with A–E using two skeletons, alternating them for inner and outer formes, and F–H using one skeleton throughout, but with the perfect regularity described by Fredson Bowers in 'Headlines in early books', *English Institute Annual, 1941* (1942), p. 190.

84 Right-hand alignment of such doubled lines occurs nowhere else in the book. Usually they are approximately centred, or given a breathing space of 1 to 1.5 cm. after the last word of the previous speech.

85 There might be a precedent for this, too, in Purfoot's practice, if Peter Davison's theory is correct that an extra compositor gave spot

help in setting A–E of *The Dutch Courtesan*. See his edition (1968), p. 13.

86 The few copies that have uncorrected inner formes for G also use the unwatermarked Q1 paper that appears nowhere else in Q2 except sheet D in some copies; D, printed from corrected standing type, was the first of A–D to be printed in Q2. Paper tests, which were made on all extant copies of the two quartos, establish also that though the first sheet of Q1 might have been set up earlier than others in A–D, the forme was kept unprinted till most if not all of Q1 was run off, a common practice at the time.

87 There is a similar clean-up at D1*v* (II.i.386). But Q2 is as often the saucier text: see the variants for IV.i.32 (F3) and IV.i.404 (G3*v*).

88 Surviving examples of Marston's handwriting are normally in italic (including sections of the *Ashby Entertainment*, Huntington E. L. 34.39), so the usual way of setting off names and foreign words in play MSS—switching from secretary hand to italic—would not apply. Though it is impossible to determine what method Marston employed, the Q1 reading clearly indicates that he had one.

89 Halstead's theory, that the purpose of Q2 was mainly to announce the forthcoming edition of Marston's *Sophonisba*, may be dismissed on typographical grounds alone. The rubric *Sophonisba* does not appear at all in the Chapin copy of Q2, and was evidently an afterthought added during the printing process, since it appears in the wrong place in some other copies. W. L. Halstead, *ibid.*, p. 32.

90 Fredson Bowers, *Principles of Bibliographical Description* (1949), p. 110. In a footnote specifically keyed to his mention of *The Fawn*, Bowers refers to Greg's article, '"The Honest Whore" or "The Converted Courtezan"', *The Library*, fourth series, XV (1935), 54–60. Greg's hypothesis is that such editions were the results of surpluses of sheets after the printing of the first edition, with new settings to make up the missing sheets for further copies. But, as Greg says, '[t]he oddments (and reprinted sheets) would naturally not be very numerous', and this makes the relevance of his hypothesis to *The Fawn* remote indeed. The two Q1 copies with F sheets from Q2 suggest quite the opposite, that extra printings of some Q2 sheets could make up for short supply in Q1.

91 Spelling differences between Q1 and Q2 in reset sections are so marked that it is unlikely that any compositor reset his former portion. Quite possibly Purfoot shifted his workmen about deliberately so that no one knew the extent of standing type. There is always the added possibility that a second printing shop was involved (which would not alter the argument; the work loads would have been split between two shops rather than between two groups in the same shop). G. K. Hunter entertains this possibility in the printing of *The Malcontent*. See his introduction to the Revels edition (1975), p. xxxii n. 1.

92 The copy of Q2 in the University of Texas Library contains a few anomalous readings which defy bibliographical analysis. On A2 recto the last line of text, the signature, and the catchword differ in form from all other copies. On A2*v* and A3*v* catchwords are provided, as in

no other copies of either quarto (but precisely as in the 1633 Sheares edition). And most of the running titles through signatures H and I are new, though there is no evidence of the type shift which normally occurs in such cases and though both formes are involved haphazardly. The copy was formerly in the library of T. J. Wise, and the sort of inquiry which it invites is, though fascinating, outside the concerns of this edition.

Copies of Q1 collated (the first seven in the original): Folger, British Library (three), Victoria and Albert Museum, Earl of Verulam, Carl Pforzheimer, Henry E. Huntington, Boston Public. Copies of Q2 collated (the first eight in the original): Folger (two), Congress, New York Public, British Library, Victoria and Albert Museum, Bodleian, Eton, Harvard, University College (London), Edinburgh University, Henry E. Huntington, University of Illinois, Chapin, Newberry, University of Texas, Boston Public.

PARASITASTER,

OR

THE FAWNE,

AS
IT HATH BENE DIVERS
times prefented at the blacke Friars, by the Children of the Queenes
Maiefties Reuels.

Written
By Iohn Marston.

AT LONDON
Printed by T. P. for W. C.
1606.

PARASITASTER,

OR

THE FAWNE,

AS

IT HATH BEEN DIVERS TIMES PRE-
fented at the blacke Friars, by the Children of the
Queenes Maiefties Reuels, and fince at Powles.

Written
By IOHN MARSTON.

And now corrected of many faults, which by reafon of the Authors abfence, were let flip in the firft edition.

AT LONDON
Printed by T. P. for W. C.
1606.

THE FAWN

To My Equal Reader

I have ever more endeavoured to know myself than to be
known of others, and rather to be unpartially beloved of all,
than factiously to be admired of a few; yet so powerfully
have I been enticed with the delights of poetry, and (I must
ingeniously confess) above better desert so fortunate in these   5
stage-pleasings, that (let my resolutions be never so fixed to
call mine eyes into myself) I much fear that most lamentable
death of him,

> *Qui nimis notus omnibus,*
> *Ignotus moritur sibi.*—Seneca.   10

But since the over-vehement pursuit of these delights
hath been the sickness of my youth, and now is grown to be
the vice of my firmer age, since to satisfy others I neglect
myself, let it be the courtesy of my peruser rather to pity my
self-hindering labours than to malice me; and let him be   15

0.1. *Equal*] impartial, fair.

1–2. *I . . . others*] Theodore Spencer quotes this passage to show that
'there is something pathetic in Marston's imitations of Montaigne' ('John
Marston', *The Criterion*, XIII [1934], 597). But the sentiment was a
Renaissance commonplace, and appears in Marston before Florio's
Montaigne was published, e.g. *CS.*, 'To Detraction . . .', 17–22, and *SV.*,
'To him that hath perused me', 24–8.

5. *ingeniously*] ingenuously.

6. *stage-pleasings*] The compound form is a nonce usage not recorded in
O.E.D., which defines 'pleasing' (sb. sense †3) as 'A source of pleasure; an
object of delight'. Marston was specially fond of this sort of coinage, but
since most are nonce usages, I gloss only those that might give difficulty.
For a more complete listing of Marston's compound words passed over by
O.E.D., see Cross, *passim*.

7. *call . . . myself*] subject myself to strict self-examination.

9–10.] 'who, but too well known to all, dies to himself unknown'
(F. J. Miller); *Thyestes*, 402–3 (Loeb Library). This is part of a passage
which Marston had already used in *AM.* (HHW, I, 44).

13. *firmer age*] the more mature age I have now reached. The contrast
between age and youth, in both its serious and comic aspects, is one of the
play's minor themes.

15. *malice*] The verb is used in Marston's *DC.* (HHW, II, 129) in the
sense of 'to malign', a meaning unrecorded in *O.E.D.* (Cross, *N&Q*, CC
[1955], 336). Yet here it may well be used in a sense more familiar in
Marston's time: 'to regard with malice', or 'to entertain with malice'.

pleased to be my reader, and not my interpreter, since I
would fain reserve that office in my own hands, it being my
daily prayer: *Absit a jocorum nostrorum simplicitate malignus
interpres.*—Martial.

If any shall wonder why I print a comedy, whose life   20
rests much in the actors' voice, let such know that it cannot
avoid publishing; let it therefore stand with good excuse that
I have been my own setter out.

If any desire to understand the scope of my comedy,
know it hath the same limits which Juvenal gives to his   25
satires:

    Quicquid agunt homines, votum, timor, ira, voluptas,
    Gaudia, discursus, nostri farrago libelli est.—Juvenal.

As for the factious malice and studied detractions of some
few that tread in the same path with me, let all know I most   30

---

21. actors'] *Dilke;* Actors *Qq;* actor's *AHB.*

18–19. Absit . . . interpres.] 'May the frankness of my jests find no
malicious interpreter' (W. C. A. Ker). From the prose preface to Book I
of the *Epigrams* (Loeb Library). Marston returns to this passage in the
Prologue.
21. *actors' voice*] When Marston wrote 'Actors voice' (Qq), I doubt whether
he firmly 'meant' the plural or the singular (any more than, say, Marvell
meant only 'the war's' *or* 'the wars' [and fortune's son] in 'An Horatian
Ode', 113). The present mix is the closest that modern spelling gets to the
original idea.
23. *setter out*] publisher.
27–8.] 'All the doings of mankind, their vows, their fears, their angers
and their pleasures, their joys and goings to and fro, shall form the motley
subject of my page' (G. G. Ramsay); Satire I, 85–6 (Loeb Library). A
century later Steele used this as the motto for *The Tatler.*
29. *studied*] *O.E.D.*'s first example of this sense ('carefully contrived, . . .
deliberate') is from *Ant.* (1606–7) IV.ii.140, which *The Fawn* antedates.
29–30. *some few*] Who these 'few' were is difficult to ascertain, since
quarrelling seems to have been one of Marston's hobbies. His changing
'minions' to 'minion' (l. 45, below), if the change is indeed his, narrows
the object of attack even more. The quarrel with Jonson, patched up by
the time Marston wrote his complimentary dedication to *Malc.* and
probably re-opened by the time of the slyly digging address to the reader
in *Soph.*, was probably exacerbated by the *Eastward Ho* affair. And the
Hall flyting was long gone. The statement may be only a manifestation of
the general stance taken by the author in this preface.

easily neglect them, and (carelessly slumbering to their
vicious endeavours) smile heartily at their self-hurting baseness. My bosom friend, good Epictetus, makes me easily to
contemn all such men's malice: since other men's tongues
are not within my teeth, why should I hope to govern them ?   35
For mine own interest for once, let this be printed: that of
men of my own addiction, I love most, pity some, hate none;
for let me truly say it, I once only loved myself for loving
them, and surely I shall ever rest so constant to my first
affection that let their ungentle combinings, discourteous   40
whisperings, never so treacherously labour to undermine my
unfenced reputation, I shall (as long as I have being) love the
least of their graces, and only pity the greatest of their vices.

And now to kill envy, know you that affect to be the only
minion of Phoebus, I am not so blushlessly ambitious as to   45
hope to gain any the least supreme eminency among you; I
affect not only the *'Euge' tuum et 'Belle' !*—'tis not my
fashion to think no writer virtuously confident that is not
swellingly impudent. Nor do I labour to be held the only

45. minion] *Q2;* Minions *Q1.*

---

33. *Epictetus*] Stoic philosopher whose inclination to resignation rather
than to firm-jawed endurance was becoming more attractive to Marston.

36. *for once*] once and for all; cf. I.ii.185.

37. *addiction*] bent, inclination. Cf. II.i.527 n., for a slightly different
sense.

42. *unfenced*] unprotected; the context implies both 'open to attack' and
'needing no defence'.

44. *envy*] ill-will, enmity.

affect] assume ostentatiously. In this sense the earliest *O.E.D.* example
is 1605; but with infinitive, with the sense 'to profess', the earliest *O.E.D.*
example is 1720.

45. *minion*] Though there are grammatical difficulties, the change from
the plural 'minions' to the singular seems to have been deliberate.
This adds an unusually harsh note to a preface otherwise remarkably
conciliatory.

47. 'Euge' tuum et 'Belle'] 'Your "Bravo!" and your "Beautiful!"'
(G. G. Ramsay); Persius, Sat. I, 49 (Loeb Library).

49. *swellingly impudent*] arrogantly shameless.

spirit whose poems may be thought worthy to be kept in   50
cedar chests:

> *Heliconidasque pallidamque Pyrenen*
> *Illis relinquo quorum imagines lambunt*
> *Hederae sequaces. . . .*—Persius.

He that pursues fame shall, for me, without any rival have   55
breath enough—I esteem felicity to be a more solid content-
ment; only let it be lawful for me, with unaffected modesty
and full thought, to end boldly with that of Persius:

> *. . . Ipse semipaganus*
> *Ad sacra vatum carmen affero nostrum.*—Persius.   60

>   JO. MARSTON.

Reader, know I have perused this copy to make some satisfaction for the first faulty impression; yet so urgent hath
been my business that some errors have still passed, which
thy discretion may amend. Comedies are writ to be spoken,   65
not read: remember the life of these things consists in action;

62–70.] *Q2; not in Q1.*

---

51. *cedar chests*] The allusion is either to Horace's *Ars Poetica*, 330–3,
or Persius's later use of the idea in Sat. 1, 41–3.

52–4.] 'The maidens of Mount Helicon, and the blanching waters of
Pirene, I give up to the gentlemen round whose busts the clinging ivy
twines' (Ramsay); Prologue to *Satires*, 4–6. The 'maidens' are the Muses;
'give up' translates 'remitto', which is the usually accepted reading, though
Marston's 'relinquo' (bequeath) also has authority. See W. V. Clausen's
preface to the Oxford edition (1959), v–xiv.

58. *full*] one of Marston's favourite words, and like some others (e.g.
'only') frequently of vague significance. Here, and again at 1.ii.86, it
seems to mean 'well-weighed', 'serious'. The closest *O.E.D.* sense is 6:
sufficient, satisfying.

59–60.] This completes the previous passage in the Prologue to
Persius's *Satires*, 6–7: 'It is but as a half-member of the community that
I bring my lay to the holy feast of the bards.' Marston reminds us that he
is a gentleman, and not, like other men of his 'addiction', one that must
write for a living.

62. *this copy*] probably no single bound copy, but unbound sheets of Q1
(mostly, but not all, in a corrected state), and perhaps also some unbound
Q2 sheets. See Introduction, pp. 43–50.

65–9. *Comedies . . . perusal.*] Besides demonstrating Marston's apprecia-
tion of the theatrical aspects of his medium, the passage shows a conventional evaluation of tragedy as a genre more worthy of serious study.

and for your such courteous survey of my pen, I will present
a tragedy★ to you which shall boldly abide the most curious
perusal.

★ *Sophonisba*

---

70. *Sophonisba.*] *so this ed.; in margin to the left of l. 68–9 Q2 corr.; in
margin to the left of l. 62 Q2 uncorr.; not in Chapin copy.*

Prologus

Let those once know that here with malice lurk,
'Tis base to be too wise in others' work.
The rest, sit thus saluted:
Spectators, know you may with freest faces
Behold this scene, for here no rude disgraces   5
Shall taint a public or a private name;
This pen at viler rate doth value fame
Than at the price of others' infamy
To purchase it. Let others dare the rope;
Your modest pleasure is our author's scope.   10
The hurdle and the rack to them he leaves
That have naught left to be accompted any

2. others'] *AHB;* others *Qq;* other's *Dilke.*

[Prologus] 2. *'Tis base . . . work.*] Really a paraphrase of the second half
of the sentence in Martial's Preface from which Marston took ll. 17–18 of
'To My Equal Reader' 'inprobe facit qui in alieno libro ingeniosus est.'
'It is a shameless business when anyone exercises his ingenuity on another
man's book' (W. C. A. Ker, Loeb Library). Though the disclaimer (some-
what disingenuous) to malice is common enough among writers of
Marston's period, he seems to have decided to employ a version close to
Martial's in the Preface to the *Epigrams.*

5. *scene*] performance.

7–9. *This pen . . . purchase it.*] 'Mihi fama vilius constet.' 'May my fame
be bought at lesser cost' (Ker). Martial's Preface again.

9. *dare the rope*] not just figuratively. Cf. Weever's *The Whipping of the
Satyre,* published five years earlier: 'Was not one hang'd of late for
libelling ? / Yes questionlesse. And you deserve the same' (ll. 331–2).

10. *modest*] moderate, temperate, as opposed to self-indulgent.

11. *hurdle*] 'A kind of frame or sledge on which traitors used to be
drawn through the streets to execution' (*O.E.D.*).

rack] instrument of torture upon which victims were stretched.

12–13. *That have . . . not being*] that have no way of asserting their
existence but through death.

12. *accompted*] accounted.

But by not being. Nor doth he hope to win
Your louder hand with that most common sin
Of vulgar pens, rank bawdry, that smells   15
Even through your masks, *usque ad nauseam*;
The Venus of this scene doth loathe to wear
So vile, so common, so immodest clothings.
But if the nimble form of comedy,
Mere spectacle of life and public manners,   20
May gracefully arrive to your pleased ears,
We boldly dare the utmost death of fears.
For we do know that this most fair-filled room
Is loaden with most Attic judgements, ablest spirits,
Than whom there are none more exact, full, strong,   25
Yet none more soft, benign in censuring;
I know there's not one ass in all this presence,
Not one calumnious rascal or base villain
Of emptiest merit, that would tax and slander
If innocency herself should write—not one, we know't.   30
O you are all the very breath of Phoebus:

14. louder] *Q2;* Laud or *Q1.*   16. through] *edd.;* thorough *Qq.*

---

14. *louder hand*] The Q1 reading, 'Laud or hand', seems acceptable, but
Q2's comparative form is typical of Marston. 'Hand' as 'applause' is
recorded only in the Supplement to the third edition of *S.O.D.*, with the
date 1890. But see *MND.*, v.i.424: 'Give me your hands, if we be friends.'

16. *masks*] The half-mask was common apparel for gentlewomen of the
day.

usque ad nauseam] quite to the point of nausea.

17. *Venus*] not simply the goddess, but the essential presiding quality
or grace. Cf. II.i.141, and III.i.37.

19–21.] Marston's attitude towards the function of comedy seems to
have gone through a continuous mellowing process. Cf. especially the
Induction to *WYW.* and the Prologue to *DC.*

20. *mere*] Elsewhere in the play this means 'absolute', 'pure'; but here
the modern sense of 'nothing more than' is probably meant.

22. *death of fears*] apparently means: the most fearful of deaths.

24. *Attic*] refined, classical. Marston here antedates the first *O.E.D.*
example. See Cross, *N&Q*, CCIII (1958) 103.

26. *censuring*] judging.

27. *presence*] assembly, company.

In your pleased gracings all the true life blood
Of our poor author lives; you are his very graces.
   Now if that any wonder why he's drawn
   To such base soothings, know his play's—*The Fawn*.   35

33. graces.] *Q2;* grace, *Q1.*   34. that] *Q2; not in Q1.*

---

32. *gracings*] gracious acceptance.
35. The Fawn] fawner, parasite, sycophant. *O.E.D.*'s only example is
from 1635. Jonson already used the word in *Poetaster* (1601): '*Horace*, that
goat-footed enuious slaue; hee's turn'd fawne now, an informer, the rogue.'
Poetaster, IV.vii.9–10. But Marston's sense seems different. The alternative name for the play, given precedence on the quarto title-page, is
Parasitaster. As Dilke pointed out, the word occurs in Terence's *Adelphi*,
as a diminutive of contempt. In English, the suffix usually produces a
pejorative connotation, as it does in *Poetaster*; but here it suggests
incomplete resemblance. Faunus is only apparently a parasite, not truly so.

INTERLOCUTORS

HERCULES, (*disguised*, FAUNUS) *Duke of Ferrara.*

GONZAGO, *Duke of Urbin, a weak lord of a self-admiring wisdom.*

TIBERIO, *son to Hercules.*

DULCIMEL, *daughter to Gonzago.*

PHILOCALIA, *an honorable learned lady, companion to the*   5
Princess Dulcimel.

GRANUFFO, *a silent lord.*

DON ZUCCONE, *a causelessly jealous lord.*

DONNA ZOYA, *a virtuous, fair, witty lady, his wife.*

SIR AMOROSO DEBILE-DOSSO, *a sickly knight.*   10

---

2. *a . . . wisdom.*] *Q2; not in Q1.*

Interlocutors] speakers, *dramatis personae.*

1. *Hercules*] The character is not based on any account of Ercole d'Este of Ferrara (e.g. that in Thomas's *Historye of Italye*, reprinted by Halliwell and Bullen), but since one of the play's subjects is the continuation of the ducal line of Ferrara, there may still be historical connotations. In 1597 Alfonso d'Este died. He was the son of Ercole and the great grandson of an earlier Ercole. All three of his marriages had been childless, as a result of which Ferrara passed to Pope Clement VIII. Since the Papacy had refused permission to Alfonso's brother to relinquish holy orders and marry, the issue was something of an international scandal at the time. For Joel Kaplan's theory that Marston is working with the myth of the labours of Hercules, see Introduction, pp. 30–1.

Faunus] Marston had used the name in *SV.*, III, 143–6, but there seems to be no relationship between the two uses. In *SV.*, Faunus is 'an insanely enthusiastic huntsman' (Davenport). See *Poems*, p. 115, and p. 297 (n.).

2. weak] lacking strength of mind; credulous.

4. *Dulcimel*] 'Dolcemelle, a musicalle instrument called a Dulcimell or Dulcimer. Also hony sweet. Also vsed for a mans pillicock [penis]' Florio (1611).

5. *Philocalia*] 'Philocalia, delight in, or loue of fairenesse' Florio (1611).

7. *Granuffo*] perhaps Florio's 'gramuffo', 'a kind of staring, stately, staulking, puffing looke'. Or 'Granfo', which apparently could be 'vsed also for a silly gull or simple foole'.

8. *Zuccone*] 'Zuccone, a shauen pate, a notted skull. Also a logarhead, a gullish pate' Florio (1611); Florio (1598) includes 'a notted poule, a pouled pate, a gull, a ninnie, a ioult-head'.

9. *Zoya*] 'Zoia, often used for Gioia' Florio (1611). 'Goia', in turn, is defined as 'a ioy, a gemme, a iewell, or any precious thing. Also iouissance, delight, hearts-ease, or comfort'.

10. *Amoroso*] '[A] he loue or louer' Florio (1611).

DONNA GARBETZA, *his lady.*

HEROD FRAPPATORE, *brother to Sir Amoroso and a vicious braggart.*

NYMPHADORO, *a young courtier and a common lover.*

DONDOLO, *a bald fool.* 15

RENALDO, *brother to Hercules.*

POVEIA,
DONETTA, } *two ladies, attendants on Dulcimel.*

PUTTOTTA, *a poor laundress of the court that washeth and diets footmen.* 20

Pages.

[CUPID.]

Debile] 'weak, feeble, faint' Florio (1611).

Dosso] 'the backe of a man or any other creature' Florio (1611). The naming of Sir Amoroso, who is sexually bankrupt, accords with the contemporary convention of associating virility with the strength of one's back.

11. *Garbetza*] Evidently only the first part of Florio's definition applies: 'Garbezza, Sowrenes, tartnes, sharpenes. Also grace comelines, neatnes, handsomenes, or decorum, featness, prettiness.'

12. *Herod Frappatore*] The first name comes from English dramatic tradition, where Herod is always the great ranter and boaster. The Italian 'frappatore' is a good match: 'a bragger, a boaster, a vanter, a craker. Also a craftie pratler, a cunnicatcher, a cheater. Also a beater, a banger' Florio (1611). Herod is twice given the surname 'Baldanzozo', which has a similar meaning: 'bold, hardie, confident, assured, saucie, presumptuous, vndanted, licentious' Florio (1611).

14. *Nymphadoro*] 'Nimfadoro, an effeminate fellow, a spruce ladies courting fellow' Florio (1611).

15. *Dondolo*] 'Dondolo, a shallow-pate, a silly gull' Florio (1611). 'A gull, a foole, a thing to make sport' Florio (1598).

17. *Poveia*] 'Poueia, a Butter-flie or a Ladie-bird' Florio (1611).

18. *Donetta*] 'Donnetta, a little woman' Florio (1611). But in the 1598 edition, the definition continues: 'also as much as goodie flurt, or goodie driggle-draggle'.

19. *Puttotta*] 'Puttotta, a handsome plum cheeked wench' Florio (1611). Marston also puns on 'potato' (and its supposed aphrodisiac qualities), IV.i.41.

washeth] washes clothes for; *O.E.D.*'s earliest example of this sense is 1795.

20. *diets*] boards, supplies food for; *O.E.D.*'s first example is 1635. Considering the proverbially bad reputation of laundresses, Puttotta's functions may have a wider range, including the treatment of venereal disease (cf. II.i.123), where Amoroso 'takes the diet', a euphemism for undergoing a cure for venereal disease).

The Fawn

Dat veniam corvis, vexat censura columbas.

Act I

[I. i.]

Enter HERCULES *and* RENALDO.

Herc. See, yonder's Urbin; those far-appearing spires rise
    from the city—you shall conduct me no further. Return
    to Ferrara: my Dukedom, by your care in my absence,
    shall rest constantly united and most religiously loyal.
Ren. My prince and brother, let my blood and love   5
    Challenge the freedom of one question.
Herc. You have't.

Dat . . . columbas] *so this ed.; in margin, Qq.*   Act I] ACTVS PRIMI
SCENA PRIMA. *Qq.*   5–6. *in verse*] *AHB; in prose Qq.*

0.1. Dat veniam corvis, vexat censura columbas] 'Our censor absolves
the crow and passes judgment on the pigeon!' (Ramsay); Juvenal, Sat. II,
63. Marston's fondness for this passage (he used part of it as the motto for
Malc. as well) undoubtedly is connected to his own experiences with
censorship. But here the motto is more likely aimed at reminding readers
of the passage's original context, which is 'Laronia's defence of women
by citing male offences: "de nobis post haec tristis sententia fertur ? dat
veniam corvis, vexat censura columbas." "After these things what evil
judgment can be put on us women ? [The criticizing male] absolves the
crows and passes judgment on the doves"' Richard C. Harrier's note to
the epigraph of *Malc.* in his edition included in *Jacobean Drama I* (1963),
p. 475.
    1. *far-appearing*] visible from afar; Cross lists this as unrecorded in
O.E.D., *N&Q.*, CCIV (1959), 254.
    4. *constantly*] steadfastly, faithfully.
    5. *blood*] close family relationship. Cf. I.ii.266 and III.i.167.
    6. *Challenge*] lay claim to.

Ren. Why, in your steadier age, in strength of life
    And firmest wit of time, will you break forth
    Those stricter limits of regardful state   10
    (Which with severe distinction you still kept)
    And now to unknown dangers you'll give up
    Yourself, Ferrara's Duke, and in yourself
    The state, and us ? O, my loved brother,
    Honour avoids not only just defame,   15
    But flies all means that may ill voice his name.

Herc. Busy yourself with no fears, for I shall rest most wary
    of our safety; only some glimpses I will give you for
    your satisfaction why I leave Ferrara. I have vowed to
    visit the court of Urbin, as thus: my son, as you can well   20
    witness with me, could I never persuade to marriage,
    although myself was then an ever-resolved widower, and
    though I proposed to him this very lady to whom he is
    gone in my right to negotiate. Now how his cooler
    blood will behave itself in this business would I have an   25
    only testimony. Other contents shall I give myself, as
    not to take love by attorney, or make my election out of
    tongues; other sufficings there are which my regard

15–16. *in italics*] *Q2; in roman Q1.*   24. his] *Q1; not in Q2.*   26. only]
Q1 corr. and Q2; on- / a *Q1 uncorr.*

---

8. *strength of life*] full powers; evidently spiritual rather than physical
since Hercules is over sixty. For *strength* cf. II.i.494.

9. *firmest wit of time*] the time of soundest and acutest intelligence.

10. *regardful state*] responsible office.

11. *still*] always, continually.

24. *in my right*] representing my claim or offer.

negotiate] Cf. II.i.478–9, 'negotiate his royal father's love'. The closest
O.E.D. sense of *negotiate* seems to be either 2.a., to conduct a matter
requiring skill or consideration, or 2.b., to arrange for, bring about something by means of negotiation. Marston antedates both senses.

26. *an only testimony*] 'I simply wish to see how . . .' Marston uses
'only' with a remarkably wide range of meanings, sometimes vague ones.

contents] assurances.

27–8. *make my election out of tongues*] make my selection from hearsay
or rumour.

28. *sufficings*] sufficient assurances. This sense is not in *O.E.D.*

would fain make sound to me. Something of much you
know: that, and what else you must not know, bids you   30
excuse this kind of my departure.

Ren. I commend all to your wisdom, and yours to the Wisest.

Herc. Think not but I shall approve that more than folly
    which even now appears in a most ridiculous expecta-
    tion. Be in this assured: *the bottom of gravity is nothing*   35
    like the top. Once more, fare you well. *Exit* RENALDO.
    And now, thou ceremonious sovereignty—
    Ye proud, severer, stateful complements,
    The secret arts of rule—I put you off;
    Nor ever shall those manacles of form   40
    Once more lock up the appetite of blood.
    'Tis now an age of man—whilst we all strict
    Have lived in awe of carriage regular
    Apted unto my place, nor hath my life
    Once tasted of exorbitant affects,   45

35–6. *italics*] *Q2; in roman Q1.*

33–5. *Think not . . . expectation*] Hercules may already suspect that the
match between him and Dulcimel is disproportionate, in which case
more than = very great (*approve* = prove). If *even now* means no more
than 'at the moment', Hercules is reassuring Renaldo that something
other than mere folly is to be expected.

35–6. *the bottom . . . top*] can mean either: beneath Hercules' dignified
demeanour is a heart turbulent with longings; or: the most weighty
matters may be found under seemingly frivolous events, which Hercules
expects to ensue. Taylor lists as proverbial, 204.

38. *stateful complements*] either his dignified habits or more probably,
his ducal robes and appurtenances.

40–1.] The restraints of custom and duty shall no longer repress the
natural expression of my passions. (As opposed to Gonzago, for whom
'arts' and 'form' are used to defeat passion and nature.)

42. '*Tis now an age of man*] 'I have now reached that stage in a man's
life when . . .'. The broken syntax of the lines that follow reflect Hercules'
inner turmoil.

43. *carriage regular*] well-ruled behaviour.

44. *apted*] suited, appropriate.

45. *exorbitant*] excessive, outrageously large. *O.E.D.*'s first example is
1621. See Cross, *N&Q*, CCV (1960), 136.

affects] appetites, passions.

Wild longings, or the least of disranked shapes—
But we must once be wild; 'tis ancient truth—
O fortunate, whose madness falls in youth!
Well, this is text, whoever keeps his place
In servile station is all low and base.   50
Shall I because some few may cry, 'Light, vain,'
Beat down affection from desirèd rule ?
He that doth strive to please the world's a fool.
To have that fellow cry, 'O mark him, grave,
See how austerely he doth give example   55
Of repressed heat and steady life,'
Whilst my forced life against the stream of blood
Is tugged along, and all to keep the god
Of fools and women, Nice Opinion,
Whose strict preserving makes oft great men fools   60
And fools oft great men. No, thou world, know thus:
There's nothing free but it is generous.   *Exit.*

58. tugged] *Q2;* lugg'd *Q1.*   61. oft] *Q2;* of *Q1.*   62. *in italics*] *Q2;* in
roman *Q1.*

---

46. *disranked shapes*] Dilke takes this to mean 'appearance unbecoming
my rank'. But disranked can mean 'to throw out of rank or into disorder',
and shape, an object in the imagination. Hercules may well mean dis-
orderly or impermissible imaginings.

48. proverbial (Tilley, F 438).

49. *this is text*] 'This is gospel', Dilke.

57–8. *my forced life . . . along*] constraints force my life to move in the
direction opposite to my natural inclinations.

59. *Opinion*] The word had attained the function of jargon amongst the
satirists, to whom it was the great bugbear—the uninformed judgement
of the multitude. See Marston's mock dedication of *CS.,* 'TO THE
WORLDS MIGHTIE MONARCH, *GOOD OPINION*',
Poems, p. 49; and cf. v.i.370.

62. There's nothing free but it is generous.] 'Free' and 'generous' are
virtually synonymous, being related to the qualities of magnanimity and
virtue in the renaissance gentleman. The two terms are often found
together in Shakespeare (e.g. *Tw.N.,* I.v.98, *Ham.,* IV.vii.136, V.ii.253).
Hercules may mean something like 'The virtuous man must be given
his head, no matter how strange the direction of his actions may at
first seem.' For *free,* cf. II.i.412 and v.i.286–8 n. For *generous,* cf. I.ii.288
and II.i.246.

[I. ii.]

Enter NYMPHADORO, HEROD [*and* PAGE].

Herod. How now, my little more than nothing, what news is stirring?

Page. All the city's afire.

Nym. On fire?

Page. With joy of the Princess Dulcimel's birthday. There's   5
show upon show, sport upon sport.

Herod. What sport, what sport?

Page. Marry, sir, to solemnise the princess' birthday.
There's first crackers which run into the air, and when
they are at the top, like some ambitious strange heretic,   10
keep a-cracking and a-cracking, and then break, and
down they come.

Herod. A pretty crab—he would yield tart juice and he
were squeezed.

Nym. What sport else?   15

Page. Other fireworks.

Herod. Spirit of wine, I cannot tell how these fireworks
should be good at the solemnising the birth of men or
women; I am sure they are dangerous at their begetting.
What more fireworks, sir?   20

Page. There be squibs, sir; which squibs, running upon

[I.ii]] SCENA SECVNDA. *Qq.*   0.1 *and* PAGE] *AHB.*   5. Princess]
Dilke; Prince *Qq.*

---

9. *crackers*] firecrackers.

10. *ambitious strange heretic*] 'Ambitious' and 'strange' seem to point to
a foreign upstart, which could be ironic in the light of 'Faunus's' success
in the court of Urbin. But Faunus is no heretic, and the phrase probably
is only a general reference to the burning of heretics at the stake.

11. *a-cracking*] both 'exploding' and 'boasting'.

13. *crab*] crab apple (or perhaps crab orange, see III.i.145–6).

and] if.

21. *squibs*] 'A species of fire-work, in which the burning of the composition is usually terminated by a slight explosion' (*O.E.D.*). Bullen
draws attention to a similar passage in Dekker and Webster's *Northward
Ho*: '[T]hey, as soon as they come to their lands, get up to London and
like squibs that run upon lines, they keep a spitting of fire and cracking

lines like some of our gaudy gallants, sir, keep a-
smother, sir, with flishing and flashing, and in the end,
sir, they do, sir—

Nym. What, sir? 25

Page. Stink, sir.

Herod. 'Fore heaven, a most sweet youth.

Enter DONDOLO.

Dond. News, news, news, news!

Herod. What, in the name of prophecy?

Nym. Art thou grown wise? 30

Herod. Doth the duke want no money?

Nym. Is there a maid found at twenty-four?

Herod. Speak, thou three-legged tripos, is thy ship of fools
afloat yet?

Dond. I ha' many things in my head to tell you. 35

Herod. Ay, thy head is always working; it rolls and it rolls,
Dondolo, but it gathers no moss, Dondolo.

Dond. Tiberio, the Duke of Ferrara's son, excellently
horsed, all upon Flanders mares, is arrived at the court

---

till they ha' spent all; and when my squib is out what says his punk? foh,
he stinks!' (IV.iii.90–3).

22–3. *a-smother*] As adverbial phrase, not recorded in *O.E.D.*; 'a-
smoulder', meaning 'smoulder' is dated 1880. The noun 'smother' is
defined as 'a smouldering or slow-burning fire'.

23. *flishing*] 'variant of flashing, probably connected with the onomato-
poeic v[erb] flisk, expressive of a sudden movement through the air. Unrecorded in *O.E.D.*' Cross, *N&Q*, CCIV (1959), 254.

33. *three-legged tripos*] oracle. There is probably a double reference to
the stool on which the Delphic priestess sat and to that on which a
Cambridge bachelor of arts sat when in comic disputation with a candidate
for the degree. Dondolo may carry a staff, cane or fool's sceptre to make
him 'three-legged'.

ship of fools] The device originates in Sebastian Brandt's *Narrenschiff*,
published in Germany in 1494 and in English translation (by Alexander
Barclay) in 1508. Only gradually during the play does it become apparent
that the ship is more than a figurative one.

36–7. *it rolls . . . moss*] proverbial (Tilley, S 885); we are reminded that
Dondolo is a 'bald fool'.

39. *Flanders mares*] much admired at the time as coach horses

this very day, somewhat late in the night-time.   40

Herod. An excellent nuntius.

Dondolo. Why, my gallants, I have had a good wit.

Herod. Yes, troth, but now 'tis grown like an almanac for
    the last year—past date; the mark's out of thy mouth,
    Dondolo.   45

Nym. And what's the prince's ambassage? Thou art private
    with the duke; thou belongest to his close stool.

Dond. Why, every fool knows that; I know it myself, man,
    as well as the next man: he is come to solicit a marriage
    betwixt his father, the Duke of Ferrara, and our Duke   50
    of Urbin's daughter, Dulcimel.

Nym. Pity of my passions, Nymphadoro shall lose one of his
    mistresses.

Herod. Nay, if thou hast more than one the loss can ne'er
    be grievous, since 'tis certain he that loves many form-   55
    ally never loves any violently.

Nym. Most trusted Frappatore, is my hand the weaker be-
    cause it is divided into many fingers? No, 'tis the
    more strongly nimble. I do now love threescore and
    nine ladies, all of them most extremely well, but I do   60
    love the princess most extremely best; but in very sigh-
    ing sadness, I ha' lost all hope, and with that hope a

50. Ferrara] *Dilke; Ferraraes Qq.*

---

41. *nuntius*] messenger; the term used in Seneca's plays.

44. *the mark's out of thy mouth*] 'A horse is often too old for use when
the mark, "a depression caused by a fold in the enamel of a horse's incisor
tooth" (*O.E.D.*), is gone from his mouth' (Smith).

46. *ambassage*] business entrusted to him.

47. *close stool*] a portable privy or 'private' (*O.E.D.* II†8)—a pun.
Montaigne (Crawford): 'Princes, who to dispatch their weightiest affaires
make often their close stoole, their regall Throne or Councel-chamber...'
I, iii, 16. The notion was not far-fetched. King James, explaining why he
had not yet given out many honours, told his first parliament: 'If euery
man had the like accesse to my Priuy or Bedchamber, then no man could
haue it, because it cannot containe all.' *The Kings Maiesties Speech*
(1604), D1v. See note on I.ii.188.

61-2. *very sighing sadness*] absolutely true seriousness.

lady that is most rare, most fair, most wise, most sweet,
most—

Herod. Anything, true; but remember still this fair, this   65
wise, this sweet, this all of excellency has in the tail of
all, a woman.

[*Enter* SIR AMOROSO.]

Nym. Peace, the presence fills against the prince approacheth. Mark who enters.

Herod. My brother, Sir Amoroso Debile-Dosso.   70

Nym. Not he.

Herod. No, not he?

Nym. How is he changed!

Herod. Why, grown the very dregs of the drabs' cup.

Nym. O Babylon, thy walls are fallen. Is he married?   75

Herod. Yes, yet still the ladies' common—or the common
ladies'—servant.

Nym. How does his own lady bear with him?

Herod. Faith, like the Roman Milo: bore with him when

67.1] *This ed.*   73. changed!] *This ed.; chang'd? Qq.*

---

66. *tail*] conclusion; with a bawdy pun.

68–9. *the presence . . . approacheth*] The presence-chamber fills, in
anticipation that the prince is approaching.

74. *the very dregs of the drabs' cup*] i.e. all that is left of him after a career
of frequenting drabs (prostitutes).

75. *O Babylon, thy walls are fallen.*] Rev., xviii, 2. Wood believes the
phrase is 'probably a snatch of a ballad'.

76–7. *common ladies'*] prostitutes'.

79. *the Roman Milo*] a famous athlete, who lifted a calf every day for
four years, and then 'at the game of *Olympus* with his bare hande slue [it],
and afterward caried him a furlong, and the same day eate him euerie
morsel' (Cooper). We may assume that Marston has the calf 'grow' into
an ox rather than a bull (as the story usually went) for reasons allied to
Amoroso's present physical state. Perhaps, however, he had read
Taverner's translation of selections from Erasmus's *Chiliades* (*Adagia*)
(1569, ed. DeWitt T. Starnes, 1956): 'He that hath borne a calfe, shal also
beare a bull, he that accustomed him selfe to litle thinges, by litle and litle
shalbe able to goe away with greater thinges. One named *Milo*, was wont
euery day to beare a certaine way on his shoulders a calf. At length the
calfe grew to a great oxe, his daily exercise made him still able to beare the

he was a calf, and now carries him when he's grown an   80
ox.

Nym. Peace, the duke's at hand.

Cornets. Enter GRANUFFO, GONZAGO, DULCIMEL, PHILOCALIA,
ZOYA.

Gon. Daughter, for that our last speech leaves the firmest
print, be thus advised. When young Tiberio negotiates
his father's love, hold heedy guard over thy passions,   85
and still keep this full thought firm in thy reason: 'tis
his old father's love the young man moves—[*to*
GRANUFFO] is't not well thought, my lord; we must
bear brain—and when thou shalt behold Tiberio's life-
full eyes and well-filled veins, complexion firm, and   90
hairs that curls with strength of lusty moisture—[*to*
GRANUFFO] I think we yet can speak, we ha' been
eloquent—thou must shape thy thoughts
To apprehend his father well in years,
A grave wise prince, whose beauty is his honour   95
And well-passed life, and do not give thy thoughts
Least liberty to shape a divers scope—

82.2 Zoya] *JOH; Loia Qq*, Poveia *Smith.*   94] *as prose Qq.*

---

oxe, when the oxe was now of an exceding great quantitie, ye see what
maistries vse worketh' (p. 11). It is just as likely, of course, that Marston
had read the *Adagia* in Latin. In any case, there is no doubt that Marston
chose *ox* here for its comic appropriateness.

83. *for that*] so that.
84. *print*] imprint.
85. *heedy*] heedful, careful.
86. *full*] See 'To My Equal Reader', 58 n.
87. *moves*] pleads, proposes.
89. *bear brain*] be shrewd, wary (Bullen).
90. *complexion*] constitution. Cf. I.ii.323 and III.i.2.
91. *lusty moisture*] strong, healthy temperament; 'moisture' = humour
(in the old physiological sense).
94. *apprehend*] understand (his father) to be; *O.E.D.*'s first example for
this sense is 1639.
97. *divers*] either 'different', or (possibly) 'differing from or opposed to
good or right; perverse' (*O.E.D.* †2).

My Lord Granuffo, pray ye note my phrase—
So shalt thou not abuse thy younger hope,
Nor afflict us, who only joy in life   100
To see thee his.

Dul.   Gracious my father, fear not;
I rest most duteous to your dispose.

Consort of music.

Gon. Set on then, for the music gives us notice
The prince is hard at hand.

[*Enter*] TIBERIO *with his train, with* HERCULES *disguised.*

Dul. You are most welcome to our long-desiring father. To   105
us you are come—
Tib. From our long-desiring father.
Dul. Is this your father's true proportion? *Shows a picture.*
Tib. No, lady, but the perfect counterfeit.
Dul. And the best graced—
Tib.   The painter's art could yield.   110
Dul. I wonder he would send a counterfeit
To move our love.

101–4.] *so AHB; prose Qq.*   108. *Shows a picture*] *Qq;* [*on previous line*]
Smith.   110–12. *so AHB; prose Qq.*

---

99. *thy younger hope*] your earlier, original expectation (of marrying the
duke).

102. *your dispose*] your command, control.

102.2. Consort of music] (performance by) a group of musicians.

105. *long-desiring*] Cross notes that this is unrecorded in *O.E.D.*; *N&Q*,
CCVI (1961), 299.

108. *proportion*] form, shape. Cf. I.ii.243 and III.i.190 for other senses
of *proportion*.

109. *counterfeit*] likeness, portrait. One is reminded of the tradition
that the Holbein portrait of Anne of Cleves influenced Henry VIII in his
decision to marry her. It is not clear who 'shows a picture'.

110.] By 'graced' Dulcimel perhaps means to compliment the conveyor
of the portrait, but Tiberio changes it to apply to the painter's art. There
is a somewhat similar association of 'grace', 'counterfeit', and courting in
DC.,I.i.50–3.

Gon. Hear, that's my wit. When I was eighteen old such a
    pretty toying wit had I, but age hath made us wise—
    has't not, my lord?   115

Tib. Why, fairest princess, if your eye dislike
    That deader piece, behold me his true form
    And livelier image; such my father hath been.

Dul. My lord, please you to scent this flower.

Tib. 'Tis withered, lady, the flower's scent is gone.   120

Dul. This hath been such as you are, hath been, sir.
    They say in England that a far-famed friar
    Had girt the island round with a brass wall,
    If that they could have catched 'Time is'; but 'Time is past'
    Left it still clipped with agèd Neptune's arm.   125

Tib. Aurora yet keeps chaste old Tithon's bed.

Dul. Yet blushes at it when she rises.

Gon. Pretty, pretty, just like my younger wit—you know it,
    my lord.

Dul. But is your father's age thus fresh; hath yet his head   130

---

115. has't] *This ed.;* hast *Qq.*   116–18.] *so AHB; prose Qq.*   121–5.] *so AHB; prose Qq.*   122. far-famed friar] *Q2;* farre found Frier *Q1 corr.;* farre found *Q1 uncorr.*   125. still] *Q1, Q2 corr.;* hill *Q2 uncorr.*

---

113. *eighteen old*] This rare locution may be caused by Marston's originally intending to fit these lines into verse (they make roughly three iambic pentameters). But this is not so clear a case for relineation as others that follow.

114. *toying*] playful, especially amorously playful.

117. *piece*] picture, painting.

122–5. *They say . . . arm.*] 'The allusion is to the well-known story of Friar Bacon and the brazen head' (Halliwell). See Robert Greene's *Friar Bacon and Friar Bungay*, sc. xi, 53–75 (ed. D. Seltzer).

122. *far-famed*] Antedates first *O.E.D.* example. See Cross, *N&Q*, CCII (1957), 66.

125. *clipped with*] embraced by.

126–7.] Aurora, goddess of the dawn, gave her lover Tithonus eternal life but forgot to give him eternal youth. The 'blushing' is of course the classical 'rosiness' of dawn, but Dulcimel is hinting at a sense of shame in the disproportionate marriage; thus the *Epithetorum Epitome* of Joannes Ravisius lists 'pudoricolor' amongst Aurora's attributes.

128. *my younger wit*] my own wit when I was young.

So many hairs?

Tib.   More, more, by many a one.

Dul. More say you?

Tib.   More.

Dul.   Right, sir, for this hath none.
Is his eye so quick as this same piece makes him show?

Tib. The courtesy of art hath given more life to that part
than the sad cares of state would grant my father.   135

Dul. This model speaks about forty.

Tib. Then doth it somewhat flatter, for our father hath seen
more years, and is a little shrunk from the full strength
of time.

Gon. Somewhat coldly praised.   140

Dul. Your father hath a fair solicitor,
And be it spoke with virgin modesty,
I would he were no elder; not that I do fly
His side for years, or other hopes of youth,
But in regard the malice of lewd tongues,   145
Quick to deprave on possibilities
(Almost impossibilities), will spread
Rumours, to honour dangerous.

DULCIMEL *and* TIBERIO *confer privately.*

Gon. What? whisper? Ay, my Lord Granuffo, 'twere fit
To part their lips. Men of discerning wit   150
That have read Pliny can discourse, or so,

131–2.] *so HHW; prose Qq.*   136. about] *Q1;* aboue *Q2.*   148.1.] *to
the right of ll. 147–8 Q2; not in Q1.*

132. *for this hath none*] Since the picture is made of paint, it of course
has no hair.
136. *about*] The Q2 reading is 'aboue'; Q1 is supported by the German
Tiberius play, quoted in Sources, p. 34: 'Irgend vierzig Jahr'.
143–4. *fly His side for years*] wish to reject him because of his (old) age.
146. *deprave*] vilify, defame, slander.
150. *discerning wit*] penetrating intelligence. Cross cites this use of
'discerning' as antedating *O.E.D.*'s first example; *N&Q*, CCIII (1958), 104,

But give me practice; well-experienced age
Is the true Delphos: I am no oracle,
But yet I'll prophesy. Well, my Lord Granuffo,
'Tis fit to interrupt their privacy,   155
Is't not, my lord? Now sure thou art a man
Of a most learned silence, and one whose words
Have been most precious to me; right, I know thy heart,
'Tis true, thy legs discourse with right and grace,
And thy tongue is constant. [*to Tiberio*] Fair my lord,   160
Forbear all private closer conference;
What from your father comes, comes openly,
And so must speak: for you must know my age
Hath seen the beings and the *quid* of things:
I know *dimensions* and the *termini*   165
Of all *existens*. Sir, I know what shapes
Appetite forms, but policy and states
Have more elected ends: your father's suit
Is with all public grace received, and private love
Embraced. As for our daughter's bent of mind,   170
She must seem somewhat nice; 'tis virgins' kind

160. S.D.] *Dilke.*   161. all private] *Q1;* all all pruat *Q2.*   171.
virgins'] *Dilke;* virgins *Qq;* virgin's *Smith.*

---

152. *practice*] practical experience.
153. *true Delphos*] the true source of oracular powers; refers to the
Delphic oracle.
164. *the beings and the* quid *of things*] the essential substance of things;
part of the jargon of scholastic philosophy.
165. dimensions] (properly *dimensiones*) extension, measure.
termini] ends; also starting point, or final cause.
166. existens] being.
167. *policy*] sagacity (especially political); Gonzago is specially proud
of his 'policy'. Cf. IV.i.620 n.
states] high rank, positions of importance. For other senses, see V.i.122.2
and V.i.156.
168. *elected*] carefully chosen, preferred.
171. *nice . . . virgins' kind*] So also in *Malc.,* V.ii.144–5: ''tis said a
squeamish affected niceness is natural to women.'
nice] shy, reluctant.
kind] nature.

To hold long out; if yet she chance deny,
Ascribe it to her decent modesty.
We have been a philosopher and spoke
With much applause; but now age makes us wise,   175
And draws our eyes to search the heart of things,
And leave vain seemings. Therefore you must know
I would be loth the gaudy shape of youth
Should one provoke, and not-allowed-of heat
Or hinder, or—for sir, I know, and so—   180
Therefore before us time and place affords
Free speech, else not: wise heads use but few words.
In short breath, know the Court of Urbin holds
Your presence and your embassage so dear
That we want means once to express our heart   185
But with our heart. Plain meaning shunneth art:
You are most welcome. (Lord Granuff, a trick,
A figure, note.) We use no rhetoric.
  Exit GONZAGO [*with* DULCIMEL, TIBERIO *and attendants*].

  Remanent HERCULES, NYMPHADORO *and* HEROD.

179. one provoke, and] *Qq;* once provoke a *AHB.*   185. express] *Q1;*
oppresse *Q2.*   188.1. *with . . . attendants.*] *This ed.*

---

178. *gaudy*] gay (with the sense of dangerous attractiveness).
178–80.] Bullen's emendation is attractive, but Marston probably makes Gonzago's syntax awkward on purpose. It is uncertain whether it is Tiberio's 'gawdy shape of youth' which may 'provoke' Dulcimel or vice versa.
182. *wise heads use but few words*] proverbial. 'A wise head makes a close mouth' (Tilley, H 276).
185. *once*] once and for all, in short.
188. *figure*] a rhetorical figure of speech. Gonzago may mean either the repetition of 'heart', which Puttenham might describe as *ploce* or 'the doubler', pp. 201–2—or the near-*paronomasia* (pun) on heart/art. Cf. II.i.552.
We use no rhetoric] Such a denial from an obvious offender reminds us of Polonius (*Ham.*, II.ii.96). It may also have been intended to remind Marston's contemporaries of King James's first speech to the English parliament on 19 March 1603/4: '. . . I will plainely and freely in my maner tell you . . . That it becommeth a King, in my opinion, to vse no other Eloquence then plainnesse and sinceritie' (*The Kings Maiesties Speech*, quarto printed by Robert Barker [1604], D2v–D3).

Herod. Did not Tiberio call his father fool ?

Nym. No, he said years had weakened his youthful quickness.   190

Herod. He swore he was bald.

Nym. No. But not thick-haired.

Herod. By this light, I'll swear he said his father had the
　　hipgout, the strangury, the fistula *in ano*, and a most
　　unabideable breath, no teeth, less eyes, great fingers,   195
　　little legs, an eternal flux, and an everlasting cough of
　　the lungs.

Nym. Fie, fie, by this light he did not.

Herod. By this light he should ha' done then. Horn on him,
　　threescore and five, to have and to hold a lady of   200
　　fifteen. O Mezentius! a tyranny equal if not above thy
　　torturing; thou didst bind the living and the dead bodies
　　together, and forced them so to pine and rot, but this
　　cruelty binds breast to breast not only different bodies,
　　but if it were possible most unequal minds together,   205
　　with an enforcement even scandalous to nature.

[*Spies* HERCULES.]

206.1. S.D.] *Dilke.*

---

194. *hipgout*] sciatica.

strangury] 'a disease of the urinary organs characterised by slow and
painful emission of urine' (*O.E.D.*).

unabideable] Unrecorded in *O.E.D.* See Cross, *N&Q*, CCVIII (1963),
312.

fistula] 'A long, narrow, suppurating canal of morbid origin in some
part of the body' (*O.E.D.*); here it is in the anus. Any or all of the three
diseases Herod lists could be taken as euphemisms for venereal disease.

196. *little legs*] skinny legs; Marston himself was apparently ridiculed
for having 'little legs'.

flux] dysentery.

199. *Horn on him*] i.e. may he be a cuckold.

201. *Mezentius*] a tyrant described by Virgil in Book VII of the *Aeneid*.
The application of this particular torture to enforced marriages is antici-
pated in Geoffrey Whitney's *A Choice of Emblems* (1586). See Mario
Praz's review of Wood's edition of Marston's plays in *English Studies*,
XXI (1939), 26, and Glenn H. Blayney's 'Enforcement of marriage in
English drama (1600–1650),' *P.Q.*, XXXVIII (1959), 459–72.

202. *torturing*] antedates *O.E.D.*'s first example; see Cross, *N&Q*,
CCVIII (1963), 311.

Now the jail deliver me, an intelligencer! Be good to
me, ye cloisters of bondage. Of whence art thou ?

Herc. Of Ferrara.

Herod. A Ferrarese—what to me! Camest thou in with the   210
Prince Tiberio ?

Herc. With the Prince Tiberio. What o' that, you will not
rail at me, will you ?

Herod. Who, I ? I rail at one of Ferrara, a Ferrazese ? No!
Didst thou ride ?   215

Herc. No.

Herod. Hast thou worn socks ?

Herc. No.

Herod. Then blessed be the most happy gravel betwixt thy
toes. I do prophesy thy tyrannising itch shall be honour-   220
able, and thy right worshipful sole shall appear in full
presence. Art thou an officer to the prince ?

210. Ferrarese—what to me!] *This ed.; Ferarees* what to mee, *Q1; Ferrares*
what to me, *Q2;* Ferrarese ? what to me ? *Dilke;* Ferrarese! what to me ?
AHB; Ferrara's what to me ? *Smith.*   212. o'] *Q1;* to *Q2.*   221. worshipful sole] *This ed.;* worshipfull soule *Q1;* worshipfull, Loue *Q2;* worshipful louse *AHB.*   222. prince] *Q2;* Princes *Q1.*

207. *the jail deliver me*] i.e., deliver me from jail.

intelligencer] informer, spy. Elizabethan England seems to have been
plagued with informers, so much so that acts were passed from time to
time to curb the practice as it disturbed the workings of the court, e.g.
31 Eliz. (1589) c. 5 'An Act concerning Informers: For that divers of the
Queen's Majesty's Subjects be daily unjustly vexed and disquieted by
divers common Informers....'

210-45.] Though several of the Q2 readings for B3 *verso* are attractive
(see collations for lines 210 to 245), the nature of the error at 221 (*Loue* for
soule) indicates that the Q2 reviser for that page was not Marston; editorial
choices here will thus inevitably seem eclectic.

214. *Ferrazese*] evidently a playful variant of Marston's, if not a typographical error.

219. *gravel*] Besides its usual sense, the word could refer to urinary
difficulties, which might suggest another location for the 'tyrannising itch'.

220. *tyrannising*] antedates *O.E.D.*'s first example; see Cross, *N&Q*,
CCVIII (1963), 312.

221. *right worshipful sole*] the old sole/soul pun, but it stumped most
editors after the Q1 compositor.

222. *an officer to*] in the employ of, given an 'office' by.

Herc. I am, what o' that?

Herod. My cap. What officer?

Herc. Yeoman of his bottles; what to that?   225

Herod. My lip. Thy name, good yeoman of the bottles?

Herc. Faunus.

Herod. Faunus? An old courtier; I wonder thou art in no
    better clothes and place, Faunus.

Herc. I may be in better place, sir, and with them of more   230
    regard if this match of our duke's intermarriage with
    the heir of Urbin proceed, the Duke of Urbin dying,
    and our lord coming in his lady's right of title to your
    dukedom.

Herod. Why then shalt thou, O yeoman of the bottles,   235
    become a maker of *magnificoes*. Thou shalt beg some
    odd suit and change thy old suit, pare thy beard, cleanse
    thy teeth, and eat apricocks, marry a rich widow, or a
    cracked lady whose case thou shalt make good. Then,

230. them] *Q1;* you *Q2.*   233. of] *Q2; not in Q1.*   237. suit] *Q1;*
shert *Q2.*

---

230. *place*] rank. Hercules is able to throw this sneering remark back at
them by II.i.114–16: 'What, ha' ye plots, projects, correspondences, and
stratagems? Why are not you in better place?'

233. *right of title*] On the husband's assuming the rights of property
belonging to his wife, see S. Clarkson and C. T. Warren, *The Law of
Property in Shakespeare and Elizabethan Drama* (1942), where this passage
is cited. 'This was the result of the concept that by marriage the personality
of the wife dissolved into that of her husband; the twain became one flesh
legally as well as biblically, but that one was the husband' (p. 201).

236. magnificoes] the title given to the magnates of Venice.

236–7. *beg some odd suit and change thy old suit*] pun on 'suit' as supplica-
tion and as set of clothing.

237. *pare thy beard*] The shape of a beard could label a man: 'What
beards ha they? Gentleman-like-beards, or broker-like-beards?', George
Wilkins, *The Miseries of Enforced Marriage* (1607), 1112–13 (Malone
Society Reprints, 1964).

238. *apricocks*] apricots; a luxury.

238–9. *a cracked lady whose case*] 'Cracked' can mean 'bankrupt', but
also 'flawed' or as Dilke euphemistically puts it: 'a lady whose character is
gone'. 'Case' puns on 'lawsuit' and 'female pudendum' (kaze) (Bullen).
Marston also uses the pun in *DC.* (I.i.117–24): 'Do you know no alderman
would pity such a woman's case? . . . and indeed, wherein should they
bestow their money better? In land, the title may be crack'd. . . .'

my Pythagoras, shall thou and I make a transmigration   240
of souls: thou shalt marry my daughter, or my wife
be thy gracious mistress. Seventeen punks shall be thy
proportion. Thou shalt beg to thy comfort of clean
linen, eat no more fresh beef at supper, or save the
broth for next day's porridge, but the flesh-pots of   245
Egypt shall fatten thee, and the grasshopper shall
flourish in thy summer.

Nym. And what dost thou think of the duke's overture of
marriage?

Herod. What do you think?   250

Herc. May I speak boldly as at Aleppo?

Nym. Speak till thy lungs ache, talk out thy teeth; here are
none of those cankers, these mischiefs of society,
intelligencers, or informers, that will cast rumour into
the teeth of some Laelius Balbus, a man cruelly eloquent   255
and bloodily learned: no, what sayest thou, Faunus?

Herc. With an undoubted breast thus, I may speak boldly.

---

244. save the] *Q2;* haue thy *Q1.*   255. Balbus] *AHB; Baldus Qq.*
257 thus, . . . boldly.] *Smith;* thus . . . boldly, *Q1;* thus, . . . boldly, *Q2;*
thus:- . . . boldly? *AHB.*

---

240. *Pythagoras*] ancient philosopher one of whose tenets was the
immortality and transmigration of souls (but after death).

242. *punks*] prostitutes.

243. *proportion*] due share.

244. *fresh beef*] unsalted beef; therefore unreliable, given sanitary
conditions of the day (?); fits *O.E.D.* sense 4.b. of *fresh.*

245. *porridge*] pottage made by stewing vegetables, meat, etc.

245–6. *the flesh-pots of Egypt*] from Exodus, xvi, 3.

246–7. *grasshopper . . . summer*] a playful, and subtle, misquotation of
Eccl., xii, 5: '. . . and the almond tree shall flourish, and the grasshopper
shall be a burden, and desire shall fail. . . .'

247. *Aleppo*] in Syria, long a centre of international trade. 'Hercules is
about to "traduce the state" in the person of the Duke. Surely the reference here is to Othello's "malignant and . . . turban'd Turk" who, "in
Aleppo once . . . traduced the state" ?' Wood. Sugden had earlier made
this suggestion, which seems somewhat strained, though possible.

255. *Laelius Balbus*] a lawyer in the reign of Tiberius who supported
his charges of treason by the use of informers. See Tacitus, *Annals,* vi, 48
(Loeb Library).

257. *With an undoubted breast*] unhesitatingly, without fear.

Herod. By this night I'll speak broadly first and thou wilt,
    man: our Duke of Urbin is a man very happily mad,
    for he thinks himself right perfectly wise, and most   260
    demonstratively learned; nay, more—
Herc. No more, I'll on. Methinks the young lord our
    prince of Ferrara so bounteously adorned with all of
    grace, feature, and best-shaped proportion, fair use of
    speech, full opportunity, and that which makes the   265
    sympathy of all, equality of heat, of years, of blood;
    methinks these lodestones should attract the metal of
    the young princess rather to the son than to the
    noisome, cold, and most weak side of his half-rotten
    father.   270
Herod. Th'art ours, th'art ours. Now dare we speak boldly
    as if Adam had not fallen, and made us all slaves. Hark
    ye, the duke is an arrant, doting ass, an ass, and in the
    knowledge of my very sense, will turn a foolish animal;
    for his son will prove like one of Baal's priests, have all   275
    the flesh presented to the idol his father, but he in the
    night will feed on't, will devour it. He will, yeoman of
    the bottles, he will.

258. night] *Qq;* light *conj. AHB.*

---

258. *By this night*] Earlier, Herod had vowed 'by this light' (I.ii.193,
199), and Bullen suggests that it should be the reading here as well. But
Marston may be using the opportunity to set the scene, and there may be a
comic touch in Herod's speaking so *broadly* under the cover of darkness.

   broadly] outspokenly, openly; antedates *O.E.D.*'s first example: Cross,
N&Q, CCIV (1959), 356.

261. *demonstratively*] 'According to clear and convincing evidence'
(*O.E.D.*); antedates *O.E.D.*'s first example (1646): Cross, *N&Q,* CC
(1955), 20.

265–6. *that which makes the sympathy of all*] what makes all of these
qualities harmonise.

266. *heat*] intensity of or capacity for feeling. 'Blood' means approximately the same—'temper, disposition'—and both are a carry-over from
the old theories of humours. For *heat,* cf. I.ii.345 n.

275–7. *one of Baal's priests . . . devour it*] 'The allusion is to the story of
Bel and the Dragon, in the Apocrypha' (Dilke).

Herc. Now gentlemen, I am sure the lust of speech hath
    equally drenched us all; know I am no servant to this   280
    Prince Tiberio.

Herod. Not?

Herc. Not, but one to him out of some private urging
    most vowed—one that pursues him but for opportunity
    of safe satisfaction. Now if ye can prefer my service to   285
    him, I shall rest yours wholly.

Herod. Just in the devil's mouth! Thou shalt have place,
    Fawn, thou shalt. Behold this generous Nymphadoro,
    a gallant of a clean boot, straight back, and beard of a
    most hopeful expectation. He is a servant of fair   290
    Dulcimel's, her very creature, born to the princess' sole
    adoration, a man so spent in time to her that pity (if no

285. safe] *Q2;* false *Q1.*   289. beard] *Q2;* head *Q1.*

---

279. *lust*] delight, appetite. This lust seems to have drenched most of
the court of Urbin. For another sense of *lust*, cf. II.i.138, n.

280. *drenched*] immersed, overwhelmed.

283. *urging*] pressing claim or need.

284. *vowed*] modifies either *urging* (in which case it means 'dedicated' or
'committed') or *to him* (in which case it means 'engaged' or 'employed').

285. *prefer*] recommend.

287. *Just in the devil's mouth*] proverbial? Some sort of reassurance,
apparently: 'Absolutely!'

288. *generous*] gallant, (or) high-born. Perhaps both.

289. *a gallant of a clean boot*] This kind of listing appears in *Eastward
Ho*, I.i.61–3: 'Gentlemen of good phrase, perfect language, passingly
behau'd, Gallants that weare socks and cleane linnen, and call me kinde
coozen Francke....'

straight back] sexually active (in contrast to the weak-backed Sir
Amoroso, for instance).

289–90. *beard of a most hopeful expectation*] Marston uses a similar
phrase to suggest Freevil's youthfulness in *DC.* (III.i.62–4): 'he has a leg
like a post, a nose like a lion, a brow like a bull, and a beard of most fair
expectation.'

290. *servant*] one dedicated to her service in love, rather than an
employee.

291. *creature*] instrument or puppet.

291–2. *born to the princess' sole adoration*] born for the express purpose
of adoring the princess. Marston is fond of the 'born to' locution. Donna
Zoya was 'created to be the affliction of' Don Zuccone, for example
(II.i.348–9).

292. *so spent in time to her*] who has spent so much time in her service.

more of grace) must follow him. When we have gained
the room, second his suit.

Herc. I'll be your intelligencer.   295

Herod. Our very heart.

Nym. And if need be work to most desperate ends.

Herod. Well urged.

Herc. Words fit acquaintance, but full actions friends.

Nym. Thou shalt not want, Faunus.   300

Herc. You promise well.

Herod. Be thou but firm, that old doting iniquity of age,
that only-eyed lecherous duke thy lord, shall be baffled

293–7. him. When . . . heart. / *Nym.* And] *This ed.;* him second, when wee
haue gayned the roome, / seru'd his suite *Hercules.* Ile be your intelligencer.
/ *Her:* Our very hart, and *Q1;* him when we haue gayned the roome,
second / his suite *Hercules.* Ile be your intelligencer. / *Her:* Our very
heart, and *Q2;* him second, when we have / gained the room, serv'd his
suit. / *Herc.* I'll be your intelligencer. / *Her.* Our very heart— / *Herc.*
And, *Dilke;* him when we have gained the room. Second his suit, Faunus; /
I'll be your intelligencer. / *Herc.* Our very heart, and, *AHB;* him when
we have gained the room, second his suit. / HERCULES. I'll be your intelligencer, your very heart, and *Smith.*   297. work] *Q2;* workes *Q1.*
303. only-eyed] *Qq;* horny-eyed *AHB;* oily-eyed *London (see note), conj.
J. C. Maxwell.*

293–4. *When . . . suit*] 'Faunus' has asked the courtiers to recommend
him to Tiberio; this will be done indirectly by his joining Nymphadoro
(seconding his suit) as he courts Dulcimel in the presence chamber (room).

297.] This line may perhaps be ascribed to Hercules, but it is Nymphadoro who later (II.i.103–12) suggests 'desperate', 'Italian' actions.

299. *Words . . . friends*] Taylor lists this as proverbial; it is a combination of 'Few words among friends are best' (Tilley, W 796) and 'Not
words but deeds' (Tilley, W 820).

302. *iniquity*] the comic figure otherwise called the Vice in the morality
plays.

303. *only-eyed*] Gerald Smith, in *N&Q,* CCVI (October 1961), 397,
hypothesises a bibliographical defence for J. C. Maxwell's suggested
emendation to 'oily-eyed' (*N&Q,* CCVI [May 1961], 195); it is a very
shaky one. 'Only-eyed' makes good sense, given Marston's wide-ranging
use (virtually abuse) of 'only'; here it means 'single'—one-eyed, i.e. half-
blind from age.

baffled] (publicly) disgraced; from the original sense of punishment of a
perjured knight. Cross lists this as being nearest *O.E.D.* sense 5.b, but
that meaning has to do with juggling and quibbling. It is possible that the
sense 'foiled, frustrated' (*O.E.D.* II.8) applies, in which case Marston
would antedate *O.E.D.*'s example (1675).

to extremest derision, his son prove his fool father's own
issue.   305

Nym. And we, and thou with us, blessed and enriched past
that misery of possible contempt, and above the hopes
of greatest conjectures.

Herod. Nay, as for wealth, *vilia miretur vulgus.* I know by
his physiognomy, for wealth he is of my addiction, and   310
bids a *fico* for't.

Nym. Why, thou art but a younger brother, but poor
Baldanzozo.

Herod. Faith, to speak truth, my means are written in the
book of fate, as yet unknown; and yet I am at my fool   315
and my hunting gelding. Come, *via*, to this feastful
entertainment.   *Exeunt. Remanet* HERCULES.

Herc. I never knew till now how old I was.

By Him by whom we are, I think a prince
Whose tender sufferance never felt a gust   320

---

307. that] *Q1;* all *Q2.*   309. *Herod.*] *London; Her. Qq; Herc. Dilke and*
the other modern edd.   313. Baldanzozo] *This ed.;* Baldazozo *Qq.*

304–5. *prove his fool father's own issue*] i.e., prove himself both lecher
and fool.

307. *that misery of possible contempt*] that state in life where it is still
possible to be open to contempt. Neither quarto reading makes very clear
sense. A very tentative conjecture: 'past all measure of possible content'.

309. vilia miretur vulgus] 'Let what is cheap excite the marvel of the
crowd' (Showerman); Ovid, *Amores*, XV, 36 (Loeb Library).

310. *physiognomy*] 'The face or countenance, especially viewed as an
index to the mind and character' (*O.E.D.*).

addiction] inclination.

311. fico] a fig. See Tilley, F 210.

313. *Baldanzozo*] For meaning, see Interlocutors, 12, n. Apparently
this is the family name, while 'Frappatore' and 'Debile-Dosso' are more
or less nicknames.

315–16. *and yet . . . gelding*] Herod later explains how he can afford
these luxuries (II.i.180–4).

316. via] 'An adverbe of encouraging, much used by riders to their
horses, and by commanders; go on, away, go to, on, forward, quickly'
(Florio).

320. *tender sufferance*] either 'gentle tolerance' or (more likely) 'touchi-
ness', 'reluctant indulgence'.

Of bolder breathings, but still lived gently fanned
With the soft gales of his own flatterers' lips,
Shall never know his own complexion.
Dear sleep and lust, I thank you: but for you,
Mortal—till now—I scarce had known myself.   325
Thou grateful poison, sleek mischief, flattery,
Thou dreamful slumber (that doth fall on kings
As soft and soon as their first holy oil),
Be thou forever damned. I now repent
Severe indictions to some sharp styles;   330
Freeness, so't grow not to licentiousness,
Is grateful to just states. Most spotless kingdom,
And men—O happy—born under good stars,
Where what is honest you may freely think,

---

321. *breathings*] utterances; *O.E.D.* sense 6 ('Of the wind: Gentle blowing' 1635) in figurative sense (unrecorded). This also antedates *O.E.D.*'s first example for sense 4, 'utterance', which is in *Ant.*, I.iii.14: 'I am sorry to give breathing to my purpose.'

323. *complexion*] his own nature or mind.

324–5. *Dear sleep and lust . . . known myself*] Montaigne (Crawford), III.v.126–7: '*Alexander* said, that he knew himselfe mortall chiefly by this action, and by sleeping: sleepe doth stifle, and suppresseth the faculties of our soule: and that both [devoureth] and dissipates them.' 'This action' is the sexual act. Marston strains somewhat to fit the passage in here.

326. *grateful*] pleasing, agreeable. Hercules returns to this description of flattery at the end of the next act: 'O mighty flattery, / Thou easiest, common'st, and most grateful venom . . .' (II.i.580–1).

sleek] oily, fawning.

328. *soon*] 'So the old eds.; but quy. "soote" (sweet)?' (Bullen).

330. *indictions*] reproofs, admonishments; or perhaps a more formal sense of 'indictments'. Marston may well have the fate of his own satires in mind (in 1598); free speech was even more chancy under James, not because of a continual repression but because of inconsistency and unpredictability.

331. *freeness*] outspoken honesty. 'Freenesse of speech, is when we speake boldly and without feare, euen to the proudest of them, whatsouer we please or haue list to speake. *Diogenes*, herein did excell, and feared no man when he sawe iust cause to say his minde. This worlde wanteth such as hee was, and hath ouer many such as neuer honest man was, that is to saie, flatterers, fauners, and soothers of mens sayings.' Wilson, p. 200.

332. *Most spotless kingdom . . .*] 'Marston probably designed this as a compliment on the constitution of his own country' (Dilke). The opposite is more likely.

Speak what you think, and write what you do speak,   335
Not bound to servile soothings! But since our rank
Hath ever been afflicted with these flies
(That blow corruption on the sweetest virtues),
I will revenge us all upon you all
With the same stratagem we still are caught,   340
Flattery itself; and sure all know the sharpness
Of reprehensive language is even blunted
To full contempt, since vice is now termed fashion,
And most are grown to ill even with defence:
I vow to waste this most prodigious heat,   345
That falls into my age like scorching flames

341. know] *TC;* knowes *Qq.*   343–4. contempt, since . . . defence:]
This ed.; contempt, since . . . defence, *Qq;* contempt: since . . . defence,
Dilke; contempt. Since . . . ill, . . . defence *AHB;* contempt. Since . . .
defence, *Smith.*

336. *soothings*] flattery. Cf. IV.i.558, n.
our rank] i.e. governors, princes.
337. *blow corruption*] Two senses of 'blow' are used here, the depositing
of eggs by flies, and the bloating of rotten meat; the connection is easily
made.
340. *the same . . . caught*] the same trick (of flattery) by which we rulers
are continually caught.
343. *since . . . fashion*] In *CS.*, III, 43–50, Marston writes:
　　　O frantick men! that thinke all villanie
　　　The compleate honors of Nobilitie.
　　　When some damn'd vice, som strange mishapen sute,
　　　Makes youths esteeme themselues in hie repute.
　　　O age! in which our gallants boast to be
　　　Slaues vnto riot, and lewd luxury!
　　　Nay, when they blush, and thinke an honest act
　　　Dooth their supposed vertues maculate!
And again in *DC.*, III.i.283: 'What old times held as crimes, are now but
fashion.' Crawford finds the source of the two later instances in Montaigne,
'Of Repenting', III,ii,25: '*Quae fuerant vitia, mores sunt. What earst were
vices are now growne fashions.*'
344. *And most . . . defence*] either (i) most of those who have spoken
against vice (defence in the sense of moral attack, prohibition) have come
into trouble; or (ii) most people have become vicious (or as they call it,
fashionable) while in fact believing they are vindicated in doing so ('euen
with defence'). The first seems more probable.
345. *this . . . heat*] the unusual, and as yet unchannelled, energy which
he described in I.i. He now sees a worthwhile way of expanding this

In depth of numbed December, in flattering all
In all of their extremest viciousness,
Till in their own loved race they fall most lame,
And meet full butt the close of vice's shame.   *Exit.*   350

349. loved (lou'd)] *Qq;* lewd (leud) *conj. HHW.*

---

energy through the correction of abuses in the court of Urbin. Note the
various connotations Marston gives the term *heat*: sexuality (IV.i.403),
alchemy (II.i.596), eloquence (II.i.484, 514), rationality (III.i.468). The
present passage suggests he sees them related to each other through a sort
of Einsteinian law of thermodynamics.

347–8. *flattering . . . viciousness*]. As Faunus, Hercules thus serves the
same function as Malevole but in the opposite manner: 'therefore does he
afflict all in that to which they are most affected.' *Malc.*, I.i.34–5.

348. *viciousness*] the general category of 'vice', rather than the modern,
more specialised sense of malice or spite.

350. *full butt*] final end, goal.

the close of vice's shame] the proper end of vice, which is shame (rather
than 'the end of that shame which belongs to vice'). This is what occurs
at the end of the play, though in an unexpectedly mild form.

Act II

[*Enter*] HEROD *and* NYMPHADORO *with napkins in their hands, followed by pages with stools and meat.*

Herod. Come, sir, a stool, boy. These court feasts are to us servitors court fasts; such scambling, such shift for to eat, and where to eat: here a squire of low degree hath got the carcass of a plover, there pages of the chamber divide the spoils of a tattered pheasant, here the sewer   5 has friended a country gentleman with a sweet green goose, and there a young fellow that late has bought his office has caught a woodcock by the nose—[*Sings*] 'with cups full ever flowing'.

Act II] ACTVS SECVNDVS SCENA PRIMA. *Qq.*   o.1. Enter] *Dilke.*
8. S.D.] *This ed.*   9. ever flowing] *Qq;* overflowing *TC.*

0.2. *meat*] food.

2. *servitors*] The function of Herod and Nymphadoro here makes their standing in the court unclear; perhaps they have been honoured by being made overseers of the proceedings rather than mere waiters.

scambling] scrambling, hasty effort. 'If ever thou beest mine, Kate, . . . I get thee with scambling. . . .' (*H5*, V.ii.218).

shift] use of expedient, contrivance. Cf. v.i.136.

3. *a squire of low degree*] i.e., an upstart. But perhaps the phrase already had the sense it has in Brome's *The City Wit* (1628): 'an Esquire of low Degree. Or in direct phrase, a Pandar' (*Works*, I, 345).

5. *sewer*] 'An attendant at a meal who superintended the arrangement of the table, the seating of the guests, and the tasting and serving of the dishes. Formerly an officer of the Royal Household' (*O.E.D.*).

6–7. *sweet green goose*] 'a young tender goose' (Wood). For *green*, cf. IV.i.47.

8. *woodcock*] a good bird for eating, but better known for its proverbial stupidity. See Tilley, W 746.

9. *'with cups full ever flowing'*] Evidently the refrain of a song, but I have been unable to locate it.

Nym. But is not Faunus preferred with a right hand?   10

Herod. Did you ever see a fellow so spurted up in a
    moment? He has got the right ear of the duke, the
    prince, princess, most of the lords, but all of the ladies;
    why, he is become their only minion, usher, and
    supporter.   15

Nym. He hath gotten more loved reputation of virtue, of
    learning, of all graces, in one hour, than all your snarl-
    ing reformers have in—

Herod. Nay, that's unquestionable, and indeed what a
    fruitless labour, what a filling of Danae's tub, is it be-   20
    come to inveigh against folly! Community takes away
    the sense, and example the shame. No,
    Praise me these fellows, hang on their chariot wheel
    And mount with them whom fortune heaves, nay drives;
    A stoical sour virtue seldom thrives.   25
    Oppose such fortune, and then burst with those are pitied.

23. *so AHB; prose Qq.*   24–6.] *so Q2; prose Q1.*   26. burst] *Q2;*
bursts *Q1.*

---

10. *preferred with a right hand*] raised (in rank) with marks of (the
duke's) friendship.

12. *the right ear of the duke*] The proverb is more properly applied to a
pig (see Tilley, S 684); it appears also in *Eastward Ho*, II.ii.278, in a
passage usually attributed to Marston.

13. *most of the lords, but . . . ladies*] one of Marston's favourite stylistic
tricks; cf. v.i.231–2, 'with the assent of some of the lords, most of the
ladies, and all the commons. . . .'

14. *usher*] attendant, chamberlain.

20. *Danae's tub*] '"Danaus' tub" is again mentioned in this act; it is an
allusion to the supposed punishment of the Danaides, who after death
were condemned to fill with water a tub *perforated with holes*, as an eternal
punishment for the murder of their husbands' (Dilke). Either Marston
confused Danaus with his daughters or he intended a strained pun on
'Danes' and their traditional capacity for drinking.

21. *Community*] commonness, ordinary occurrence.

22. *sense*] the ability to perceive (folly). Cf. IV.i.701.

23–9.] By the image of the chariot wheels (23 and 29) Marston produces
an interestingly concrete variation of the commonplace of Fortune's
wheel.

24. *heaves*] raises (without the modern connotation of effort).

26. *Oppose . . . pitied*] The sense seems to be: if you neglect to take the
opportunity to associate yourself with the man that rises to power, expect

The hill of chance is paved with poor men's bones,
And bulks of luckless souls, over whose eyes
Their chariot wheels must ruthless grate, that rise.

Enter HERCULES, *freshly suited.*

Nym. Behold that thing of most fortunate, most prosperous   30
impudence, Don Faunus himself.

Herod. Blessed and long-lasting be thy carnation ribbon,
O man of more than wit, much more than virtue, of
fortune! Faunus, wilt eat any of a young spring sallet?

Herc. Where did the herbs grow, my gallant, where did   35
they grow?

Herod. Hard by in the city here.

Herc. No, I'll none—I'll eat no city herbs, no city roots; for
here in the city a man shall have his excrements in his
teeth again within four and twenty hours; I love no city   40
sallets: hast any canary?

Nym. How the poor snake wriggles with this sudden
warmth.   *Herod drinks.*

27–9. *Q2; not in Q1.*   31. impudence] *Q2; not in Q1.*   34. Faunus]
Q2; not in Q1.   42. *Aside*] *conj. this ed.*   snake] *Q2;* snayle *Q1.*
this] *Qq;* his *AHB.*

---

to achieve only ruin ('burst'), like the lowest of humanity (characterised
by Epictetus as those who are the object of pity).

28. *bulks*] bodies.

31. *impudence*] Since Faunus gets ahead by flattery, it seems odd that
he could be thought of at this early stage as insolently disrespectful, in-
delicate or shamelessly forward. What is chiefly meant, apparently, is a
kind of presumption; whether this is the cause, result, or summation of
the nature of his quick social climb is uncertain.

32. *carnation*] flesh-pink. 'How much carnation ribbon may a man buy
for a remuneration?' (*LLL.*, III.i.146–7). It was apparently popular in
courtly dress; see Linthicum, pp. 37–8.

34. *sallet*] salad.

39–40. *a man shall have his excrements . . . four and twenty hours*] a poke
at unsanitary conditions in London. See Stow's *Survey of London*, ed.
H. B. Wheatley (1956), pp. 14 and 16.

42–3.] Apparently Nymphadoro is accusing Faunus of ungratefulness
or snobbery. Cf. Webster's *The Duchess of Malfi*, II.iii.38–9 (and Lucas's
note): 'You are an impudent snake indeed, sir, / Are you scarce warm,
and do you shew your sting?' On the other hand, Faunus may have been

Herod. Here, Faunus, a health as deep as a female.

Herc. 'Fore Jove, we must be more endeared.   45

Nym. How dost thou feel thyself now, Fawn?

Herc. Very womanly, with my fingers: I protest I think I
    shall love you. Are you married? I am truly taken with
    your virtues. Are you married?

Herod. Yes.   50

Herc. Why, I like you well for it.

Herod. No, troth, Fawn, I am not married.

Herc. Why, I like you better for it; 'fore heaven, I must
    love you.

Herod. Why, Fawn, why?   55

Herc. 'Fore heaven, you are blest with three rare graces:
    fine linen, clean linings, a sanguine complexion, and I
    am sure, an excellent wit, for you are a gentleman born.

Herod. Thank thee, sweet Fawn, but why is clean linen
    such a grace, I prithee?   60

Herc. O my excellent and inward dearly approved friend—

---

57. fine … linings] *Qq;* clean linen *conj. this ed.*

---

given a draught of wine, though no such stage direction is extant; this
could have done the warming.

44. *a health as deep as a female*] possibly a pun on *deep* as 'cunning'
(*O.E.D.* sense 18), but more probably an obscene physical suggestion.

45. *endeared*] close, held mutually dear; antedates first *O.E.D.* example:
see Cross, *N&Q,* CCII (1957), 222.

46–7.] punning on 'feel thyself' as 'regard yourself' and 'excite yourself
(sexually)'.

57. *fine linen, clean linings.*] Almost certainly the compositor has printed
both what Marston first wrote and the correction. 'Fine linen' and 'clean
linings' are virtually synonymous; Herod picks up the phrase 'clean *linen*'
rather than 'clean linings'; and Hercules spoke of *three* graces, while the
text as it stands has four.

61. *inward*] (= inwardly) intimately, fervently. A remarkable piece of
comic balloon-pricking when it turns out that the gushingly warm and
intimate friend can't quite remember Herod's name.

approved] esteemed. This is *O.E.D.* sense 3 (for some reason *O.E.D.*
does not list a sense 2), for which the first example is 1667 (Milton's
Paradise Lost, VI, 36). Sense 1 is 'proved by experience'; there has been
no real proof of friendship so far—though a flatterer can be given leeway.
Sense 3 seems more likely.

what's your name, sir? Clean linen is the first our life
craves, and the last our death enjoys.

Herod. But what hope rests for Nymphadoro? Thou art now
within the buttons of the prince: shall the duke his   65
father carry the lady?

Herc. 'Tis to be hoped not.

Nym. That's some relief, as long as there's hope.

Herc. But sure, sir, 'tis almost undoubted the lady will
carry him.   70

Nym. O pestilent air, is there no plot so cunning, no surmise
so false, no way of avoidance?

Herod. Hast thou any pity, either of his passion or the
lady's years—a gentleman in the summer and hunting
season of his youth, the lady met in the same warmth?   75
Were't not to be wept that such a sapless chafing-dish-
using old dotard as the Duke of Ferrara, with his
withered hand, should pluck such a bud, such a—oh,
the life of sense!

---

66. carry] *This ed.;* marry *Qq.*   73. *Herod.] London; Herc. Q1; Her: Q2.*
75. his] *Q1;* hir *Q2.*

---

65. *within the buttons of*] intimate with.

66. *carry*] i.e. win her. This emendation makes sense of Hercules' first
reply (a joke shared with the audience; the elderly 'groom' has doubts
about his strength) and his second, which completes a pun.

71. *surmise*] libellous allegation or rumour (which would prevent the
wedding); the 'malice of lewd tongues' which Dulcimel anticipates in
I.ii.145. The choice of the word shows the influence of Marston's legal
training.

72. *avoidance*] Whether the sense is 'escape', 'prevention', or 'invalida-
tion', the usage antedates *O.E.D.*'s first example. See also Cross, *N&Q*,
CCIII (1958), 5.

76. *sapless*] 'lacking the vital juices, hence strengthless' (*O.E.D.*).
Marston uses the word often.

76–7. *chafing-dish-using*] 'Humorous compound unrecorded in
O.E.D.', Cross, *N&Q*, CCI (1956), 331. Cross is perhaps making too
much of a nonce word. The chafing-dish is 'A vessel to hold burning
charcoal or other fuel, for heating anything placed upon it; a portable
grate' (*O.E.D.*). The duke would use it to warm his old bones as well as his
food.

Nym. Thou art now a perfect courtier of just fashion, good   80
    grace; canst not relieve us?
Herc. Ha' ye any money?
Nym. Pish, Fawn, we are young gallants.
Herc. The liker to have no money. But, my young gallants,
    to speak like myself: I must hug your humour. Why   85
    look you, there is fate, destiny, constellations, and
    planets (which though they are under nature, yet they
    are above women). Who hath read the book of chance?
    No, cherish your hope, sweeten your imaginations
    with thoughts of—ah, why, women are the most giddy,   90
    uncertain motions under heaven; 'tis neither propor-
    tion of body, virtue of mind, amplitude of fortune,
    greatness of blood, but only mere chanceful appetite
    sways them; which makes some one like a man, be it
    but for the paring of his nails. *Via*! As for inequality art   95
    not a gentleman?
Nym. That I am, and my beneficence shall show it.
Herc. I know you are, by that only word beneficence, which

80–1. fashion, good grace;] *This ed.;* fashion, good grace, *Qq;* fashion:
good grace, *Dilke.*   98. that] *Q1;* the *Q2.*

80–1. *just fashion, good grace*] correct style (and) in favour (with the
right people).

83–4. *gallants . . . no money*] The expense of keeping up with fashion
kept most young gallants in constant debt; one thinks of Witgood in
Middleton's *A Trick to Catch the Old One.*

85. *to speak like myself: I must hug your humour*] To speak honestly
(but also: to speak like a Faunus, a flatterer) I must embrace your opinion
on this subject.

86–7. *constellations, and planets*] i.e. one must always take into consideration astrological influences; there may be hope there, and at least
they are more dependable than women. (We should not expect the utmost
coherence in Faunus's squibs. In this passage, as in others, he switches
between reassuring and teasing the courtiers.)

91. *motions*] may have the sense here of 'puppets', easily manipulated
(as in *DC.,* III.i.122–3); or continuing the astrological imagery, the most
unpredictable bodies that move under heaven.

95. Via] See note for I.ii.316.

inequality] i.e., the difference in rank between Nymphadoro and
Dulcimel (or, perhaps, Tiberio).

only speaks of the future tense ('*shall* show it'); but may
I breathe in your bosoms? I only fear Tiberio will   100
abuse his father's trust, and so make your hopes
desperate.

Nym. How, the prince? Would he only stood cross to my
wishes, he should find me an Italian.

Herc. How, an Italian?   105

Herod. By thy aid, an Italian. Dear Faunus, thou art now
wriggled into the prince's bosom, and thy sweet hand
should minister that nectar to him should make him
immortal.

Nym. In direct phrase, thou shouldst murder the prince, so   110
revenge thine own wrongs, and be rewarded for that
revenge.

Herc. Afore the light of my eyes, I think I shall admire,
wonder at you. What, ha' ye plots, projects, correspondences, and stratagems? Why are not you in better   115
place?

Enter SIR AMOROSO.

Who's this?

Herod. My eldest brother, Sir Amoroso Debile-Dosso.

99. show] *Deighton;* know *Qq.*   101. his] *Q1;* your *Q2.*   109–10. immortal. / *Nym.* In] *London;* immortall; *Nymphadoro* in *Qq.*   117–18.
this? / *Herod.* My . . . Debile-Dosso.] *Dilke;* this? *Herod . . . Debilidoso?*
Q1; this *Herod . . . Debilidoso? Q2;* this *Herod, . . . Debili-Doso? TC.*

---

103. *Would he only stood cross to*] should he just stand opposed to, or
thwarting (my desire).

105. *an Italian*] a Macchiavellian, a conspirator, a murderer. 'A
poisoner' (Wood). For the Elizabethan view of 'Macchiavellian' Italy, see
Mario Praz, *The Flaming Heart* (1958), 90–145, and G. K. Hunter,
'English folly and Italian vice', *Jacobean Theatre* (1960).

110. S.H. Nym.] The ascription to Nymphadoro is obvious enough; the
two gallants are trying to persuade Hercules to do the dirty work.

114–15. *correspondences*] 'intercourse or communications of a secret or
illicit nature' (*O.E.D.* †5.†b.). Marston antedates *O.E.D.*'s first example,
which is 1639.

115–16. *Why . . . place?*] Perhaps Hercules emphasises 'you' to remind
them of I.ii.228–9.

Herc. Oh I know him. God bless thine eyes, sweet Sir
Amoroso: a rouse, a *vin de monte*, to the health of thy   120
chine, my dear sweet signior.

Sir Amor. Pardon me, sir, I drink no wine this spring.

Herod. Oh no, sir, he takes the diet this spring always.
Boy, my brother's bottle.

Sir Amor. Faith, Fawn, an odd unwholesome cold makes   125
me still hoarse and rheumatic.

Herod. Yes, in troth, a paltry murr; last morning he blew
nine bones out of his nose with an odd unwholesome
murr. How does my sister, your lady ? What, does she
breed ?   130

Herc. I perceive, knight, you have children. O, 'tis a blessed
assurance of heaven's favour, and long-lasting name, to
have many children.

Sir Amor. But I ha' none, Fawn, now.

Herc. O that's most excellent, a right special happiness. He   135
shall not be a drudge to his cradle, a slave to his child; he

121. chine] *Q2;* chin *Q1.*   122. *Q1; not in Q2.*   125. unwholesome]
Q1 corr., Q2; wholesome *Q1 uncorr.*   129. what,] *AHB;* what *Qq.*

---

120. *a rouse*] a full draught of liquor, a toast.

vin de monte] 'Vino del monte, *the best kind of wine in Italie*', Florio
(1598). Dilke silently emends to 'a vin de menton', and Bullen suggests it
is 'possibly a corrupt abbreviation of Ital. *Vino di Montepulciano*'.

121. *chine*] As Bullen notes, Q1 and TC have 'chin'. Since this is
addressed to the amorous knight of the weak back, 'chine' seems more
likely. Hercules has first given a blessing to the knight's eyes (which can
still be amorous), and now gives a health to his back (which can do with
some help).

123. *takes the diet*] i.e. is undergoing treatment for venereal disease.

always] continually.

127. *murr*] severe form of catarrh. Wood notes that it was often identified
with venereal disease, and gives this example from Chapman's *Monsieur
D'Olive*: 'Or that he had some gentlemanly humour, / The murr, the
headache, the catarrh, the bone-ache' (II.ii.292–3).

129. *sister*] sister-in-law, as at II.i.178.

129–30. *does she breed ?*] Is she with child ? *O.E.D.*'s first example for
this sense of 'breed' is 1629.

136. *a drudge to his cradle*] Cf. *JDE.* (HHW, III, 184): 'Ha, I was not
borne to be my Cradles drudge. . . .'

shall be sure not to cherish another's blood, nor toil to
advance peradventure some rascal's lust; without
children a man is unclogged, his wife almost a maid.
Messalina, thou criedst out, 'O blessed barrenness!'   140
Why, once with child, the very Venus of a lady's
entertainment hath lost all pleasure.

Sir Amor. By this ring, Faunus, I do hug thee with most
passionate affection, and shall make my wife thank thee.

Herod. Nay, my brother grudgeth not at my probable in-   145
heritance. He means once to give a younger brother
hope to see fortune.

Nym. And yet I hear, Sir Amorous, you cherish your loins
with high art, the only engrosser of eringoes, prepared

148. Amorous] *Q1; Amorosus Q2;* Amoroso *AHB.*

---

138. *lust*] Here *lust* seems to mean 'the effect or result of lust', illicit
progeny; so also at II.i.292. This sense is not recorded in *O.E.D.*

unclogged] unfettered.

140. *Messalina, thou criedst out, 'O blessed barrenness!'*] Marston had
already mentioned the legendary lasciviousness of Messalina, wife of the
Emperor Claudius, in *SV.*, III, 90, and *SV.*, IX, 121–6. The exclamation
credited to her is apparently unhistorical, but Marston might have confused her story with that of Agripinna: 'Oh barrennes, of all most happy,
sure / Which wordes with griefe, did AGRIPPINA grone'; Geoffrey
Whitney, *A Choice of Emblems* (1586), Y3*v*, ed. Green, p. 174.

141–2. *the very Venus of a lady's entertainment*] the very essence of a
lady's ability to delight men; but also, specifically, the female pudendum.
See Prologus, 17, and III.i.37. Here it is more than the *quality* that excites
love (*O.E.D.* sense †3) rather the *essence*.

143. *By this ring*] perhaps Sir Amoroso makes him a gift of it.

146. *once*] i.e. for once here is an elder brother willing to provide for his
younger brother.

148. *cherish*] care for tenderly, pamper.

149.ff.] Similar lists of aphrodisiacs appear in *Malc.*, II.iii.6–15, and
II.ii.19–23.

149. *engrosser*] 'One who buys in large quantities, especially with the
view of being able to secure a monopoly' (*O.E.D.* †1). Davenport, in a
note on *SV.*, XI, 81, notes that 'engross' 'was a word in bad odour in
1598. . . . Proclamations against engrossing were issued several times'
(p. 363). Evidently the practice was still sufficiently notorious for Marston
to exploit its comic possibilities here and in the trial scene (see V.i.196).

eringoes] the candied root of the sea-holly, used as an aphrodisiac. See
Wiv., V.v.20–3: 'Let the sky rain potatoes; . . . and snow eringoes; let
there come a tempest of provocation'. See also *SV.*, III, 69–70, and VIII, 112.

cantharides, cullisses made of dissolved pearl and   150
bruised amber; the pith of parkets and candied lambstones are his perpetual meats. Beds made of the down
under pigeons' wings and goose necks, fomentations,
baths, electuaries, frictions, and all the nurses of most
forcible excited concupiscence, he useth with most nice   155
and tender industry.

Herc. Pish, *zoccoli.* No, Nymphadoro, if Sir Amorous

157. *zoccoli*] *Q1; Zuccoli Q2.*   Amorous] *Qq; Amoroso AHB.*

---

150. *cantharides*] Spanish fly. *O.E.D.*'s first example of the sense
'aphrodisiac' is 1611.

cullisses] 'A cullis was a strong meat broth (Fr. coulis), but in Elizabethan use it is most commonly a broth in which gold and other precious
ingredients have been dissolved. Nares and Bullen quote from Middleton's *A Mad World My Masters*: "Let gold, amber, and dissolved pearl
be common ingrediences, and that you cannot compose a cullice without
'em."' (Wood). *A Mad World* (*c.* 1606), II.vi.49–51.

151. *bruised*] ground to a powder.

amber] either ambergris (a morbid secretion of whales) or the fossil
resin.

pith] marrow, or core of the horn in an animal.

parkets] apparently a variant spelling of 'porkets', pig; supposed to
have health-giving and aphrodisiac powers. See B. Nicholson's note in
N&Q, LXIX (2 February 1884), 93–4. Bullen conjectures 'parroquets' and
Wood (followed by Smith) 'parakeets'.

candied] preserved or incrusted with sugar. Cross notes that *O.E.D.*'s
first example is for 1616; *N&Q*, CCI (1956), 331.

151–2. *lambstones*] the testicles of a lamb. Cross notes Marston's use
of the word in *Malc.* (HHW, I, 167) as antedating *O.E.D.*'s first example,
(1613); *N&Q*, CC (1955), 427.

153. *fomentations*] the application of hot, soaked cloths; from the
figurative sense (first recorded for 1612), it was evidently used as a sexual
stimulant.

154. *electuaries*] medicines consisting of a powder or other ingredient
mixed with honey, jam or syrup.

frictions] rub-downs.

nurses] the figurative sense, of whatever nourishes or cares for something.

155. *forcible*] either 'strong, powerful', or quasi-adverbially, 'forcibly'.

157. zoccoli] '*Zoccoli Zoccoli, tush tush, awaie, in faith sir no, yea in my
other hose, we vse also to say so, when speaking of any body in secrecie and
the partie comes in, as the Latins say, Lupus est in fabula*', Florio (1598). In
the 1611 edition, Florio adds, at the beginning of the definition, 'as we say

would ha' children, let him lie on a mattress, plow or
thresh, eat onions, garlic, and leek porridge. Pharaoh
and his council were mistaken; and their device to   160
hinder the increase of procreation in the Israelites with
enforcing them to much labour of body, and to feed
hard with beets, garlic, and onions (meats that make the
original of man most sharp and taking), was absurd.

163. meats] *Q1;* meat *Q2.*

---

in mockery'; and at the end, 'so the Italians say, Zoccoli, Zoccoli'. It
would be interesting to know how much of his Italian Marston learned
from his mother. He was evidently comfortable enough in the language to
compose the duet for Antonio and Mellida in Act IV of the first *Antonio*
play (IIIW, I, 48).

158. *mattress*] evidently a mat or very rough sleeping support, as
opposed to the soft 'beds' described on ll. 152–3; as with his prescription
of food, Hercules calls upon the traditional opposition of the fertility of
the working classes and the infertility of the effete well-to-do. For the
leeks, onions and garlic, see Numbers, xi. 4–5, and for the general source
of 'Pharaoh and his council', Exodus, i. 8–12: '. . . But the more they vexed
them, the more they multiplied and grew.' Jürgen Schäfer exaggerates
somewhat in saying that 'Hercules's words are nothing but a condensed
paraphrase of a paragraph in Huarte' (*N&Q*, ccxvi [1971], 16). In *The
Examination of Mans Wit* (1594, repr. 1969), Richard Carew's rendering
of an Italian translation of Juan Huarte de San Juan's *Examen de Ingenios
para las Ciencias* (1575), appears the following: 'This point of Philosophy
was not vnderstood by *Pharao*, nor by his councell . . . And the remedie
which he vsed, to hinder that the people of Israel should not encrease so
fast, or at least that so many male children might not be borne (which he
most feared) was to keepe them vnder with much toile of body, and to
cause them for to eat leeks, garlicke, and onions, . . . VVhich preuailed so
litle, as if to quench a great fire, he should throw thereinto much oile or
grease: but if he or any of his counsellors, had been seen in this point of
naturall Philosophy, he should haue giuen them barly bread, lettice,
melons, cucūbers, & citrons to eat, and haue kept them well fed and well
filled with drinke, and not haue suffered them to take anie paine. For by
this means, their seed would haue become cold and moist, & thereof more
women than men bin begotten; and in short time their life haue been
abridged' (293–4).

163. *meats*] Here again it means 'food' generally.

164. *original*] O.E.D. does not record this sense, which seems to be
'source of generation', i.e. the efficacy of the seed.

taking] effective.

No, he should have given barley bread, lettuce, melons,   165
cucumbers, huge store of veal and fresh beef, blown up
their flesh, held them from exercise, rolled them in
feathers, and most severely seen them drunk once a day:
then would they at their best have begotten wenches,
and in short time their generation enfeebled to nothing.   170

Sir Amor. O divine Faunus, where might a man take up
forty pound in a commodity of garlic and onions?
Nymphadoro, thine ear.

Herc. [*to Herod*] Come, what are you fleering at? There's
some weakness in your brother you wrinkle at thus;   175
come, prithee impart; what, we are mutually incorporated, turned one into another, brewed together. Come,
I believe you are familiar with your sister, and it were
known.

Herod. Witch, Faunus, witch. Why, how dost dream I   180
live? Is't fourscore a year, thinkst thou, maintains my

---

168. severely] *Q1;* s.uerely *Q2;* surely *AHB.*   174. S.D.] *This ed.*
177. brewed (brued)] *Qq;* brued [*sic*] *AHB.*

---

165. *barley bread, lettuce*] These and the foods that follow are 'cooling'
foods and thus antaphrodisiacs. See John Gerard's *Herbal* (1597), *passim,*
for these and the 'hot' foods preceding.

168. *feathers*] i.e. soft bedding made of feathers. *O.E.D.*'s only example
of this sense (II.9) is dated 1649.

drunk . . . begotten wenches] 'Who goes drunk to bed begets but a girl'
(Tilley, B 195). Tilley cites this passage.

170. *generation*] capacity to procreate (?); or simply, offspring. Cf.
II.i.279 n., and IV.i.108.

172. *commodity*] a quantity of wares, a 'lot'. 'I would thou and I knew
where a commodity of good names were to be bought' (*1H4*,I.ii.93).

174. *fleering*] grinning contemptuously, sneering.

175. *wrinkle*] 'The wrinkles here meant were caused by the sneering
smiles of Herod' (Dilke). One of Dilke's example is from *Troil.*: 'Buried
this sigh in wrinkle of a smile' (I.i.38).

177. *brewed*] Bullen, who prints 'brued [sic]', evidently did not recognise
the word in its quarto spelling.

178. *sister*] sister-in-law.

180. *Witch, Faunus, witch*] Proverbial, for one who has made a good
guess; 'I think you are a witch' (Tilley, W 585).

geldings, my pages, foot-cloths, my best feeding, high
play, and excellent company? No, 'tis from hence,
from hence, I mint some four hundred pound a year.

Herc. Dost thou live like a porter, by thy back, boy?   185

Herod. As for my weak-reined brother, hang him, he
has sore shins. Damn him—heteroclite! his brain's
perished. His youth spent his fodder so fast on others'
cattle that he now wants for his own in winter. I am
fain to supply, Fawn, for which I am supplied.   190

185. thy] *Q1;* the *Q2.*   188. others'] *AHB;* others *Qq;* other's *Dilke.*
189. in]*Q1; not in Q2.*

181–3. *my geldings . . . excellent company*] Cf. Quicksilver's high living
in *Eastward Ho,* IV.ii.228–33.

182. *foot-cloths*] richly-ornamented cloths, laid over the back of a horse
and reaching to the ground on either side; a 'status-symbol'.

best feeding] first-class food, or dining places.

182–3. *high play*] hard gambling (?).

183–4. *hence*] This evidently requires a gesture, probably obscene.

185. *live like a porter, by thy back*] Cf. III.i.232–3: 'what burden is there
so heavy to a porter's back as virginity . . .' In the present passage, the joke
is of course connected to the sexual connotation of 'back'. See Montaigne,
III, v, 102.

boy] Hercules evidently feels secure enough as the successful 'Faunus'
to address Herod familiarly; the word 'boy' still had possible connotations
of contempt or at least condescension, e.g. in *Cor.*

186. *weak-reined*] weak-loined; impotent.

187. *sore shins*] perhaps there is a comic hesitation before Herod says
'shins'; any part of the skeleton will do, since the reference is to 'bone-
ache', venereal disease.

heteroclite] a person or thing that deviates from the ordinary rule, an
anomaly. *O.E.D.*'s first example is dated 1605.

187–8. *his brain's perished*] probably from the disease itself, but
perhaps from the cure: 'Hang him, a gilder that hath his brains perish'd
with quick-silver is not more cold in the liver.' Webster's *The White Devil*
(1612), I.ii.27–8.

188–9. *His youth . . . in winter*] In Act IV of Wilkins's *The Miseries of
Enforced Marriage,* Butler describes the sexually bankrupt Ilford as 'Kex,
dryde Kex [a sapless husk or stem], that in summer ha bin so liberal to
fodder other mens cattle, and scarce haue inough to keepe your owne in
Winter' (Q1, F4*v*). As Richard Levin points out (*N&Q,* CCXVII [1972],
453), the image is more coherent in Wilkins; but Wilkins's play cannot be
earlier than 1605 because of its source, and neatness does not prove
originality.

190. *supply . . . supplied*] supply = do sexual service; supplied = paid
(by Garbetza) or possibly, am well provided for (in sexual prowess).

Herc. Dost branch him, boy ?

Herod. What else, Fawn ?

Herc. What else ? Nay, 'tis enough. Why, many men
      corrupt other men's wives, some their maids, others
      their neighbours' daughters; but to lie with one's   195
      brother's wedlock, O, my dear Herod, 'tis vile and un-
      common lust.

Herod. 'Fore heaven, I love thee to the heart. Well, I may
      praise God for my brother's weakness, for I assure thee
      the land shall descend to me, my little Fawn.   200

Herc. To thee, my little Herod ? O, my rare rascal, I do
      find more and more in thee to wonder at, for thou art
      indeed—if I prosper, thou shalt know what. Who's
      this ?

                    Enter DON ZUCCONE.

Herod. What! Know you not Don Zuccone, the only   205
      desperately railing lord at's lady that ever was confid-
      ently melancholy; that egregious idiot, that husband

---

196. vile] *Qq;* royal *conj. AHB.*   203–4. Who's this ?] *Q2;* not in *Q1.*
206. lord] *Q2; not in Q1.*

---

191. *branch*] cuckold. The 'branch' refers to the horns of the cuckold,
sometimes depicted as branching antlers. This image merges with that of
grafting plants; see IV.i.100–1. Cross notes that this antedates *O.E.D.*'s first
example, which is 1633, as do two instances in *Insatiate C.*, I.i.461
(HHW, III, 18), and II.iii.109–10 (HHW, II, 164); *N&Q*, CXCIX (1954),
426.

196. *wedlock.*] wife.

196–7. *vile and uncommon lust*] 'This must be a misprint—should we
read "royal" ?' (Bullen). No. 'Since vice is now termed fashion' (I.ii.343),
Hercules can offer, and Herod can accept, such a statement as a compliment. Wood points to a similar passage in Act II of *DC.*, where Frances-
china calls her bawd a 'vile woman, reprobate woman, naughtie woman',
with a tone almost of endearment, after the bawd reminds her how she
had praised Freevill to her as 'a fool, an unthrift, a true whoremaster, . . .
a constant drab keeper' (HHW, II, 88).

206–7. *confidently*] thoroughly; perhaps 'dogmatically', in which case it
would antedate *O.E.D.*'s first example for that sense (1611).

207. *melancholy*] affected by the disease or 'humour' of melancholy,

of the most witty, fair, and (be it spoken with many
men's true grief) most chaste Lady Zoya? But we have
entered into a confederacy of afflicting him.   210

Herc. Plots ha' you laid, inductions dangerous?

Nym. A quiet bosom to my sweet Don. Are you going to
visit your lady?

Zuc. What o'clock is't, is it past three?

Herod. Past four, I assure you, sweet Don.   215

Zuc. Oh, then I may be admitted; her afternoon's private
nap is taken. I shall take her napping. I hear there's one
jealous that I lie with my own wife, and begins to withdraw his hand. I protest, I vow—and you will, on my
knees I'll take my sacrament on it—I lay not with her   220
this four year, this four year; let her not be turned upon
me, I beseech you.

Herc. My dear Don!

Zuc. O Faunus, dost know our lady?

Herc. Your lady?   225

Zuc. No, our lady. For the love of charity, incorporate with
her; I would have all nations and degrees, all know our
lady, for I covet only to be undoubtedly notorious.

Herc. For indeed, sir, a repressed fame mounts like

---

221. her this four] *Q2;* her this long *Q1.*   223. Don!] *AHB;* Don? *Qq.*

---

more particularly love-melancholy. For the connection between love-
melancholy and jealousy see Burton's *The Anatomy of Melancholy* (1621),
Part III, section 3. Zoya makes the connection as well at II.i.406–7:
'Prove such a melancholy jealous ass as he is?'

211.] 'Plots have I laid, inductions dangerous' (*R3*, I.i.32).

217. *I shall take her napping.*] I shall catch her in adultery. 'Nay, I have
ta'en you napping, gentle love, / And have forsworn you with Hortensio'
(*Shr.*, IV.ii.46–7). 'Qy. "I shall *not* take her napping"?' (Deighton, p. 8).
This is rather too literal-minded. Zuccone is only vaguely threatening.

218. *jealous*] suspicious.

218–19. *begins to withdraw his hand*] 'either ceases to pay as much
attention to her as he did formerly, or begins to look cool on me; it holds
good either way' (Dilke).

226. *incorporate*] copulate. As Cross notes, *O.E.D.* has only one example
of this usage, and that is 1622; *N&Q*, CCVI (1961), 125.

camomile, the more trod down, the more it grows; 230
    things known common and undoubted, lose rumour.

Nym. Sir, I hope yet your conjectures may err; your lady
    keeps full-face, unbated roundness, cheerful aspect.
    Were she so infamously prostitute, her cheek would fall,
    her colour fade, the spirit of her eye would die. 235

Zuc. O, young man, such women are like Danae's tub; and
    indeed all women are like Achelous, with whom
    Hercules wrestling, he was no sooner hurled to the
    earth but he rose up with double vigour. Their fall
strengtheneth them. 240

Enter DONDOLO.

Don. News, news, news, news! O, my dear Don, be raised,
    be jovial, be triumphant, ah, my dear Don!
Nym. To me first in private, thy news, I prithee.
Don. Will you be secret?
Nym. O' my life. 245

233. full-face] *Qq;* full face *Dilke.*   236. Danae's] *Smith;* Danaus *Qq;*
Danaus' *Dilke.*   237. Achelous] *AHB; Achilleus Q1; Achillous Q2;*
Antaeus *Dilke.*   240.1. *Enter] Q1; Exit Q2.*   242. jovial] *TC;* joviald
Qq.

---

230. *camomile*] a creeping herb. 'For though the camomile, the more it
is trodden the faster it grows, yet youth, the more it is wasted the
sooner it wears' (*1H4*, II.iv.441). See Tilley (C 34): 'The more camomile
is trodden down the more it spreads.'

231. *rumour*] the fact of being talked about.

233. *full-face*] The only difference the hyphen makes is to have the two
words modify 'roundness', rather than have them parallel to the two
phrases that follow. The hyphenated compound is not recorded in *O.E.D.*

234. *prostitute*] licentious.

236. *Danae's tub*] Cf. II.i.20.

237. *Achelous*] Zuccone is of course describing Hercules' battle with
Antaeus, and Dilke accordingly emends silently. Though Marston is
subtler than many scholars would admit, I think it is too much to ask that
he has created a deliberate confusion in Zuccone's mind because Achelous
lost a horn in *his* fight with Hercules. The error is probably Marston's,
and may be explained by the fact that in Book VII of Natalis Comes's
Mythologia (from which 'practically all the mythology is taken' in Marston's
satires, as Davenport tells us, *Poems*, p. 29), only a few lines separate the
accounts of the two battles.

Don. As you are generous?

Nym. As I am generous.

Don. Don Zuccone's lady's with child.

Herod. Nymphadoro, Nymphadoro, what is't? What's the
news?   250

Nym. You will be secret?

Herod. Silence itself.

Nym. Don Zuccone's lady's with child apparently.

Herc. Herod, Herod, what's the matter prithee, the news?

Herod. You must tell nobody.   255

Herc. As I am generous—

Herod. Don Zuccone's lady's with child apparently.

Zuc. Fawn, what's the whisper? What's the fool's secret news?

Herc. Truth, my lord, a thing—that beauty—that—well,
i' faith, it is not fit you know it. Now, now, now.   260

Zuc. Not fit I know it? As thou art baptised, tell me, tell me.

Herc. Will you plight your patience to it?

Zuc. Speak, I am a very block. I will not be moved, I am a
very block.

Herc. But if you should grow disquiet (as I protest, it would   265
make a saint blaspheme), I should be unwilling to
procure your impatience.

249. Nymphadoro, Nymphadoro,] *This ed.;* Nymph: Nymph: *Qq.*   259.
beauty] *Q1; not in Q2.*   260. it.] it? *Qq.*   Now, now, now.] *Q1; not
in Q2; (aside)* Now! now! now! *Dilke.*

---

246. *generous*] high-born. The modern senses of magnanimity and
munificence are apparently later (*O.E.D.* has 1623 for the first and 1696
for the second), but it is possible that Dondolo has his hand out for a
bribe.

249. *Nymphadoro, Nymphadoro*] Though no previous editor expands
the name, the colons in Qq are almost certainly indications of abbreviation
for the printed page only.

253. *apparently*] visibly, manifestly. The more modern sense, 'seemingly', *may* be right; in any case, it is all a put-up job, since they are all in
on the pretence.

263. *a very block*] Zuccone means he is impervious to being 'moved' as
a wooden log; but 'block' also meant a stupid person. Cf. *Gent.*, II.v.27:
'What a block art thou that thou canst not [understand me]!'

267. *procure*] (rather generally) to produce, cause.

Zuc. Ye do burst me, burst me, burst me with longing.

Herc. Nay, faith, 'tis no great matter. Hark ye, you'll tell
    nobody ?   270

Zuc. Not.

Herc. As you are noble ?

Zuc. As I am honest.

Herc. Your lady wife is apparently with child.

Zuc. With child ?   275

Herc. With child.

Zuc. Fool!

Herc. My Don.

Zuc. With child! By the pleasure of generation, I proclaim I
    lay not with her this—give us patience, give us patience.   280

Herc. Why ? My lord, 'tis nothing to wear a fork.

Zuc. Heaven and earth!

Herc. All things under the moon are subject to their
    mistress' grace. Horns! Lend me your ring, my Don.

268. Ye do burst me, burst me,] *TC;* Ye doe, burst me burst me, *Q1;* Yes
doe, burst me, burst me, *Q2;* Yes, do! Burst me! burst me! *AHB.*   274.
is] *Q1; not in Q2.*   281. fork] *Q1;* forker *Q2.*   284. grace. Horns!]
AHB; grace; horns; *Qq;* grace; horns ? *Dilke.*

268. *Ye do burst me . . . with longing.*] Cross notes that *burst* (a word
which Marston uses often) first appears with *O.E.D.*'s sense I.3.b. in
J.D.E. (1600), though *O.E.D.*'s first example is 1633. However, Cross
incorrectly includes the present passage, which demonstrates a transitive
use of the verb, with his other examples, which are all intransitive. *O.E.D.*
gives no figurative sense, and the closest seems to be III.11.a. See *N&Q*,
CCIII (1958), 356. Cf. *DC.*, II.ii.171: 'Stay, let not [m]y desire burst me.'
A parallel to the Q2 reading ('Yes doe, burst me, . . .') may be found in
Dekker's *Satiromastix:* '*Tuc[ca]*. Sting me, doe' (III.i.250). And see *Malc.*,
I.iii.79, where Pietro, also on the subject of cuckolding, demands, 'Who ?
By whom ? I burst with desire.'

273. *honest*] honourable, virtuous. Cf. IV.i.333.

279. *generation*] the act of procreation.

281. *fork*] This reading was chosen partly on bibliographical grounds
(Q1 is more authoritative on C4 than Q2), partly on logical grounds. At
IV.i.32, those who wear the horn are referred to as 'court forkers'; it seems
reasonable that the horn or 'branch' itself would be referred to as a 'fork'.
But see *Prince d'Amour*, p. 43: '*Item, It shall be lawful for any Knight to
shoot Forkers (though that be a Woodmans weapon) against any weak Knight
that weareth two white Feathers in his Helmet hornwise.*'

283–4. *All things . . . grace*] referring to the proverbial waywardness of

I'll put it on my finger. Now 'tis on yours again. Why, is   285
the gold now e'er the worse in lustre or fitness ?

Zuc. Am I used thus ?

Herc. Ay, my lord, true. Nay, to be—(look ye, mark ye)—to
be used like a dead ox—to have your own hide plucked
on, to be drawn on with your own horn; to have the   290
lordship of your father, the honour of your ancestors,
maugre your beard, to descend to the base lust of some
groom of your stable, or the page of your chamber—

Zuc. O Phalaris, thy bull!

Sir Amor. Good Don, ha' patience, you are not the only   295
cuckold. I would now be separated.

Zuc. 'Las, that's but the least drop of the storm of my
revenge. I will unlegitimate the issue. What I will do
shall be horrible but to think.

Herc. But sir—   300

---

286. e'er] *Dilke;* ere *Qq.*   298. unlegitimate] *Q2;* vnlegittimall *Q1.*

---

the moon (usually depicted as woman-like): '. . . the fortune of us that are
the moon's men doth ebb and flow like the sea' (*1H4*, I.ii.35). Note the
theatricality of Hercules' business with the ring; it is akin to Dulcimel's
asking Tiberio to smell the withered flower.

289–90. *plucked on*] either 'swindled' or 'humiliated'; literally, 'skinned'.
292. *maugre your beard*] i.e. despite anything you might do.
292–3. *the base lust of some groom*] See II.i.138 n.
294. *Phalaris, thy bull*] 'A cruell tyraunt of Agrigentine, who maruay-
lously delighted in the deuise of new and strange punishments. Wherefore
one *Perillus* a cunning workeman thinking to haue great thankes and a large
rewarde, inuented a Bul of brasse, into the which if one were put, and a
fire made underneath, the voyce of his crying should be like the bellowing
of a Bull. The tyrant in steede of rewarde, to trye this new deuise, first
burned in it *Perillus* himself, and after him many other. But in the ende,
when hiz tyrannie became so outragious, as no longer might be suffred, his
owne Citizens fell upon him, and putting him in the same brazē bull, with
like torment as he had vexed other, made him to ende his life' (Cooper).
296. *I would now be separated*] Note that this is suggested by Sir
Amoroso, not Hercules–Faunus. The fools support each other's folly.
298. *unlegitimate*] disown, declare illegitimate.
298–9. *What I will do shall be horrible but to think.*] The common source
of this and a similar passage in *Lr.* may be the lines in Golding's translation of Ovid's *Metamorphoses* (1567), VI, 784–5: 'The thing that I doe
purpose on, is great what ere it is. / I know not what it may be yet.' See
Kenneth Muir's note to II.iv.282–5 of *Lr.* in the Arden edition.

Zuc. But sir! I will do what a man of my form may do; and—
laugh on, laugh on, do, Sir Amorous: you have a lady,
too.

Herod. But, sweet my lord—

Zuc. Do not anger me, lest I most dreadfully curse thee, and   305
wish thee married. O, Zuccone, spit white, spit thy gall
out. The only boon I crave of heaven is—but to have
my honours inherited by a bastard! I will be most
tyrannous, bloodily tyrannous in my revenge, and most
terrible in my curses. Live to grow blind with lust,   310
senseless with use, loathed after, flattered before, hated
always, trusted never, abhorred ever; and last, may she
live to wear a foul smock seven weeks together, heaven,
I beseech thee!   *Exit.*

Enter ZOYA *and* POVEIA.

314.1.] *so Dilke; after 316 Qq.*

---

301. *form*] quality, rank.

306. *spit white*] i.e. spit out whatever phlegm is in you, rouse yourself
to anger (?). Spitting white may have been associated with a less voluntary
condition, however, as suggested at IV.i.3, where Hercules associates Sir
Amoroso's habitually spitting white with his generally bad health.
That the meaning of the phrase may include a combination of the factors
mentioned is suggested by the following passage from Nashe: 'The
Rhomish rotten *Pithagoreans*, or *Carthusian* friers, that mumpe on nothing
but fishe, in what a flegmatique predicament would they be, did not this
counterpoyson of the spitting sickenesse (sixtiefolde more restoratiue then
Bezer) patch them out and preserue them; which, being dubble rosted and
dryde as it is, not onely sucks vp all rhewmatique inundations, but is a
shooing-horne for a pinte of wine ouer-plus' ('The Prayse of the Red
Herring' [1599], *Works*, III, 184). Partridge suggests that Falstaff's 'I
would I might never spit white again' in *1H4* (I.ii.237) 'apparently refers
to seminal emission' (Partridge, p. 87). But even Partridge seems un-
comfortable with this explanation.

311. *use*] employment for sexual purposes.

313. *foul smock*] Perhaps the two words together simple mean 'shift,
chemise', with *foul* having somewhat the same force as in 'foul papers'.
'May she be left with only an undergarment to wear.' This is suggested by
the passage at V.i.341–2: 'I will never pick their trunks for letters, search
their pockets, ruffle their bosoms, or tear their foul smocks.' See Linthicum, pp. 189–91.

Zoya. Is he gone—is he blown off? Now out upon him,   315
    unsufferably jealous fool.

Don. Lady—

Zoya. Didst thou give him the famed report? Does he
    believe I am with child? Does he give faith?

Don. In most sincerity, most sincerely.   320

Herod. Nay, 'tis a pure fool. I can tell ye he was bred up in
    Germany.

Nym. But the laughter rises, that he vows he lay not in your
    bed this four year, with such exquisite protestations.

Zoya. That's most full truth. He hath most unjustly severed   325
    his sheets ever since the old Duke Pietro (heaven rest
    his soul)—

Don. Fie, you may not pray for the dead; 'tis indifferent to
    them what you say.

Nym. Well said, fool.   330

Zoya. Ever since the old Duke Pietro, the great devil of hell
    torture his soul—

Don. O, lady, yet charity!

Zoya. Why? 'Tis indifferent to them what you say, fool. But
    does my lord ravel out, does he fret? For pity of an   335

321. *Herod.*] *London; Her: Qq; Herc. Dilke; Zoy. AHB.*

---

315. *blown off*] i.e., 'blown over'; said of a storm (*O.E.D.* v.1 12.c).
This sense pretty well takes care of it, but Cross makes it specifically 'to
go away,' and lists it accordingly; *N&Q*, CCIII (1958), 5.

318. *the famed report*] the well-spread rumour.

321–2. *bred up in Germany*] 'As Praz . . . has said, the reward of the
scientist who discovers or defines a disease is often to have it called after
him. Machiavelli's anatomy of policy earned an unenviable reputation for
his countrymen; Sebastian Brandt's anatomy of folly may be responsible
for that estimate of his countrymen which evoked the indignation of
Koeppell' (from Wood's note on this passage).

323. *that*] from the fact that.

324. *exquisite*] precise.

325–6. *severed his sheets*] cut off conjugal relations, not slept with me.

328. *you may not pray for the dead*] A poke at the Puritans; cf. *JDE.*
(HHW, III, 201): 'Hush, hush, leaue praying for the dead, tis no good
Calvianisme, puritanisme.'

335. *ravel out*] fray out, disintegrate. *O.E.D.*'s first example for this
sense is 1611.

afflicted lady, load him soundly, let him not go clear
from vexation: he has the most dishonourably, with the
most sinful, most vicious obstinacy, persevered to
wrong me that, were I not of a male constitution, 'twere
impossible for me to survive it. But in madness' name,   340
let him on. I ha' not the weak fence of some of your soft-
eyed whimpering ladies, who, if they were used like me,
would gall their fingers with wringing their hands, look
like bleeding Lucreces, and shed salt water enough to
powder all the beef in the duke's larder. No, I am   345
resolute Donna Zoya. Ha, that wives were of my metal!
I would make these ridiculously jealous fools howl like
a starved dog before he got a bit. I was created to be the
affliction of such an unsanctified member, and will boil
him in his own syrup.   350

Enter ZUCCONE *listening.*

Herc. Peace, the wolf's ear takes the wind of us.

336. go] *Q2;* work *Q1.*   341. fence] *Qq;* sense *AHB.*   344. Lucreces]
AHB; Lucresses Qq; Lucretias *Dilke.*   346. resolute] *Q2;* resolued *Q1.*

---

336. *load*] burden, oppress.

341. *let him on*] let him continue (on = go on).

fence] 'Means or method of defence; protection, security' (*O.E.D.* 3).
Here it means approximately 'stalwartness', as in 'To My Equal Leader',
42, 'unfenced reputation'. It may be another instance of Marston's legal
training influencing his diction, since '"fence and ward" is a common set
phrase': see Davenport's note to *SV.*, Sat. II, 64–5, in *Poems.*

344. *bleeding Lucreces*] alluding to the often-told tale, first appearing in
Ovid's *Fasti*, of the rape of Lucrece by Tarquin.

345. *powder all the beef*] The usual way of curing beef was sprinkling
with salt or powdered spices.

346. *metal*] i.e., mettle; they were apparently interchangeable.

348. *a bit*] food to bite, victuals. The earliest *O.E.D.* example for this
sense is 1719 (*O.E.D.* sb.1 †I.4).

349. *unsanctified member*] Member = private organ; but since the
context is punishment for sinfulness, perhaps the figurative use, 'member
of Satan', is implied as well.

349–50. *boil him in his own syrup*] 'stew him in his own juice'; but
'syrup' can also mean his 'humour' of jealousy.

351. *the wolf's ear takes the wind of us*] (defined by the next line: 'The
enemy is in ambush'). If this is a proverb, it is not recorded in Tilley. But

Herod. The enemy is in ambush.

Zoya. If any man ha' the wit, now let him talk wantonly, but
    not bawdily. [*Louder*] Come, gallants, who'll be my
    servants? I am now very open-hearted, and full of   355
    entertainment.

Herc. Grace me to call you mistress.

Nym. Or me.

Herod. Or me.

Sir Amor. Or me.   360

Zoya. Or all, I am taken with you all, with you all.

Herc. As indeed, why should any woman only love any one
    man, since it is reasonable women should affect all
    perfection, but all perfection never rests in one man;
    many men have many virtues, but ladies should love   365
    many virtues; therefore ladies should love many men.
    For as in women, so in men, some woman hath only a
    good eye, one can discourse beautifully (if she do not
    laugh), one's well favoured to her nose, another hath
    only a good brow, t'other a plump lip, a third only   370
    holds beauty to the teeth, and there the soil alters; some,

354. S.D.] *This ed.*   357. to] *Dilke;* too *Qq, TC.*   362–3. any one man]
Q2; such a one *Q1.*   364–6. but . . . many men] *Q2;* yea, all should couet
many vertues, therefore Ladies should couet many men *Q1.*

---

cf. Wilson, p. 199: '[W]e say whisht, the Woulfe is at hand, when the same
man cometh in the meane season, of whom we spake before.'

   353–4. *wantonly, but not bawdily*] The fine distinction preserves Zoya's
image, a woman who can hold her own with men for wit, but who is
essentially chaste. Dulcimel (and Crispinella before her) is an off-shoot of
this favourite type of Marston's, a man's woman. Cross notes that
'bawdily' here antedates *O.E.D.*'s first example of the word (1628);
N&Q, CCIV (1959), 254.

   355. *open-hearted*] This antedates *O.E.D.* in both possible senses, 'frank'
(1611) and 'full of kindly feeling' (1617).

   356. *entertainment*] willingness to accommodate, or eagerness to be
entertained.

   362 ff.] The chop-logic here and elsewhere in the play is tailor-made for
the Inns of Court men in the audiences at the private theatres.

   371. *and there the soil alters*] i.e. teeth are her only attribute of beauty
(the rest of her soil is good for weeds only).

peradventure, hold good to the breast, and then down-
ward turn like the dreamt-of image, whose head was
gold, breast silver, thighs iron, and all beneath clay and
earth; one only winks eloquently, another only kisses   375
well, t'other only talks well, a fourth only lies well. So
in men: one gallant has only a good face, another has
only a grave methodical beard and is a notable wise
fellow (until he speaks), a third only makes water well
(and that's a good provoking quality), one only swears   380
well, another only speaks well, a third only does well—
all in their kind good; goodness is to be affected; therefore they. It is a base thing, and indeed an impossible,
for a worthy mind to be contented with the whole
world, but most vile and abject to be satisfied with one   385
point or prick of the world.

Zoya. Excellent Faunus, I kiss thee for this, by this hand.

Sir Amor. I thought as well; kiss me too, dear mistress.

Zoya. No, good Sir Amorous, your teeth hath taken rust,
your breath wants airing, and indeed I love sound   390
kissing. Come, gallants, who'll run a coranto, or leap a

386. or prick] *Q1; not in Q2.*

---

373. *the dreamt-of image*] Dilke was the first to point the source out as
Daniel ii (31–3). In *SV.*, VI, 52–4, Marston writes of 'that dreamed of
Imagerie, / Whose head was gold, brest siluer, brassie thigh, / Lead leggs,
clay feete . . .' (*Poems*, p. 136). Cross notes that 'dreamt-of' is unrecorded
in *O.E.D.*, and that 'the first recorded use of dreamed, ppl. a. in O.E.D. is
dated 1611' (*N&Q*, CCIII [1958], 104).

376. *lies*] punning on 'tells falsehoods' and 'makes love'.

378. *methodical*] carefully trimmed.

381. *only does well*] (ambiguous, but with bawdy innuendo ?)

386. *point or prick*] It may not be the most savoury joke possible, but
without 'prick' there is not much purpose to the sentence. Whoever was
responsible for the omission in Q2 (and it may not have been Marston)
was adjusting the text for a reading version; there seems no reason to
doubt that the word was meant to be retained in performance.

390. *airing*] i.e., freshening. The first *O.E.D.* example is from 1610
(Jonson's *The Alchemist*); Cross, *N&Q*, CCIII (1958), 5.

391. *coranto*] = courante, 'A kind of dance formerly in vogue, characterised by a running or gliding step (as distinguished from leaping)'
(*O.E.D.*).

levalto?

Herc. Take heed, lady, from offending or bruising the hope
of your womb.

Zoya. No matter, now I ha' the sleight, or rather the fashion   395
of it, I fear no barrenness.

Herc. Oh, but you know not your husband's aptness.

Zoya. Husband? husband? as if women could have no
children without husbands.

Nym. Ay, but then they will not be so like your husband.   400

Zoya. No matter, they'll be like their father; 'tis honour
enough to my husband that they vouchsafe to call him
father, and that his land shall descend to them. (Does
he not gnash his very teeth in anguish?) Like our
husband? I had rather they were ungroaned for. Like   405
our husband? Prove such a melancholy jealous ass as he
is? (Does he not stamp?)

Nym. But troth, your husband has a good face.

Zoya. Faith, good enough face for a husband. Come,
gallants, I'll dance to my own whistle: I am as light now   410
as—Ah! (*She sings and dances.*) A kiss to you, to my
sweet free servants; dream on me, and adieu.

                                              Exit ZOYA.

                ZUCCONE *discovers himself.*

393. *Herc.*] *TC;* H*e: Qq.*

---

392. *levalto*] (mod. *lavolta*) 'consisted in a turn of the body with two
steps, a high spring, and a pause with feet close together.' *Shakespeare's
England*, II, 448. Cited by Davenport in *Poems*, p. 315.

393. *offending*] harming. 'Bruising' means much the same here.

hope] i.e. the object or source of hope or expectation; offspring.

395. *sleight*] knack, trick.

397. *aptness*] ability (to father another child if this is lost).

402. *vouchsafe*] deign, condescend.

405. *ungroaned for*] The buck's cry at rutting-time was referred to as its
'groan' till near the end of the seventeenth century. Here, however, the
reference is apparently to a woman's labour pains.

412. *free servants*] servants in the sense of suitors in the tradition of
courtly love; *free* = noble, of gentle birth or breeding.

Zuc. I shall lose my wits.

Herc. Be comforted, dear Don, you ha' none to leese.

Zuc. My wife is grown like a Dutch crest, always rampant, 415
rampant. 'Fore I will endure this affliction, I will live by
raking cockles out of kennels, nay, I will run my
country, forsake my religion, go weave fustians, or roll
the wheelbarrow at Rotterdam.

Herc. I would be divorced, despite her friends, or the oath 420
of her chambermaid.

Zuc. Nay, I will be divorced, in spite of 'em all; I'll go to law
with her.

Herc. That's excellent; nay, I would go to law.

Zuc. Nay, I will go to law.   425

414. [*Aside*]] *conj. London.*   leese] *AHB;* leeze *Qq;* lose *Dilke.*

---

414. *leese*] lose. The line is possibly an aside. But 'Faunus' is perpetually
smiling, and he may practise this kind of 'brinkmanship' with those he
mocks, until they finally see their folly. As Zuccone later says (IV.i.544-5),
'Fawn, thou art a scurvy bitter knave, and dost flout Dons to their faces.'

415. *like a Dutch crest, always rampant*] 'A lion rampant appears in the
coats of arms of most of the Dutch provinces' (Sugden; who, however,
attributes this passage to the wrong play and renames the speaker 'Zucco').
'Rampant' can mean 'lustful' as well as 'standing on hind legs'. Cf. *DC.*,
II.ii.87 and IV.iii.16, where the Dutch courtesan is herself addressed as
'punk rampant'. Marston twice before used the phrase 'Dutch ancient'
(i.e. Dutch ensign) as a disparaging description of women, in *SV.*, VII, 182,
and in *JDE.* (HHW, III, 212). See Davenport's note, *Poems*, p. 337.

417. *cockles*] darnel, 'tares', weeds.
kennels] gutters.
run] flee (from).
418. *fustians*] coarse cloth.

418-19. *roll the wheelbarrow at Rotterdam*] Smith adopts Wood's
anachronistic suggestion, 'Turn a Jew (?)'. Perhaps 'Rotterdam' gives the
clue: the Italian, Catholic nobleman will change his country for Holland,
become a Protestant, a cloth-maker, or a porter or pedlar in a country
generally associated at the time with commerce and cloth-making—a sort
of thought-cluster.

422-3. *I'll go to law with her*] Zuccone here is one of the 'litigious men'
that Donne wrote of in 'The Canonisation'. As in the case of informers,
the Elizabethan courts were overloaded with legalistic athletes, so much
so that 'An Act to avoid trifling and frivolous Suits in Law, in her
Majesty's Courts at Westminster' was passed 43 Eliz. (1601) c.6; a similar
law was passed in 1605.

Herc. Why, that's sport alone. What though it be most
    exacting; wherefore is money?
Zuc. True, wherefore is money?
Herc. What though you shall pay for every quill, each drop
    of ink, each minim, letter, tittle, comma, prick, each   430
    breath, nay, not only for thine own orator's prating, but
    for some other orator's silence—though thou must buy
    silence with a full hand ('tis well known Demosthenes
    took above two thousand pound once only to hold his
    peace); though thou a man of noble gentry, yet you   435
    must wait and besiege his study door, which will prove
    more hard to be entered than old Troy, for that was got-
    ten into by a wooden horse, but the entrance of this may
    chance cost thee a whole stock of cattle, *Oves et boves, et*
    caetera pecora campi; though then thou must sit there,   440
    thrust and contemned, bare-headed to a grograine
    scribe, ready to start up at the door creaking, pressed

---

430. *minim*] stroke of the pen.

    tittle] 'Used here in its exact sense—a small stroke or point in writing
or printing; as, for example, the dot over the letter "i"' (Wood).

    prick] punctuation mark.

431. *breath*] mark for a pause; *O.E.D.* does not record such a sense, but
the context suggests it. Cf. IV.i.246.

433. *with a full hand*] with great expenditure.

433–5. *Demosthenes . . . peace*] As Bullen notes, the source is Plutarch's
Lives (Demosthenes, xxv); in North's translation, the amount is twenty
talents.

435. *though thou . . . yet you*] Throughout this scene Hercules shifts
between the formal *you* and intimate *thou*, perhaps testing the efficacy of
his flattery, but this phrase is specially awkward. Perhaps it should read
'though thou be a man . . .' or simply 'though a man . . .'.

439–40. Oves et boves, et caetera pecora campi] Sheep and cows and
other beasts of the field; roughly from the Vulgate version of Psalm viii,
8. The expression was apparently not unusual as a whimsical equivalent
of 'wealth of livestock'. Sir John Harrington uses it in *The Metamorphosis
of Ajax* (ed. E. S. Donno, 1962, p. 239): 'Oh these same *oves, & boves, &
pecora campi*, a flocke of white sheepe in a greene field, and a new house on
a high hill; I tell you, they be perillous tempting markes to shoot at.'

    441. *thrust*] either physically or figuratively forced (to sit waiting).

    bare-headed] i.e. showing respect.

441–2. *a grograine scribe*] Grograine (= grogram) was a coarse fabric,
sometimes made of silk, sometimes more cheaply made of other fabrics

to get in, 'with your leave, sir', to some surly groom,
the third son of a ropemaker: what of all this ?

Zuc. To a resolute mind these torments are not felt.   445

Herc. A very arrant ass, when he is hungry, will feed on,
though he be whipped to the bones, and shall a very
arrant ass be more virtuously patient than a noble Don ?

Zuc. No, Fawn, the world shall know I have more virtue
than so.   450

Herc. Do so and be wise.

Zuc. I will, I warrant thee. So I may be revenged, what care
I what I do ?

Herc. Call a dog worshipful—

---

448. ass be] *Smith;* Asse / *Zuccone,* be *Qq.*   noble Don ?] *Smith;* noble.
Qq.   449. *Zuc.*] *Dilke; Don. Qq.*   454. worshipful—] *This ed.;* worshipfull, *Qq;* worshipfull. *TC, Dilke;* worshipful ? *JOH, AHB, London;*
worshipful! *Smith.*

(including wool) mixed with silk; clothing made of the material was
regarded as cheaply flashy; hence the association with a lowly scribe, a
'poor grogaran poet' (*DC.*, III.ii.37–8), or simply a 'poore grogran-rascal'
(Jonson's *Cynthia's Revels,* III.ii.6). Cross, in citing the *DC.* example,
notes that the figurative sense is unrecorded in *O.E.D.*; but Jonson's use
is even earlier (1601); *N&Q,* cc (1955), 58.

442. *pressed*] hard-pressed.

443. *groom*] perhaps 'servant, attendant', but more probably the
contemptuous 'fellow'.

444. *the third son of a ropemaker*] probably means no more than 'the
lowest of the low'. Wood adopts Bullen's suggestion that this is a reference
to Gabriel Harvey, whom Nashe often reminded of his origins; but in any
case Gabriel was the fourth son, not the third. The whole comic attack on
lawyers gets special colour from Marston's background as a son of a
lawyer, a student of law, and a playwright producing plays for a theatre
heavily reliant on law-men for its audiences.

448–9. *ass . . . Zuc.*] The emendations are sound. The compositor was
undoubtedly confused by the positioning of the name and title in the MS.

virtuously . . . virtue] A small study in two kinds of stoicism: Hercules is
thinking of patient, humble apathy or acquiescence; Zuccone's 'virtue' is
belligerent fortitude.

454. *Call a dog worshipful*] All editors have ignored this difficult line. It
ends with a comma and at the bottom of the page in Qq, so possibly a line
is missing. More probably this is another of the quasi-proverbial phrases
Marston is fond of. 'Worshipful' is the term of address to those of

Zuc. Nay, I will embrace—nay I will embrace a jakes-   455
    farmer after eleven o'clock at night; I will stand bare
    and give wall to a bellows-mender, pawn my lordship,
    sell my foot-cloth, but I will be revenged. Does she
    think she has married an ass?

Herc. A fool?   460

Zuc. A coxcomb?

Herc. A ninny-hammer?

Zuc. A woodcock?

Herc. A calf?

Zuc. No, she shall find that I ha' eyes.   465

Herc. And brain.

Zuc. And nose.

Herc. And forehead.

Zuc. She shall, i'faith, Fawn, she shall, she shall, sweet
    Fawn, she shall, i'faith, old boy—it joys my blood to   470
    think on't—she shall, i'faith; farewell, loved Fawn,
    sweet Fawn, farewell. She shall, i'faith, boy.

Exit ZUCCONE.

Enter GONZAGO *and* GRANUFFO *with* DULCIMEL.

Zuccone's rank. The implication is that though one calls a dog 'worshipful', he is still a dog. The closest proverb in Tilley is D 508, 'To call a dog
a dog'. Puttenham, illustrating '*Ploche*, or the Doubler', gives a similar
example: 'And this is spoken in common Prouerbe. | *An ape vvilbe an ape,
by kinde as they say,* | *Though that ye clad him all in purple array*' (p. 201).
Cf. *SV.*, VI, 72: '*What though in veluet cloake, yet still an Ape.*' A version
that appears in *Lr.* (1604–5) does not make quite the same point: 'a dog's
obeyed in office' (IV.vi.163). Hercules probably makes the comment as an
aside.

    455–6. *jakes-farmer*] privy cleaner.
    456–7. *stand bare and give wall*] stand bare-headed, and give up the
inner side of the walk (closest to the wall, and thus protected by the
building's overhanging upper storeys when slops and worse were thrown
out the window); i.e., demean to. *O.E.D.*'s first example for this sense of
'wall' is 1606. But see *Rom.*,I.i.15: 'I will take the wall of any man. . . .'
    458. *foot-cloth*] See II.i.182 n.
    462–4. *ninny-hammer . . . woodcock . . . calf*] all synonyms for 'gull, fool',
though 'calf' sometimes signified a meek, inoffensive person.
    468. *forehead*] This could mean 'command of countenance, assurance',
or perhaps 'memory'; but of course, chiefly 'a place to plant horns'.

Gon. We would be private: only Faunus stay. (He is a wise
    fellow, daughter, a very wise fellow, for he is still just
    of my opinion.) My Lord Granuffo, you may likewise   475
    stay, for I know you'll say nothing. Say on, daughter. *Exeunt.*
Dul. And as I told you, sir, Tiberio being sent,
    Graced in high trust as to negotiate
    His royal father's love, if he neglect
    The honour of his faith, just care of state,   480
    And every fortune that gives likelihood
    To his best hopes, to draw our weaker heart
    To his own love (as I protest he does)—
Gon. I'll rate the prince with such a heat of breath
    His ears shall glow; nay, I discovered him;   485
    I read his eyes, as I can read an eye,
    Though it speak in darkest characters I can.
    Can we not, Fawn? Can we not, my lord?
    Why, I conceive you now, I understand you both:
    You both admire, yes, say is't not hit?   490
    Though we are old, or so, yet we ha' wit.
Dul. And you may say (if so your wisdom please,
    As you are truly wise) how weak a creature
    Soft woman is to bear the siege and strength

476. *Exeunt.*] *so TC; opposite 473 after* stay, *Qq.*   484. rate] *Q2;* hate *Q1.*
486. an] *Qq;* any *AHB.*   492. so] *Q2; not in Q1.*

478–9. *negotiate . . . love*] See I.i.24 n.

479–82. *if he neglect . . . To his best hopes*] Dulcimel is using her father's
kind of high-blown language, the terms of which are general enough to be
understood but rather too vague to define strictly; they add up to 'if he
shuns his duty. . . .'

482. *weaker*] not really comparative; Marston indulged in this form
often, possibly only because of the extra syllable it provided.

484. *rate*] chide, scold.

heat of breath] energy of speech.

487. *darkest characters*] either 'darkest, most illegible letters' (referring
perhaps to black-letter type); or, more probably, 'most obscure symbols'.

489. *conceive*] = understand. Cf. III.i.369.

490. *admire*] are filled with astonishment.

491. *wit*] here, = perspicacity. Cf. III.i.126.

494. *strength*] power or resources, in the military sense (to fit with
'siege').

Of so prevailing feature and fair language   495
As that of his is ever. You may add
(If so your wisdom please, as you are wise)—
Gon. As mortal man may be.
Dul.   I am of years
Apt for his love, and if he should proceed
In private suit, how easy 'twere   500
To win my love, for you may say (if so
Your wisdom please) you find in me
A very forward passion to enjoy him;
And therefore you beseech him seriously
Straight to forbear with such close cunning art   505
To urge his too well gracèd suit: for you
(If so your lordship please) may say I told you all.
Gon. Go to, go to, what I will say or so,
Until I say, none but myself shall know;
But I will say go to. Does not my colour rise?   510
It shall rise, for I can force my blood
To come and go, as men of wit and state
Must sometimes feign their love, sometimes their hate:
That's policy, now. But come, with this free heat,
Or this same *Estro* or *Enthusiasm*   515

498–9.] *lineation AHB;* I . . . proceed *continuous Qq.*   505. close cunning] *Qq;* close-cunning *AHB.*   510. not] *Q2; not in Q1.*

---

495. *prevailing*] strong enough to be victorious.

499. *Apt*] suited, suitable.

500. *In private suit*] i.e., on his own behalf, as opposed to the 'public suit' on behalf of Ferrara and its duke.

503. *forward*] eager.

505. *close . . . art*] close-hidden, secretive . . . artfulness.

506. *gracèd*] favoured, acceptable.

512. *state*] high rank.

514. *policy*] diplomacy, political sagacity (see I.ii.167); a favourite term of Gonzago's kindred soul Gostanzo, in Chapman's *All Fools.*

free heat] noble vehemence (in eloquence); perhaps 'free' means 'unimpeded, spontaneous' here.

515. Estro] 'The oestrum or gadfly is here meant, which extremely torments cattle in the summer. It is metamorphically used for inspired fury of any kind' (Dilke).

Enthusiasm] poetical fervour.

(For these are phrases both poetical),
Will we go rate the prince, and make him see
Himself in us; that is, our grace and wits
Shall show his shapeless folly: vice kneels whiles virtue sits.

Enter TIBERIO.

But see, we are prevented: daughter, in!   520
It is not fit thyself should hear what I
Must speak of thy most modest, wise, wise, mind;
For th'art careful, sober, in all most wise,
And indeed our daughter. *Exit* DULCIMEL.
      My Lord Tiberio,
A horse but yet a colt may leave his trot,   525
A man but yet a boy may well be broke
From vain addictions; the head of rivers stopped,
The channel dries; he that doth dread a fire
Must put out sparks, and he who fears a bull
Must cut his horns off when he is a calf;   530
Principiis obsta, saith a learned man

524. S.D.] *so AHB; on 523 after* wise, *Qq.*

518–19. *our grace . . . virtue sits*] The conventional alliance of reason and virtue against folly and vice has ironic overtones when formulated by a fool.

520. *prevented*] anticipated, met beforehand.

525–30.] Gonzago shares with Polonius a euphuistic love of listed proverbs.

525. *may leave his trot*] apparently means 'may be trained not to run off on his own whim', since all the wise saws Gonzago gives are illustrations of *principiis obsta*, 'resist beginnings'. The source may be Horace, *Epistles*, I.ii.64–5: *Fingit equum tenera docilem cervice magister / ire viam qua monstret eques.* 'While the colt has a tender neck and is able to learn, the groom trains him to go the way his rider directs' (H. R. Fairclough, Loeb Library).

527. *addictions*] habits. Cross classifies this use of *addiction* as *O.E.D.*'s sense 2, 'The state of being given to a habit or pursuit', for which *O.E.D.*'s first example is dated 1641; *N&Q*, CCIII (1958), 5. Cf. 'To My Equal Reader', 37.

531. Principiis obsta] 'Resist beginnings' (J. H. Mozley); Ovid, *Remedia Amoris*, l. 91 (Loeb Library). See Davenport's note to *SV.*, IV, 93–8, where Marston paraphrases the passage from which this phrase comes.

Who, though he was no duke, yet he was wise,
And had some sense or so.
Tib.   What means my lord?
Gon. La, sir! thus men of brain can speak in clouds
          Which weak eyes cannot pierce. But, my fair lord,   535
          In direct phrase, thus: my daughter tells me plain,
          You go about with most direct entreats
          To gain her love, and to abuse your father.
          O, my fair lord, will you, a youth so blest
          With rarest gifts of fortune and sweet graces,   540
          Offer to love a young and tender lady?
          Will you, I say, abuse your most wise father,
          Who, though he freeze in August and his calves
          Are sunk into his toes, yet may well wed our daughter,
          As old as he in wit? Will you, I say   545
          (For by my troth, my lord, I must be plain)?
          My daughter is but young, and apt to love
          So fit a person as your proper self,
          And so she prayed me tell you. Will you now
          Entice her easy breast to abuse your trust,   550
          Her proper honour, and your father's hopes?
          I speak no figures, but I charge you check
          Your appetite and passions to our daughter
          Before it head, nor offer conference
          Or seek access but by and before us.   555

534. *Gon.*] *Q2; not in Q1.*   538. your] *Dilke;* her *Qq.*

---

537. *entreats*] entreaties.
538. *abuse your father*] Dilke's emendation is corroborated by Gonzago's repetition of the question on l. 542: 'Will you, I say, abuse your most wise father … ?'
543–4. *his calves | Are sunk into his toes*] i.e., his legs have lost their shapeliness.
548. *proper*] own.
550. *easy*] yielding, credulous.
551. *proper*] perhaps again = own; but more likely 'fitting, expected'.
552. *figures*] generally, any obvious rhetorical formes; but here specifically 'metaphors', since he immediately uses one.
554. *head*] come to a head.

What, judge you us as weak, or as unwise?
No, you shall find that Urbin's duke has eyes—
And so think on't.

Exeunt GONZAGO *and* GRANUFFO.

Tib. Astonishment and wonder, what means this?
Is the duke sober?

Herc.   Why, ha' not you endeavoured   560
Courses that only seconded appetite,
And not your honour, or your trust of place?
Do you not court the lady for yourself?

Tib. Fawn, thou dost love me: if I ha' done so
'Tis past my knowledge, and I prithee, Fawn,   565
If thou observest I do I know not what,
Make me to know it, for by the dear light
I ha' not found a thought that way. I apt for love?
Let lazy idleness, filled full of wine,
Heated with meats, high fed with lustful ease,   570
Go dote on colour. As for me, why, death o' sense,

---

557. Urbin's] *London;* Venice *Qq.*   561. only] *Q2;* haue *Q1.*   570.
Heated] *Q2;* Heau'd *Q1;* Heav'd up *Dilke.*   571. death o' sense] *Q2;*
earth a sence *Q1;* earth's as sensible *Dilke.*

---

556. *weak*] See Interlocutors, 2 n.

557. *that Urbin's duke has eyes*] Cf. v.440, where Hercules throws this
back at Gonzago: 'For we all know that Urbin's duke has eyes.' The only
other editor to make the obvious emendation from Qq's 'Venice' is
London. An easy enough error for a compositor to make from MS.

560. *sober*] probably the ordinary sense 'not drunk'; but perhaps 'sane,
rational', for which *O.E.D.*'s first example is 1638.

560–1. *endeavoured / Courses . . . seconded*] attempted lines of action . . .
furthered.

562. *your trust of place*] the obligations of your position.

564. *Fawn, thou dost love me*] deep irony, since Tiberio can only say this
because he, like the rest, has been taken in by Faunus's flattery; yet the
father within the 'Fawn' does indeed love Tiberio.

570. *Heated with meats*] stimulated with (special) foods.

high fed] fed (perhaps figuratively) richly (with the sense of 'stimula-
tion'); cf. *2H4*, I.i.9–10: '. . . contention, like a horse / Full of high
feeding, madly hath broke loose'.

lustful ease] lust-provoking comfort.

571. *Go dote on colour*] The first problem is what Qq mean by 'culler';
that it is the same as 'colour' is supported by *O.E.D.*'s listing it as a

I court the lady ? I was not born in Cyprus.
I love! when ? how ? whom ? Think, let us yet keep
Our reason sound. I'll think, and think, and sleep.   *Exit.*
Herc. Amazed, even lost in wond'ring, I rest full   575
      Of covetous expectation: I am left
      As on a rock, from whence I may discern
      The giddy sea of humour flow beneath,
      Upon whose back the vainer bubbles float

---

variant spelling of 'colour', and by its appearance in *JDE.* (HHW, III, 222)
and the *Ashby Entertainment* (spelt *Cullo^rs*), both times meaning 'colour'.
In *Satiromastix*, at the end of a passage in which he has discussed hair,
Horace says:

> I thus conclude,
> Cullors set cullors out; our eyes iudge right,
> Of vice or vertue by their opposite:
> So, if faire haire to beauty ad such grace,
> Baldnes must needes be vgly, vile and base.   (IV.i.97–101)

There may also be an influence of Marston's attitude toward 'colours' of
rhetoric, as mere ornament. So Smith's note is probably close enough:
'outward appearance.'

death o' sense] 'a sort of meaningless oath' (Bullen); but not altogether
so, since it fits Tiberio's rejection of the 'life of sense' (which Herod
apostrophises at II.i.79).

572. *I was not born in Cyprus*] best explained by the last stanza of
Marston's *The Metamorphosis of Pigmalion's Image*:

> Let this office, that that same happy night
> So gracious were the Gods of marriage
> Mid'st all there pleasing and long wish'd delight
> *Paphus* was got: of whom in after age
>   *Cyprus* was *Paphos* call'd, and euermore
>   Those Ilanders do *Venus* name adore.   (*Poems*, p. 61)

It is a frequent allusion in Marston's works, e.g. *SV.*, III, 143, and
VIII, 56.

575. *Amazed*] From the context, this suggests 'lost as in a maze'. The
noun was often so written (to be in amaze, a maze).

576. *covetous*] eager; this sense (and construction) not in *O.E.D.*

576–80. *I am left . . . break*] In *Tit.* (*c.* 1592), Titus also stands 'as one
upon a rock, / Environ'd with a wilderness of sea' (III.i.93–4), but unlike
him, Hercules does not take the image as betokening personal danger.

578. *The giddy sea of humour*] i.e. the bewilderingly varied range of
human foibles.

579. *the vainer bubbles*] Marston's typical comparative construction of
adjectives is here less vague than usual: it is the more vain or light
'bubbles' that rise to the surface; the others remain safely within the sea.

And forthwith break. O mighty flattery,   580
Thou easiest, common'st, and most grateful venom
That poisons courts and all societies,
How grateful dost thou make me! Should one rail
And come to sear a vice, beware leg-rings
And the turned key on thee, when, if softer hand   585
Suppling a sore that itches (which should smart)—
Free speech gains foes, base fawnings steal the heart.
Swell, you impostumed members, till you burst;
Since 'tis in vain to hinder, on I'll thrust,
And when in shame you fall, I'll laugh from hence,   590
And cry, 'So end all desperate impudence.'
Another's court shall show me where and how
Vice may be cured; for now beside myself,
Possessed with almost frenzy, from strong fervour

583. me!] *This ed.;* me, *Q1;* me ? *Q2;* me; *Dilke.*   584. sear] *Qq, this ed.;*
feare *or* fear *all other edd.*

581. *grateful*] See I.ii.326 n.

584. *sear*] brand, stigmatise (*O.E.D.* 3. †d.). Though the first letter in
Qq is unquestionably a long 's', all previous editors have followed TC in
printing 'fear' (glossed as 'frighten'), as does Cross in his note on leg-
rings.

leg-rings] 'A shackle or fetter for the leg. Unrecorded in O.E.D.';
Cross, *N&Q,* CC (1955), 335.

586. *Suppling*] softening or mollifying (a wound, etc.) usually by apply-
ing an unguent (*O.E.D.*).

587. *Free speech*] frank, plain-spoken speech; it is not insignificant that
Marston antedates the first *O.E.D.* example for this sense of 'free' (1611).

fawnings] flatteries.

588. *impostumed*] purulent, abscessed, festering.

members] See II.i.349 n. But here it vaguely refers to any parts of the
body, figuratively representing persons.

589. *Since 'tis in vain to hinder, on I'll thrust*] This is in fact the rationale
of Hercules' role in the play. He does not so much initiate action as further
it once it has started.

590. *from hence*] (as a result) from this. *O.E.D.*'s first example of the
phrase used in this sense is 1608.

591. *desperate impudence*] outrageous, extreme shamelessness, insolence.

594. *fervour*] vehemence, with the underlying sense of intense heat; it is
this 'heat' which is the physiological and psychological source of Hercules'
actions.

I know I shall produce things mere divine: 595
Without immoderate heat, no virtues shine.
For I speak strong, though strange: the dews that steep
Our souls in deepest thoughts are fury and sleep.   *Exit.*

595. mere] *Qq;* near *Smith.*

---

595. *mere*] absolutely, altogether. Smith's reading, 'near', has support in
Marston's source for this passage. As Crawford pointed out, most of lines
593–8 can be traced to 'An Apologie of *Raymond Sebond*', in Florio's
Montaigne, II, xii, 348–9. '[N]*o eminent or glorious vertue, can be without
some immoderate and irregular agitation.* . . . Does [some editions: Dares]
not Philosophie thinke that men produce their greatest effects, and neerest
approching to divinity, when they are besides themselves, furious and
madde? We amend our selves by the privation of reason, and by her
drooping. The two naturall waies, to enter the cabinet of the Gods, and
there to foresee the course of the destinies, are furie and sleepe.' But Q1's
standing type is carefully corrected for Q2 on this page, and both Qq read
meere.
    597. *strong*] = with good sense; truly. Cf. IV.i.202.

Act III

Nym. Faith, Fawn, 'tis my humour, the natural sin of my
    sanguine complexion: I am most enforcedly in love with
    all women, almost affecting them all with an equal
    flame.

Herc. An excellent justice of an upright virtue: you love all   5
    God's creatures with an unpartial affection.

Nym. Right, neither am I inconstant to any one in particu-
    lar.

Herc. Though you love all in general, true, for when you
    vow a most devoted love to one, you swear not to tender   10
    a most devoted love to another; and indeed why should
    any man overlove anything? 'Tis judgement for a man to
    love everything proportionally to his virtue: I love a
    dog with a hunting pleasure, as he is pleasurable in
    hunting; my horse after a journeying easiness, as he is   15

Act III] ACTVS TERTIVS. *Qq.*   0.1.] *Hercules] Smith; Faunus Qq.*
Nymphadoro] TC; Nymphador Qq.

[III.i.] 2. *sanguine complexion*] amorous temperament. The sanguine
complexion, according to the old physiology, resulted from the dominance
of blood over the other three humours, creating a ruddy countenance
(leading to the modern sense of 'complexion'), and a courageous, hopeful,
and amorous disposition. (See *O.E.D.* for 'sanguine'.) Since he was born
that way (it is his 'natural' sin), Nymphadoro has a built-in excuse for his
weakness. It was the kind of dilemma that made difficulties for moralists
like Marston; this play is one of his attempts to deal with it.

    enforcedly] compulsively.

    3. *affecting*] loving.

    5. *upright virtue*] (probably a bawdy pun here; each word can be taken
two ways).

    12. *judgement*] discretion, good sense. Cf. III.i.126.

    13. *proportionably to his virtue*] in proportion to its (practical) value.

easy in journeying; my hawk, to the goodness of his
wing; and my wench—

Nym. How, sweet Fawn, how?

Herc. Why, according to her creation. Nature made them
pretty, toying, idle, fantastic, imperfect creatures; even   20
so I would in justice affect them, with a pretty, toying,
idle, fantastic, imperfect affection; and as indeed they
are only created for show and pleasure, so would I only
love them for show and pleasure.

Nym. Why, that's my humour to the very thread; thou dost   25
speak my proper thoughts.

Herc. But sir, with what possibility can your constitution be
so boundlessly amorous as to affect all women of what
degree, form, or complexion soever?

Nym. I'll tell thee: for mine own part, I am a perfect   30
Ovidian, and can with him affect all. If she be a virgin
of a modest eye, shamefaced, temperate aspect, her very
modesty inflames me, her sober blushes fires me; if I
behold a wanton, pretty, courtly, petulant ape, I am

25. the] *Q2;* a *Q1.*

---

19. *creation*] purpose (or) manner of her creation.

20. *toying*] See I.ii.114 n.

fantastic] fanciful, capricious; the sense is not so strong as today.

25. *to the very thread*] 'Hair' and 'thread' were often used interchangeably. Tilley records the proverb, 'To hit (fit) it to a hair' (H 26); and Cross points out that Marston had used the phrase 'to a haire' in *JDE.* (HHW, III, 191), antedating *O.E.D.*'s first example for this use of 'hair' (1606): *N&Q,* CCVI (1961), 123.

28. *boundlessly*] *O.E.D.*'s first record of this adverb is dated 1674. Cross, *N&Q,* CXCIX (1954), 426.

31. *Ovidian*] 'A disciple of Ovid. Unrecorded in O.E.D. which lists only the adj., for which its earliest ex. is 1617'; Cross, *N&Q,* CCVI (1961), 388. As Bullen implies, the passage that follows is heavily dependent on the fourth elegy of book II of Ovid's *Amores.*

32. *modest eye*] 'Eye' comes at the end of a line in Qq; perhaps it should read 'eyed'. The syntax is somewhat awkward as it stands.

shamefaced] modest, bashful.

34. *wanton*] capricious, flirtatious.

courtly] i.e., affected, following the fashions of the court.

petulant] pert. *O.E.D.*'s first example of this sense is 1605.

ape] *O.E.D.* neglects the touch of affectionateness often present in the

extremely in love with her, because she is not clownishly   35
rude, and that she assures her lover of no ignorant, dull,
unmoving Venus; be she sourly severe, I think she
wittily counterfeits, and I love her for her wit; if she be
learned and censures poets, I love her soul, and for her
soul her body; be she a lady of professed ignorance, oh,   40
I am infinitely taken with her simplicity, as one assured
to find no sophistication about her; be she slender and
lean, she's the Greek's delight, be she thick and plump,
she's the Italian's pleasure; if she be tall, she's of a
goodly form, and will print a fair proportion in a large   45
bed; if she be short and low, she's nimbly delightful,
and ordinarily quick-witted; be she young, she's for
mine eye, be she old she's for my discourse, as one
well knowing there's much amiableness in a grave
matron; but be she young or old, lean, fat, short, tall,   50
white, red, brown, nay, even black, my discourse shall

---

37. unmoving *Q2;* moving *Q1.*   41. as one] *Q2;* I am *Q1.*   48–9. discourse, . . . knowing] *JOH (and AHB);* discourse . . . knowing, *Qq;* discourse, . . . knowing; *Dilke.*

Elizabethan and Jacobean use of this word. Here it amounts to 'little
monkey'. Cf. *Rom.,* II.i.16, where Mercutio tries to call Romeo but finally
concludes, 'The ape is dead, and I must conjure him.'

    35. *clownishly*] clumsily, ignorantly.
    36. *rude*] uncultured, unrefined.
    37. *Venus*] See notes to 'Prologus', 17, and II.i.141.
    39. *censures*] gives opinions on, judges. Cf. v.i.485.
    40. *professed*] openly admitted.
    42. *sophistication*] disingenuousness.
    45. *proportion*] shape, form (i.e. silhouette).
    47. *ordinarily*] likely, as a rule.
    48. *discourse*] conversing, conversation; cf. l. 51 below.
    48–9. *as one well knowing*] If Dilke's punctuation were followed, *as one*
would refer to the old woman, and knowing would mean 'intelligent'. But
the construction at l. 41, 'as one assured', persuades me that Halliwell is
right and that 'one' refers to Nymphadoro.
    49. *amiableness*] amability (i.e. rather than merely amiability); 'much to
be loved'.
    51. *discourse*] here, = reasoning, argumentation.

find reason to love her, if my means may procure
opportunity to enjoy her.

Herc. Excellent, sir. Nay, if a man were of competent
means, were't not a notable delight for a man to have   55
for every month of the year?

Nym. Nay, for every week of the month?

Herc. Nay, for every day of that week?

Nym. Nay, for every hour of that day?

Herc. Nay, for every humour of a man in that hour, to have   60
a several mistress to entertain him; as, if he were
saturnine, or melancholy, to have a black-haired, pall-
faced, sallow, thinking mistress to clip him; if jovial
and merry, a sanguine, light-tripping, singing—indeed
a mistress that would dance a coranto as she goes to   65
embrace him; if choleric, impatient, or ireful, to have a
mistress with red hair, little ferret eyes, a lean cheek,
and a sharp nose to entertain him. And so of the rest.

62–3. pall-faced] *Qq;* pale-faced *AHB.*   65. a] *Q2;* and *Q1.*

52–3. *if my means may procure opportunity*] i.e. if it is possible for me in
some way to arrange an opportunity. *Means* here is not exclusively
financial, though when Hercules picks up the word in the next line, that is
evidently what he stresses.

61. *several*] separate, different.

62–8.] The underlying psychology here is a mixture of humours and
astrological influence: Saturn and melancholy are contrasted to Jupiter
(jovial) and blood (sanguine), and these again to the hot, dry humour of
choler.

62–3. *pall-faced*] Having a deathly look; looking like a pall-bearer.
Unrecorded in *O.E.D.*

63. *sallow, thinking*] The sallowness is caused by the melancholy; and
we know from Burton's *Anatomy of Melancholy* (Part I, sec. ii, subsect. xv)
that melancholy can be caused by too much study, or 'thinking'. It is
therefore possible that Dilke's hyphenated form 'sallow-thinking' is right,
though it would be an unusually tortured compound even for Marston;
the compound 'book-thinking' (III.i.218) is straightforward, and suggests
the sense that 'thinking' might take in a genuine Marston compound.
(*O.E.D.*'s first example of 'thinking' as a verbal adjective is dated 1678.)

65. *coranto*] See II.i.391 n. If Q1 is right, *coranto* is a verb here; *O.E.D.*
does not record it, but for the verb 'courant' or 'carant' the earliest date
is 1625.

66. *choleric*] hot-tempered. See Lawrence Babb, *The Elizabethan
Malady* (1951), 6–9 and *passim.*

Enter DONETTA.

Nym. O, sir, this were too great an ambition. Well, I love
    and am beloved of a great many, for I court all in the   70
    way of honour, in the trade of marriage, Fawn; but
    above all I affect the princess—she's my utmost end.
    Oh, I love a lady whose beauty is joined with fortune,
    above all; yet one of beauty without fortune, for some
    uses; nay one of fortune without beauty, for some ends;   75
    but never any that has neither fortune nor beauty, but
    for necessity: such a one as this is Donna Donetta.
    Here's one has loved all the court just once over.

Herc. Oh, this is the fair lady with the foul teeth. Nature's
    hand shook when she was in making, for the red that   80
    should have spread her cheeks, nature let fall upon her
    nose, the white of her skin slipped into her eyes, and the
    gray of her eyes leapt before his time into her hair, and
    the yellowness of her hair fell without providence into
    her teeth.   85

Nym. By the vow of my heart, you are my most only
    elected, and (I speak by way of protestation) I shall no
    longer wish to be, than that your only affection shall
    rest in me, and mine only in you.

Don. But if you shall love any other— ?   90

69. Well,] *Dilke;* well *Qq, Smith.*   82. skin] *Q1;* chinne *Q2.*

    79–85.] Wood brings attention to a similar passage in Donne's elegy
'The Anagram', written probably in the 1590s:
            For, though her eyes be small, her mouth is great,
            Though they be Ivory, yet her teeth are jeat,
            Though they be dimme, yet she is light enough,
            And though her harsh haire fall, her skinne is rough;
            What though her cheeks be yellow, 'her haire is red,
            Give her thine, and she hath a maydenhead. . . .
            Though all her parts be not in th'usuall place,
            She'hath yet an Anagram of a good face.
    The Elegies and the Songs and Sonnets, ed. Helen Gardner (1965), p. 21.
81. *spread*] covered.
86–7. *most only elected*] absolutely sole chosen (one).
87. *protestation*] formal public asseveration.
88. *only*] exclusive.

Nym. Any other ? Can any man love any other that knows
you, the only perfection of your sex, and astonishment
of mankind ?

Don. Fie, ye flatterer; go wear and understand my favour,
this snail: slow, but sure.   95

Nym. This kiss.

Don. Farewell.

Nym. The integrity and only vow of my faith to you ever
urged your well-deserved requital to me.

                                        Exit DONETTA.

Herc. Excellent.   100

                Enter GARBETZA.

Nym. See, here's another of—

Herc. Of your most only elected.

Nym. Right, Donna Garbetza.

Herc. Oh, I will acknowledge this is the lady made of cutwork, and all her body like a sand-box, full of holes,   105
and contains nothing but dust. She chooseth her
servants as men choose dogs, by the mouth; if they

---

94. flatterer] *Q1;* flatter me *Q2;* flatter *TC.*   95. snail:] *Smith;* snayle
Qq; snail's *TC.*   97. Farewell.] *Q1;* Farewell. *Exit. Q2.*   99. urged]
Q1; urge *Q2.*   100.1. S.D.] *location this ed.; after* of *on 101 Qq.*

---

92. *astonishment*] object of amazement. *O.E.D.*'s first example for this
sense is 1611, from the King James Bible, Deut., xxviii. 37: 'Thou shalt
become an astonishment, a prouerbe, and a by-worde.'

94. *favour*] a gift that is the mark of a lady's favour.

98. *The integrity and only vow*] 'Integrity' here is something like 'single-
centredness'; *only vow* is the vow made 'only', exclusively, to her.

98–9. *ever urged*] have always argued in favour of.

100.1 GARBETZA] London suggests that the speech head should read
Poveia throughout this scene because Poveia would otherwise appear for
the first time in the fifth act and Garbetza would be doing double duty
in the Herod/Amoroso and Nymphadoro sub-plots. But Poveia is actually
visible frequently, as an attendant to Dulcimel; and if an error is involved
in naming the characters, the error is undoubtedly Marston's own.

104–5. *cutwork*] embroidery with cut-out edges, or a kind of openwork
embroidery or lace.

105. *sand-box*] a box with a perforated top for sprinkling sand as a blotter
upon wet ink.

open well and full, their cry is pleasing. She may be
chaste, for she has a bad face, and yet questionless she
may be made a strumpet, for she is covetous.   110

Nym. By the vow of my heart, you are my most only elected,
and (I speak it by way of protestation) I shall no longer
wish to be, than all your affections shall only rest in me,
and all mine only in you.

Herc. Excellent. This piece of stuff is good on both sides; he   115
is so constant, he will not change his phrase.

Gar. But shall I give faith? May you not love another?

Nym. Another? Can any man love another that knows you,
the only perfection of your sex, and admiration of
mankind?   120

Gar. Your speech flies too high for your meaning to follow,
yet my mistrust shall not precede my experience: I
wrought this favour for you.

Nym. The integrity and only vow of my faith to you ever
urged your well-deserved requital to me.   125

Exit GARBETZA.

Herc. Why, this is pure wit, nay, judgement.

Nym. Why, look thee, Fawn, observe me.

Herc. I do, sir.

Nym. I do love at this instant some nineteen ladies, all in the
trade of marriage. Now sir, whose father dies first, or   130
whose portion appeareth most, or whose fortune betters
soonest, her with quiet liberty at my leisure will I elect;
for if my humour love—

125. urged] *Qq;* urge *JOH.*   125.1. S.D.] *Q2; not in Q1.*   131.
fortune] *Q1;* fortunes *Q2.*   133. if my humour love—] *TC;* if my
humour loue. *Q1;* that's my humour. *Q2.*

---

116. *constant*] punning on the meanings 'faithful in love' and 'consistent'.

119. *admiration*] object of admiration. He used 'astonishment' the last
time (II.i.92). Though there are several such repetitions of phrases through
the play, Marston takes no great pains to check the accuracy of the repetitions; this probably indicates hasty composition.

126. *pure wit, nay, judgement*] here, *wit* = brilliant invention, and
judgement = the highest, most considered employment of reason.

131. *portion*] dowry, marriage portion.

Enter DULCIMEL *and* PHILOCALIA.

Herc. You profess a most excellent mystery, sir.

Nym. 'Fore heaven, see the princess, she that is—   135

Herc. Your most only elected, too.

Nym. Oh ay, oh ay, but my hopes faint yet. [*to Dulcimel*] By
    the vow of my heart, you are my most only elected,
    and—

Dul. There's a ship of fools going out. Shall I prefer thee,   140
    Nymphadoro? Thou mayst be master's mate; my
    father hath made Dondolo captain, else thou shouldst
    have his place.

Nym. By Jove, Fawn, she speaks as sharply and looks as
    sourly as if she had been new squeezed out of a crab   145
    orange.

Herc. How term you that lady with whom she holds
    discourse?

Nym. O, Fawn, 'tis a lady even above ambition, and like the
    vertical sun, that neither forceth others to cast shadows,   150
    nor can others force or shade her. Her style is Donna
    Philocalia.

Herc. Philocalia! What, that renowned lady, whose ample

---

137. hopes] *Qq;* hope's *Dilke.*   S.D.] *Dilke.*   146. orange] *Q2; not in*
Q1.   153. renowned] *Q2;* renowmed *Q1.*

---

134. *mystery*] trade, calling; Nymphadoro has already referred to his
pursuit of lucrative marriage as a 'trade' (III.i.71, 130).

137. *my hopes faint yet*] Old-spelling editions retain the ambiguity of
Qq. Of the new-spelling editions since 1816, only this one interprets *hopes*
as the plural noun and *faint* as a verb; Bullen and Smith both follow Dilke
in printing 'my hope's faint'. Cf. *The Case is Altered* (I.vi.9–10): 'And yet
my thoughts cannot propose a reason, / Why I should feare, or faint thus
in my hopes. . . .'

140. *prefer*] See I.ii.285 n.

145–6. *squeezed out of a crab orange*] See I.ii.13 n.

149–50. *the vertical sun*] the sun when directly overhead. 'When the sun
is highest he casts the least shadow' (Tilley, S 989).

151. *nor can others force or shade her*] 'Qy. "nor can *others' force* shade
her" ?' (Deighton, p. 8).

style] name, official title.

153–4. *ample report*] widespread fame.

report hath struck wonder into remotest strangers, and
yet her worth above that wonder? She whose noble   155
industries hath made her breast rich in true glories and
undying habilities? She that whilst other ladies spend
the life of earth, Time, in reading their glass, their
jewels, and (the shame of poesy) lustful sonnets, gives
her soul meditations, those meditations wings that   160
cleave the air, fan bright celestial fires, whose true
reflections makes her see herself and them? She whose
pity is ever above her envy, loving nothing less than
insolent prosperity, and pitying nothing more than
virtue destitute of fortune?   165

Nym. There were a lady for Ferrara's duke: one of great
blood, firm age, undoubted honour, above her sex,
most modestly artful, though naturally modest; too
excellent to be left unmatched, though few worthy to
match with her.   170

Herc. I cannot tell—my thoughts grow busy.

Phil. The princess would be private. Void the presence.

Exeunt [HERCULES *and* NYMPHADORO].

---

154. struck] *Dilke;* stroke *Qq;* strook *TC.*   172.1. *Hercules and Nymphadoro*] *Dilke.*

---

156. *industries*] skill, works, accomplishments.
breast] heart, soul. Cf. IV.i.683.
157. *habilities*] powers (mental and spiritual)
159. *lustful sonnets*] Marston dedicates much of Satire VIII of *SV.* to
demolishing the love poetry of his contemporaries. His attacks on his own
exercise in erotic poetry, *The Metamorphosis of Pigmalion's Image*, have
long been the subject of controversy. See Davenport's introduction to
Poems, and Gustav Cross's article, 'Marston's *Metamorphosis of Pigmalions
Image*: a mock epyllion', *Etudes anglaises,* XIII (1960), 331–6.
166. *There were a lady for Ferrara's duke*] Though apparently nothing is
made of this suggestion (on the basis of dialogue), it seems reasonable to
assume that at the end of the performance of the play some indication was
made that Philocalia and Hercules would make a match.
166–7. *of great blood*] of noble lineage.
167. *firm age*] maturity. Cf. 'To My Equal Reader', 13 n.
above her sex] i.e., not subject to the limitations one would expect of
women. These were no days for feminists.
172. *Void the presence*] withdraw from the (presence-)chamber.

Dul. May I rest sure thou wilt conceal a secret?

Phil. Yes, madam.

Dul. How may I rest truly assured?   175

Phil. Truly thus: do not tell it me.

Dul. Why, canst thou not conceal a secret?

Phil. Yes, as long as it is a secret, but when two know it, how
    can it be a secret? And indeed with what justice can you
    expect secrecy in me that cannot be private to yourself?   180

Dul. Faith, Philocalia, I must of force trust thy silence, for
    my breast breaks if I confer not my thoughts upon thee.

Phil. You may trust my silence; I can command that. But if
    I chance to be questioned I must speak truth. I can
    conceal but not deny my knowledge: that must com-   185
    mand me.

Dul. Fie on these philosophical discoursing women! Prithee
    confer with me like a creature made of flesh and blood,
    and tell me if it be not a scandal to the soul of all being,
    proportion, that I, a female of fifteen, of a lightsome   190
    and civil discretion, healthy, lusty, vigorous, full, and

---

184. be] *Q1;* he *Q2.*   189. all being,] *AHB;* all being *Qq;* all-being *TC.*
190. fifteen] *Q2;* 13 *Q1.*

184–5.] Montaigne (Crawford), III, v, 78–9): 'It is a paine for me to
dissemble: so that I refuse to take charge of other mens secrets, as wanting
hart to disavow my knowledge. I [can] conceal it; but deny it I cannot,
without much a do and some trouble.' Several short phrases in this scene
are from the same passage.

190. *proportion*] here, = the modern sense of due and harmonious
relation of things to each other.

lightsome] lively. 'I love a lightsome and civill discretion. . . .' Montaigne,
III, v, 77.

191. *civil*] educated, refined.

discretion] faculty of judgement; perhaps with the phrase 'age of
discretion' implied; in English law this was the age of fourteen, so
Dulcimel may be demanding the ancient right of teenagers to be 'treated
as an adult'.

lusty] could mean 'merry, lively'; but in the context, probably 'strong,
healthy'. 'A health youthfull, lusty, vigorous, full, idle. . . .' Montaigne,
III, v, 76.

191–2. *full, and idle*] This is something of a stock phrase, suggesting
'full of energy and looking for something to do'.

idle, should forever be shackled to the crampy shins of
a wayward, dull, sour, austere, rough, rheumy, threescore and four.

Phil. Nay, threescore and ten at the least.   195

Dul. Now, heaven bless me, as it is pity that every knave is
not a fool, so it is shame that every old man is not, and
resteth not a widower. They say in China, when women
are past child-bearing, they are all burnt to make gunpowder. I wonder what men should be done withal,   200
when they are past child-getting? Yet upon my love,
Philocalia (which with ladies is often above their
honour), I do even dote upon the best part of the duke.

Phil. What's that?

Dul. His son; yes, sooth, and so love him, that I must   205
marry him.

Phil. And wherefore love him, so to marry him?

Dul. Because I love him, and because he is virtuous, I love
to marry—

Phil. His virtues?   210

Dul. Ay, with him his virtues.

Phil. Ay, with him. Alas, sweet princess, love or virtue are
not of the essence of marriage.

208. him,] *Qq;* him; *Dilke.*   is] *Q1;* his *Q2.*   209. marry—] *London;*
marry. *Qq.*   210. virtues?] *Dilke;* virtues. *Qq.*

---

193. *wayward*] self-willed, intractable.

rheumy] suffering from catarrh.

196–7. *as it is pity . . . fool*] The play contradicts Dulcimel's complaint.
See Montaigne, III, v, 79.

198–200. *They say in China . . . gun-powder*] 'What should be done with
an old woman (wife) but make gunpowder of her?' (Tilley, W 639). The
addition of China is probably due to the tradition that '[t]he Chinese are
supposed to have discovered gunpowder in a remote antiquity . . .'
(Sugden). In Chapman's *The Widow's Tears* there is a suggestion that
poor old widows 'shall be burnt to make soap-ashes' (v.iii.317–18).

201. *child-getting*] 'The begetting of children. Unrecorded in O.E.D.';
Cross, *N&Q,* CCI (1956), 331.

205–11.] Though the general drift is plain enough, the passage is
awkward and evidently acts chiefly as a 'set-up' for the exchange beginning
with l. 212.

212–13. *love . . . marriage*] Crawford returns us to Montaigne's 'Upon

Dul. A jest upon your understanding! I'll maintain that
    wisdom in a woman is a most foolish quality. A lady of   215
    a good complexion, naturally well witted, perfectly
    bred, and well exercised in discourse of the best men,
    shall make fools of a thousand of these book-thinking
    creatures. I speak it by way of justification. I tell thee
    (look that nobody eavesdrop us), I tell thee, I am truly   220
    learned, for I protest ignorance; and wise, for I love
    myself; and virtuous enough for a lady of fifteen.
Phil. How, virtuous?
Dul. Shall I speak like a creature of a good healthful blood,

214. A jest] *Q2;* I iest *Q1;* I rest *TC.*   215. is a most] *Q1;* is most *Q2.*
221. protest] *Q1;* prote *Q2.*   ignorance] *Q2;* ignorant *Q1.*   223.
How,] *This ed.;* How *Qq.*

Some Verses of Virgil': 'Those who thinke to honour marriage, by
joyning love unto it, (in my opinion) doe as those, who to doe vertue a
favour, holde, that nobilitie is no other thing then Vertue. Indeed these
things have affinitie; but therewithall great difference: their names and
titles should not thus be commixt: both are wronged so to be confounded'
(III, v, 85). Marston also uses the passage for one of Crispinella's outbursts
in *DC.*: 'Virtuous marriage! There is no more affinity betwixt virtue and
marriage than betwixt a man and his horse' (III.i.88–90). Cf. *SV.*, v, 56–61,
where the satirist mistakenly tries to help a wooer by praising his virtues
to the lady.

    214. *A jest upon your understanding*] = oh bother your understanding.
But the phrase seems to have worried some readers. Deighton suggests
A'y, pest, or *A pest* and Wood accepts the latter in his notes but prints
A jest.
    I'll maintain] i.e., in formal debate.
    216. *good complexion*] balanced temperament.
    well witted] intelligent; *witted* alone could mean this, cf. v.i.456.
    218. *book-thinking*] 'Pedantic, full of thoughts gathered from books.
Unrecorded in O.E.D.'; Cross, *N&Q*, CCi (1956), 331.
    219. *justification*] verification, proof (in debate).
    220. *eavesdrop*] secretly listen to. Marston had used the verb in *AM.*,
II.i.310: 'The jealous ear of night eave-drops our talk.' O.E.D.'s first
record of the verb is 1606; Cross, *N&Q*, CC (1955), 186. As Dilke notes,
the word appears frequently in the plays of the day; but Marston's seems
the first use.
    220–1. *I am truly learned, for I protest ignorance*] alluding to Socrates,
who knew he knew nothing.

and not like one of these weak, green sickness, lean,   225
phthisic starvelings? First, for the virtue of magnanimity, I am very valiant, for there is no heroic action
so particularly noble and glorious to our sex as not to
fall to action; the greatest deed we can do is not to do
(look that nobody listen). Then am I full of patience,   230
and can bear more than a sumpter-horse, for (to speak
sensibly) what burden is there so heavy to a porter's
back as virginity to a well-complexioned young lady's
thoughts? (Look nobody hearken.) By this hand, the
noblest vow is that of virginity, because the hardest. I   235
will have the prince.

Phil. But by what means, sweet madam?

Dul. O, Philocalia, in heavy sadness and unwanton phrase,
there lies all the brain-work: by what means? I could
fall into a miserable blank verse presently.   240

232. burden] *Dilke;* burthen *Qq.*

---

225. *green sickness*] 'Greensickness is the anaemia of young women, and
it was popularly ascribed to virginity—"a malady most incident to maids" '
Poems, p. 378 (Davenport's note to *Ashby Entertainment,* 437).

225–6. *lean, phthisic starvelings*] Phthisis is pulmonary consumption,
though sometimes it was used loosely to mean a severe cough or asthma.
Marston probably picked up the phrase from Florio's Montaigne. 'Drie
pthisicke starveling' occurs in 'Upon Some Verses of Virgil', III, v, 109.

226–7. *magnanimity*] courage, fortitude.

229. *the greatest . . . do*] '*There is no point of doing more thorny, nor more
active, then this of not doing.*' Montaigne (Crawford), III, v, 102. (The
sententiae in Florio's Montaigne are italicised, as here and in other notes
to this scene.

231. *sumpter-horse*] pack-horse.

232. *sensibly*] clearly.

232–4. *what burden . . . lady's thoughts*] '*I finde it easier, to beare all ones
life a combersome armour on his backe, then a maidenhead.*' Montaigne
(Crawford), *loc. cit.*

234–5. *the noblest vow . . . hardest*] '*And the vow of virginity, is the noblest
of all vowes, because the hardest.*' Montaigne (Crawford), *loc. cit.*

238. *in heavy sadness*] in grave earnest.

[*in*] *unwanton phrase*] i.e., 'joking aside'.

239. *brain-work*] Cross lists this as unrecorded by *O.E.D.; N&Q,* CCII
(1957), 284.

240. *fall . . . verse*] a charming example of a character conscious of what
is expected of one in a play.

presently] immediately.

Phil. But, dear madam, your reason of loving him?

Dul. Faith, only a woman's reason: because I was expressly
forbidden to love him. At the first view I liked him, and
no sooner had my father's wisdom mistrusted my liking
but I grew loth his judgement should err; I pitied he   245
should prove a fool in his old age, and without cause
mistrust me.

Phil. But when you saw no means of manifesting your
affection to him, why did not your hopes perish?

Dul. O, Philocalia, that difficulty only enflames me: when   250
the enterprise is easy, the victory is inglorious. No, let
my wise, aged, learned, intelligent father, that can
interpret eyes, understand the language of birds,
interpret the grumbling of dogs and the conference of
cats, that can read even silence, let him forbid all inter-   255
views, all speeches, all tokens, all messages, all (as he
thinks) human means, I will speak to the prince, court
the prince, that he shall understand me. Nay, I will so
stalk on the blind side of my all-knowing father's wit
that, do what his wisdom can, he shall be my only   260
mediator, my only messenger, my only honourable
spokesman; he shall carry my favours, he shall amplify

242–3.] '*To forbid us any thing, is the ready way to make us long for it.*'
Montaigne (Crawford), II, xv, 416. See also Tilley: 'A woman does that
which is forbidden her' (W 650); and 'Because is a woman's reason'
(B 179).

244. *mistrusted*] suspected the intentions or motives of.

250. *that difficulty only enflames me*] '[Love is] a pleasure inflamed by
difficulty...' Montaigne (Crawford), III, v, 90.

250–1. *when the enterprise . . . inglorious*] '*The price of honor of the
conquest is rated by the difficultie.*' Montaigne (Crawford), III, v, 103.

252–3. *can interpret eyes*] Cf. II.i.486–7.

254. *grumbling*] growling. Cross notes that this antedates *O.E.D.*'s first
example for this verbal noun (1610). *N&Q*, CC (1955), 186.

256. *tokens*] keepsakes, given as an expression of affection.

257. *means*] i.e., means of communication.

259. *stalk on the blind side*] (an image from hunting); to act stealthily.

all-knowing] (antedates *O.E.D.* [1612]); Cross, *N&Q*, CCIV (1959),
355.

261. *mediator*] go-between, messenger.

262. *amplify*] expatiate, enlarge upon.

my affection, nay, he shall direct the prince the means,
the very way to my bed; he and only he, when he only
can do this, and only would not do this, he only shall do   265
this.

Phil. Only you shall then deserve such a husband. O love,
how violent are thy passages!

Dul. Pish, Philocalia, 'tis against the nature of love not to be
violent.   270

Phil. And against the condition of violence to be constant.

Dul. Constancy? Constancy and patience are virtues in no
living creatures but sentinels and anglers. Here's our
father.

      Enter GONZAGO, HERCULES *and* GRANUFFO.

Gon. What, did he think to walk invisibly before our eyes?   275
And he had Gyges' ring, I would find him.

Herc. 'For Jove, you rated him with emphasis.

Gon. Did we not shake the prince with energy?

---

268. *passages*] acts, proceedings.

269–70.] '[*I*]*t is against the nature of love, not to be violent, and against the
condition of violence, to be constant.*' Montaigne (Crawford), III, v, 137.

276. *Gyges' ring*] As Dilke noted, the story of the ring that rendered the
wearer invisible originated with Plato (*Republic*, ii, 359–60). By this time
it was proverbial (see Tilley, R 132).

277. *emphasis*] The word is capitalised in both Qq, suggesting that it
carries the weight here that it did in formal rhetoric, i.e. a figure of speech
in which more is implied than is actually said, meaning that is conveyed by
implication. The more general sense of 'vigorous, passionate expression'
is probably also present.

278. *energy*] The word is spelled 'enargie' in both Qq, but it is doubtful
that Marston is making the fine distinction that Puttenham does in his
section on 'ornament': 'This ornament then is of two sortes, one to
satisfie & delight th' eare onely by a goodly outward shew set vpon the
matter with wordes, and speaches smothly and tunably running: another
by certaine intendments or sence of such wordes & speaches inwardly
working a stirre to the mynde: that first qualitie the Greeks called *Enargia*,
of this word *argos* because it geueth a glorious lustre and light. This latter
they called *Energia* of *ergon*, because it wrought with a strong and vertuous
operation; and figure breedeth them both . . .' (pp. 142–3). Puttenham
goes on to say that sometimes the appeal is only to the ear, sometimes only
to the mind, but that they can sometimes be found together.

Herc. With Ciceronian elocution ?

Gon. And most pathetic piercing oratory ?   280

Herc. If he have any wit in him, he will make sweet use of it.

Gon. Nay, he shall make sweet use of it ere I have done.
    Lord, what overweening fools these young men be, that
    think us old men sots.

Herc. Arrant asses.   285

Gon. Doting idiots, when we, God wot—ha ha! 'Las, silly
    souls.

Herc. Poor weak creatures to men of approved reach.

Gon. Full years.

Herc. Of wise experience.   290

Gon. And approved wit.

Herc. Nay, as for your wit—

Gon. Count Granuffo, as I live, this Faunus is a rare under-
    stander of men, is 'a not ? Faunus, this Granuffo is a
    right wise good lord, a man of excellent discourse, and   295
    never speaks; his signs to me, and men of profound
    reach, instruct abundantly. He begs suits with signs,
    gives thanks with signs, puts off his hat leisurely, main-

---

294. not ? Faunus,] *TC;* not, *Fawnus, Q1;* not *Faunus* ? *Q2.*   296.
speaks;] *Dilke;* speakes, *Q1;* speakes *Q2.*

---

279. *Ciceronian*] worthy of Cicero (in style). *O.E.D.*'s first example for
this adjective is dated 1661.

    elocution] eloquence, oratory.

280. *pathetic*] stirring, moving (or) arising from strong emotion, passionate; probably a mixture of the two. Marston always uses it mockingly of
love poetry: 'O frantick fond pathetique passion!' (*SV.*, VIII, 110). See
also *SV.*, VIII, 25.

284. *sots*] dolts; without the connotation of overdrinking, though this
sense had also become current by then.

288. *approved reach*] proven powers of comprehension.

296–7. *men*] 'Mr. Daniel suggests that we should . . . read "His signs to
me and mien of profound reach"' (Bullen). Interesting, but unnecessary.
'Men' here implies 'other such men'.

298–9. *maintains his beard learnedly*] 'Learnedly' is probably only a
variation of 'methodically', carefully, (Cf. II.i.378, 'grave methodical
beard'); but the suggestion is that the beard shows the wisdom of the
wearer.

tains his beard learnedly, keeps his lust privately, makes
a nodding leg courtly, and lives happily.   300

Herc. Silence is an excellent modest grace, but especially
before so instructing a wisdom as that of your excellency's. As for his advancement, you gave it most
royally, because he deserves it least duly; since to give
to virtuous desert is rather a due requital than a princely   305
magnificence, when to undeservingness it is merely all
bounty and free grace.

Gon. Well spoke, 'tis enough. Don Granuffo, this Faunus is
is a very worthy fellow, and an excellent courtier, and
beloved of most of the princes of Christendom, I can   310
tell you; for howsoever some severer dissembler grace
him not when he affronts him in the full face, yet if he
comes behind or on the one side, he'll leer and put back
his head upon him, be sure. Be you two precious to each
other.   315

Herc. Sir, myself, my family, my fortunes, are all devoted, I

---

300. *leg*] bow.

306. *magnificence*] sovereign bounty or munificence.

307. *free grace*] The irony of the passage is summed up by this phrase, which is properly used theologically of the free and unmerited favour of God; here it appears in the context of reward for services to the state, where merit *should* prevail.

308. *'tis enough*] Gonzago's frequent use of this phrase is part of his rich characterisation; verbose himself, he makes a point of breaking off others' speeches, both to save the court's valuable time and to display how quickly he catches on to things.

311–14. *for howsoever ... be sure*] Dilke seems to have made sense of this difficult passage: 'The meaning is, that *flattery is so universally acceptable, that though some pretend to dislike it, when it is too* gross and direct, yet if it be artfully covered, or indirectly offered, they who seem to hate it most will smile upon and countenance him who offers it.' If this is correct (which seems likely), *some severer dissembler* means 'one who dissembles even more than Faunus', suggesting that Gonzago, though he likes Faunus's flattery, does recognise him as a flatterer. Also *affront* would mean simply 'Meet, confront', without the connotation of insult or defiance; indeed, the 'affronting' would here include flattery.

313. *leer*] glance (and smile ?) obliquely, slyly.

313–14. *put back his head*] raise his head proudly (?).

316–21.] Marston was always fond of (and good at) the mock encomium. See his 'dedications' to the first part of *AM.*, to *CS.*, and to *SV.* Lampatho

protest, most religiously to your service. I vow my
whole self only proud in being acknowledged by you
but as your creature, and my only utmost ambition is by
my sword or soul to testify how sincerely I am con-   320
secrated to your adoration.

Gon. 'Tis enough. Art a gentleman, Fawn?

Herc. Not uneminently descended; for were the pedigrees
of some fortunately mounted searched, they would be
secretly found to be of the blood of the poor Fawn.   325

Gon. 'Tis enough. You two I love heartily, for thy silence
never displeaseth me, nor thy speech ever offend me.
[DULCIMEL *comes forward.*] See, our daughter attends
us. My fair, my wise, my chaste, my duteous, and indeed, in all my daughter (for such a pretty soul for all   330
the world have I been): what, I think we have made the
prince to feel his error.

What, did he think he had weak fools in hand?
No, he shall find, as wisely said Lucullus,
Young men are fools that go about to gull us.   335

Dul. But sooth, my wisest father, the young prince is yet
forgetful, and resteth resolute in his much unadvised
love.

Gon. Is't possible?

Dul. Nay, I protest, whate'er he feign to you (as he can   340
feign most deeply)—

Gon. Right, we know it; for if you marked, he would not

323. uneminently] *Q1;* oneminently *Q2.*   328. S.D.] *Dilke.*   333–5.
verse] *AHB; prose Qq.*

Doria has a similar one in *WYW.* (II.i.37–43): 'Sir, I protest I not
only take distinct notice of your dear rarities of exterior presence, but
also I protest I am most vehemently enamour'd, and very passionately
dote on your inward adornments and habilities of spirit! I protest I shall
be proud to do you most obsequious vassalage.'

325. *of the blood . . . Fawn*] i.e., flatterers.
334. *Lucullus*] There is no evidence that the Roman statesman said
anything of the sort, but his name was very handy for the rhyme.

once take sense of any such intent from him. O impudence, what mercy canst thou look for!

Dul. And as I said, royally wise and wisely royal father—   345

Gon. I think that eloquence is hereditary.

Dul. Though he can feign, yet I presume your sense is quick
enough to find him.

Gon. Quick, is't not, Granuffo ? Is't not, Fawn ? Why, I did
know he feigned; nay I do know (by the just sequence   350
of such impudence) that he hath laid some second siege
unto thy bosom, with most miraculous conveyances of
some rich present to thee.

Dul. O bounteous heaven, how liberal are your graces to my
Nestor-like father!   355

Gon. Is't not so, say ?

Dul.   'Tis so, oraculous father.
He hath now more than courted with bare phrases.
See, father, see, the very bane of honour,
Corruption of justice and virginity:
Gifts hath he left with me. O view this scarf;   360
This—as he called it—most envied silk,
That should embrace an arm, or waist, or side,

---

349. Granuffo] *so Dilke; Gra.* [speech head] *Qq.*   350. he] *Dilke;* you *Qq.*
353. to] *Qr;* on *Q2.*   356–7.] *so this ed.; prose Qq.*

---

343. *take sense of*] acknowledge.

346. *I think that eloquence is hereditary*] an interesting anticipation of
the biological principle; *O.E.D.*'s first record of *hereditary* in that sense is
dated 1863.

349. *Granuffo*] There is no doubt that Dilke's emendation is correct;
Granuffo must not speak till the trial scene. The original error must have
been caused either by Marston's abbreviating the name (so that it appeared
to be a speech head), or by the coincidental coming together of the name
and the beginning of a new line in the MS, or both.

350. *just sequence*] logical consequence. *O.E.D.*'s first example of this
sense of sequence is dated 1613.

355. *Nestor-like*] extremely wise; after Nestor, the oldest of the Greek
leaders in *The Iliad*.

356. *oraculous*] i.e., as wise as an oracle. Cross notes that this antedates
O.E.D.'s first example of this sense (1617); *N&Q*, CCVI (1961), 388.

Which he much feared should never—this he left,
Despite my much resistance.

Gon. Did he so? Give't me. I'll give't him, I'll re-give his   365
token with so sharp advantage—

Dul. Nay, my worthy father, read but these cunning letters.

Gon. Letters? Where? [*Reads*]
'Prove you but justly loving and conceive me,
Till justice leave the gods, I'll never leave thee,   370
For though the duke seem wise, he'll find this strain:
Where two hearts yield consent, all thwarting's vain.'
And darest thou then aver this wicked writ?
O world of wenching wiles, where is thy wit?

Enter TIBERIO.

Dul. But other talk for us were far more fit,   375
For see, here comes the prince Tiberio.

Gon. Daughter, upon thy obedience, instantly take thy
chamber.

Dul. Dear father, in all duty, let me beseech your leave, that
I may but—   380

Gon. Go to, go to, you are a simple fool, a very simple
animal.

368. S.D.] *AHB ad. Dilke.*   372. yield] *Q2;* find *Q1.*   373. wicked]
Q2; not in Q1.

---

363. *Which . . . never*] which he much feared *he* should never (be able
to do).

364. *much*] great.

366. *advantage*] interest.

369. *justly*] properly, i.e. in good faith.
conceive me] understand me.

371–2.] There are probably musical connotations here for *strain* (tune,
musical 'statement'), and *consent* (harmony).

373. *aver*] acknowledge as your own. *O.E.D.* does not record a sense
exactly the same. *Thou* refers to the absent Tiberio.
writ] letter, written communication.

374. *wenching wiles*] love tricks.

382. *animal*] i.e., lacking rational powers; one in whom the animal
nature has the ascendancy (*O.E.D.* sense 3. *O.E.D.* gives as an example
LLL., IV.ii.27–8: '. . . he is only an animal, only sensible in the duller
parts').

Dul. Yet let me (the loyal servant of simplicity)—

Gon. What would you do ? What, are you wiser than your

    father ? Will you direct me ?   385

Dul. Heavens forbid such insolence, yet let me denounce my

    hearty hatred.

Gon. To what end ?

Dul. Though't be but in the prince's ear (since fits not

    maiden's blush to rail aloud)—   390

Gon. Go to, go to.

Dul. Let me but check his heat.

Gon. Well, well—

Dul. And take him down, dear father, from his full pride of

    hopes.   395

Gon. So, so, I say once more, go in.

                       Exeunt DULCIMEL *and* PHILOCALIA.

I will not lose the glory of reproof.

Is this th' office of ambassadors, my lord Tiberio,

Nay, duty of a son, nay, piety of a man

(A figure called in art *gradatio*—   400

383. me (the . . . simplicity)] *Q2;* me be the . . . simplicitie *Q1*.   392. but]
Q2; not in Q1.   396.1. *Exeunt*] *AHB; Exit Qq*.   399. piety] *Q1;*
pittie *Q2*.   400. (A] *Q2; A Q1*.

---

383. *the loyal servant of simplicity*] ironic undertones here: she is
'dedicated to innocence'; she also owes obedience (ll. 377) to a fool. There
may be an anticipation of *simplicity* as 'simpleton' (for which *O.E.D.*'s
first example is 1633.)

386. *insolence*] In the sense of 'impertinence, presumption, sauciness',
this antedates *O.E.D.*'s first example (dated 1668).

denounce] proclaim, announce. But *O.E.D.*'s first example for the sense
'to proclaim by way of a threat or warning' is dated 1632.

389. *fits*] it befits.

390. *maiden's blush*] Here *blush* = 'modesty'; *O.E.D.* does not record
this metonymy. Cf. *H5*, v.ii.253: 'Put off your maiden blushes.'

400–1. gradatio . . . climax] 'Gradation, is when we rehearse the word
that goeth next before, and bring an other word thereupon that encreaseth
the matter, as though one should goe vp a paire of stayres and not leaue
till he come at the top.' Wilson, p. 204. Another 'learned', Puttenham,
uses only the term *Climax*, which he calls 'the *marching figure*, for after the
first steppe all the rest proceede by double the space . . . [I]t may as well
be called the *clyming* figure, for *Clymax* is as much to say as a ladder. . . .'
Puttenham, p. 208.

With some learned, *climax*), to court a royal lady
For's master, father, or perchance his friend,
And yet intend the purchase of such beauty
To his own use?

Tib.   Your Grace doth much amaze me.

Gon. Ay, feign, dissemble, 'las, we are now grown old,   405
weak-sighted, alas, anyone fools us.

Tib. I deeply vow, my lord—

Gon. Peace, be not damned, have pity on your soul.
I confess, sweet prince,
For you to love my daughter, young and witty,   410
Of equal mixture both of mind and body,
Is neither wondrous nor unnatural;
Yet to forswear and vow against one's heart
Is full of base, ignoble cowardice,
Since 'tis most plain, such speeches do contemn   415
Heaven, and fear men (that's sententious now).

Tib. My gracious lord, if I unknowingly have erred—

Gon. Unknowingly? Can you blush, my lord?
Unknowingly? Why, can you write these lines,
Present this scarf, unknowingly, my lord,   420
To my dear daughter—um, unknowingly?
Can you urge your suit, prefer your gentlest love
In your own right, to her too easy breast

---

401. With] *Q2;* Which *Q1.*   *climax*)] *Q2;* (*Climax*) *Q1.*   403. such]
Q1; his *Q2.*   408–11. *lineation*] *This ed.;* I . . . daughter, / Young . . .
bodie, *Qq;* I . . . daughter, / Young and witty, / Of . . . body, *AHB;*
Peace . . . damnde, / Haue . . . Prince [,] / For . . . wittie, *London.*   416.
sententious] *Q1;* sentious *Q2.*

---

403. *purchase*] obtaining, acquisition. According to *O.E.D.*, this sense
was obsolete when Marston used it (the last example is dated 1589). His
legal training may have had some influence here, since it was (and is)
current in a related sense in law. Shakespeare uses it ironically in *1H4,*
II.i.101, where it is applied to (anticipated) stolen goods.

415–16. *such speeches do contemn / Heaven, and fear men*] Crawford
found the source in Montaigne, 'Of Giving the Lie': '. . . *whosoever lieth,
witnesseth that he contemneth God and therewithall feareth men*' (II, xviii,
491).

422. *prefer*] Cf. I.ii.285 n.

That, God knows, takes too much compassion on ye
(And so she prayed me say), unknowingly, my lord?   425
If you can act these things unknowingly,
Know we can know your actions so unknown,
For we are old, I will not say in wit
(For even just worth must not approve itself)—
But take your scarf, for she vows she'll not wear it.   430
Tib. Nay, but my lord—
Gon.   Nay, but my lord, my lord,
You must take it, wear it, keep it,
For by the honour of our house and blood,
I will deal wisely, and be provident;
Your father shall not say I panderised,   435
Or fondly winked at your affection.
No, we'll be wise: this night our daughter yields
Your father's answer; this night we invite
Your presence therefore to a feastful waking;
Tomorrow to Ferrara you return,   440
With wished answer to your royal father.
Meantime, as you respect our best relation
Of your fair bearing (Granuffo, is't not good?)—
Of your fair bearing, rest more anxious

429. even] *Q2;* euery *Q1.*

---

427. *so unknown*] which you claim not to know about; or, so unheard of;
probably the first.

429.] For even true worthiness must not commend itself.

435. *panderised*] acted as a pander, pimp. *O.E.D.*'s first example of the
word is from Florio's Montaigne, again the essay 'Upon Some Verses of
Virgil': 'Might it not be *Venus* her selfe, who so cunningly enhanced the
market of her ware, by the brokage or panderizing of the lawes?' (III, v,
116).

436. *fondly*] foolishly.

affection] bent, inclination.

439. *waking*] festival; festive vigil.

442. *respect our best relation*] expect, look for our good report (to your
father).

443. *fair bearing*] = good behaviour.

444–5. *anxious*] concerned. *O.E.D.*'s first example for this word is dated
1623. The poetic process is self-mockingly caught in action.

(No, anxious is not a good word)—rest more vigilant   445
Over your passion; both forbear and bear,
Anechou e apechou (that's Greek to you now),
Else your youth shall find
Our nose not stuffed, but we can take the wind
And smell you out—I say no more but thus—   450
And smell you out. What, ha' not we our eyes,
Our nose and ears, what, are these hairs unwise ?
Look to't, *quos ego*—(a figure called *aposiopesis* or
increpatio).

Exeunt GONZAGO *and* GRANUFFO.

TIBERIO *reads the embroidered scarves.*

447. *Anechou e apechou*] *AHB; Anechon, e apechon, Q1; Anexou è ampexou
Q2.*   (that's . . . now),] *Q2;* thats . . . now, *Q1.*   454.2. S.D.] *so
London; left margin opposite ll. 453–5 Q2; not in Q1.*

447. Anechou e apechou] = forbear and bear, as in l. 446, or 'sustain
and abstain'. The motto was a by-word for Epictetan philosophy, though
it does not appear in any of the works ascribed to him (or his amenu-
enses). The source is Book XVII, xix, of Aulus Gellius's *Attic Nights*,
where they are credited to Epictetus. The *e* is a survival of the Latin *et*
which appears between the two Greek words in many Renaissance editions of Aulus Gellius; in others the Greek *kai* sign is used.
    that's Greek to you now] 'It is Greek to me' (Tilley, G 439). Shakespeare
was not above using this all-too-popular phrase in *Caes.*, I.ii.287.
    449. take the wind] sniff the air and catch the scent; a hunting metaphor.
    453. quos ego] '*Quos ego* is a well-known passage in the "First Book of
the Aeneid [I, 135]," where Neptune threatens the winds with punishment for the commotions raised in the sea without his leave. It is a very
striking instance of the figure Aposiopesis, where a person through anger
or some other passion, breaks off his speech abruptly, and yet so as to be
understood' (Dilke).
    453–4. aposiopesis *or* increpatio] For definition, see previous note.
Wood calls this '[a] figure all too frequently used by Marston himself',
and in a note to *Soph.*, Bullen called it a 'horrid figure'. Marston probably
liked it because of the emotional realism it suggested, but there is no doubt
that the dangers of abusing the trick were already apparent in the 1580s:
'This figure is fit for phantasticall heads and such as be sodaine or lacke
memorie. I know of one of good learning that greatly blemisheth his
discretion with this maner of speech: for if he be in the grauest matter of
the world talking, he will vpon the sodaine for the flying of a bird our-
thwart the way, or some other such sleight cause, interrupt his tale and
neuer returne to it again' (Puttenham, p. 167).

Tib. 'Prove you but justly loving and conceive me,   455
    Justice shall leave the gods before I leave thee,'—
    Imagination prove as true as thou art sweet—
    'And though the duke seem wise, he'll find this strain:
    When two hearts yield consent, all thwarting's vain.'
    O, quick, deviceful, strong-brained Dulcimel,   460
    Thou art too full of wit to be a wife.
    Why dost thou love ? Or what strong heat gave life
    To such faint hopes ? O woman, thou art made
    Most only of, and for, deceit; thy form
    Is nothing but delusion of our eyes,   465
    Our ears, our hearts, and sometimes of our hands;
    Hypocrisy and vanity brought forth,
    Without male heat, thy most, most monstrous being.
    Shall I abuse my noble father's trust,
    And make myself a scorn, the very food   470
    Of rumour infamous ? Shall I, that ever loathed
    A thought of woman, now begin to love
    My worthy father's right, break faith to him
    That got me, to get a faithless woman ?
Herc. True, my worthy lord, your grace is *verè pius*.   475
Tib. To take from my good father the pleasure of his eyes,
    And of his hands, imaginary solace of his fading life.

---

476. take] *Q2;* rake *Q1.*

456.] Cf. III.i.370. The 'letters' have changed.
460. *deviceful*] ingenious.
    strong-brained] intelligent, brilliant. Not recorded in *O.E.D.*
463–8.] Tiberio's about-turn from the conventional anti-feminism of this passage to the encomium of 512 ff. is a lighter version of Malheureux's 'conversion' in *DC.*, and a healthier one.
468. *without male heat*] i.e. lacking the masculine (rational) principle. Cf. Milton's *Il Penseroso*, ll. 1–2: 'Hence, vain deluding Joys, / The brood of Folly without father bred.'
473. *right*] object of (my father's) rightful claim. *O.E.D.* does not record a sense close enough to this to fit.
475. verè pius] truly dutiful. Cf. III.i.399 for a like sense of 'piety'.
477. *imaginary*] imagined, hoped-for. This sense is not recorded in *O.E.D.*

Herc. His life that only lives to your sole good.

Tib. And myself good, his life's most only end.

Herc. Which, O, may never end!   480

Tib. Yes, Fawn, in time. We must not prescribe to nature
    everything. There's some end in everything.

Herc. But in a woman. Yet as she is a wife, she is oftentimes
    the end of her husband.

Tib. Shall I, I say—   485

Herc. Shall you, I say, confound your own fair hopes,
    Cross all your course of life, make your self vain
    To your once steady graveness, and all to second
    The ambitious quickness of a monstrous love,
    That's only out of difficulty born,   490
    And followed only for the miracle
    In the obtaining? I would ha' ye now
    Tell her father all.

Tib.   Uncompassionate, vild man,
    Shall I not pity, if I cannot love?
    Or rather shall I not for pity love   495
    So wondrous wit in so most wondrous beauty,
    That with such rarest art and cunning means
    Entreats what I (thing valueless) am not

483–4. *so AHB;* But . . . she is, / Oftentimes *Qq.*   493–4.] *so TC;*
Vncompassionate . . . loue *continuous Qq.*   498. Entreats what I (thing
valueless) am] *AHB;* Entreates? what I thinke valules, and *Q1;* Entreates?
what (I thing valules) am] *Q2.*

---

478. *to*] for.

479.] The only goal of his life is that I be good.

480–4. *end! . . . end in everything . . . end of her husband*] This is an odd
time for punning, since there is *some* seriousness to the scene. We may
perhaps sympathise with Johnson's concluding remarks on *Rom.*: 'His
persons, however distressed, *have a conceit left them in their misery, a
miserable conceit.*'

487. *Cross all your course of life*] thwart your prospects, your chosen
direction in life.

487–8. *vain To*] foolish in the face of.

489. *ambitious quickness*] improperly aspiring eagerness.

491. *miracle*] With this one word, Hercules cleverly undercuts his
pretended admonition.

493. *vild*] vile; a common variant at the time.

Worthy but to grant, my admiration ?
Are fathers to be thought on in our loves ?   500
Herc. True, right, sir.
    Fathers or friends, a crown and love hath none,
    But all are allied to themselves alone.
    Your father, I may boldly say, he's an ass
    To hope that you'll forbear to swallow   505
    What he cannot chew; nay, 'tis injustice, truly,
    For him to judge it fit that you should starve
    For that which only he can feast his eye withal,
    And not digest.
Tib. O, Fawn, what man of so cold earth   510
    But must love such a wit in such a body ?
    Thou last and only rareness of heaven's works,
    From best of man made model of the gods—
    Divinest Woman: thou perfection
    Of all proportions, Beauty—made when Jove was blithe,   515
    Well filled with nectar, and full friends with man:

499. grant,] *Q2;* grant *Q1.*   501–3. *lineation] London;* True . . . crowne,/
And . . . alone, *Qq.*   503. all] *Q1; not in Q2.*   509. digest] *Dilke;*
disgest *Qq.*   515. proportions, Beauty—] *This ed.;* proportions, bewty
Q1; proportions *Beutie, Q2;* proportion's beauty, *Dilke.*

502–3.] 'Probably our poet had a view to the adage, "*Non bene con-
venient, nec in una sede | Morantur majestas, et amor*"' (Dilke). Wilhelm
Creizenach noted the resemblance of this passage to one in Seneca's
Agamemnon, 259; *The English Drama in the Age of Shakespeare* (1916),
p. 74.
    508. *For that . . . withal*] Cf. *Ant.* (1607), II.ii.230–1, where Antony
'for his ordinary pays his heart / For what his eyes eat only'.
    510. *earth*] i.e. 'clay', constitution; also, of the four elements, earth was
cold and dry.
    512–13.] Eve, made from Adam (*best of man*) and after him is thus the
last . . . of heaven's works. *Model* here probably means 'image', 'replica',
rather than 'pattern (for)', 'exemplar', which *O.E.D.* indicates is a later
usage.
    515. *Beauty*] i.e. Woman is Beauty itself. Cf. Quadratus's libertine
encomium of woman in IV.i. of *WYW.*, followed by Lampatho's 'O
beautie feminine!'; in HHW, II, 279.
    516. *full friends with*] in perfect friendship with.

Thou dear as air, necessary as sleep
To careful man—Woman! Oh, who can sin so deeply
As to be cursed from knowing of the pleasures
Thy soft society, modest amorousness,   520
Yields to our tedious life! Fawn,
The duke shall not know this.

Herc.   Unless you tell him;
But what hope can live in you,
When your short stay, and your most shortened
    conference,
Not only actions, but even looks observed,   525
Cut off all possibilities of obtaining?

Tib. Tush, Fawn, to violence of women's love and wit,
Nothing but not obtaining is impossible.
    Notumque furens quid foemina possit.

Herc. But then how rest you to your father true?   530
Tib. To him that only can give dues, she rests most due.   *Exit.*
Herc. Even so? He that with safety would well lurk in courts
To best elected ends, of force is wrung
To keep broad eyes, soft feet, long ears, and most short
    tongue:
For 'tis of knowing creatures the main art   535

521–2. *lineation*] *TC;* Yeelds . . . this *one line, Qq.*   522–4. *lineation*] *This
ed.;* Vnlesse . . . in you; / When . . . conference, *Qq;* Vnlesse . . . him, /
But . . . stay, / And . . . conference, *London.*   532. so?] *Q2;* so *Q1;* so;
Dilke; so. *JOH.*

---

517. *dear as air*] proverbial: 'As loved (dear) as the air I breathe'
(Tilley, A 91). See also *Malc.*, v.iii.113, and *DC.*, II.ii.194.
    necessary as sleep] Taylor lists as proverbial, but it is not in Tilley.
    518. *careful*] full of cares.
    524. *conference*] conversation(s) (with Dulcimel).
    529. Notumque furens quid foemina possit] This is from the *Aeneid,*
v, 6, but Crawford is probably correct in suggesting that Marston got it
from Montaigne, III, v, 107, where it is quoted. Florio translates, 'It is
knowne what a woman may, / Whose raging passions have no stay.'
    531. *dues*] the toll, fee, i.e. the physical requirements of love.
    533. *To best elected ends*] for the best chosen purposes.
    534. *broad*] wide open.

To use quick hams, wide arms, and most close heart.

536. heart.] heart. / *Actus tertii Finis. Qq.*

536. *quick hams*] promptitude in bowing. The 'wide arms' may be part of an elaborate bow, or it may mean a readiness to embrace people in pretence of friendship. There might be an echo here of Gilbert Dugdale's (or ghost-writer Robert Armin's) advice to the crowds who annoyed King James at the Exchange during his unsuccessful attempt to spy on his subjects: 'doe as they doe in *Scotland* stand still, see all, and vse silence . . .' (*The Time Triumphant* [1604] sig. B2).

Act IV

Enter HERCULES *and* GARBETZA.

Herc. Why, 'tis a most well-in-fashion affection, Donna
Garbetza. Your knight, Sir Amorous, is a man of a most
unfortunate back, spits white, has an ill breath, and at
three after dinner goes to the bath, takes the diet, nay,
which is more, takes tobacco; therefore with great   5
authority you may cuckold him.

Gar. I hope so, but would that friend my brother discover
me, would he wrong himself to prejudice me?

Herc. No prejudice, dear Garbetza: his brother your
husband, right; he cuckold his eldest brother, true; he   10
gets her with child, just.

Gar. Sure there's no wrong in right, true, and just.

Act IV] ACTVS QVARTVS. *Qq.*   2. Amorous] *Amoros Qq.*   3. and]
Q1; not in Q2.

---

1. *affection*] either (i) feeling, impulse, or (ii) style of conduct (basically
'affectation'). Hercules is talking about Garbetza's wish, or habit, of
cuckolding Sir Amoroso.

3. *spits white*] Cf. II.i.306 n.

4. *takes the diet*] Cf. II.i 123 n.

5. *takes tobacco*] King James 'anonymously' published *A Counter-Blaste
to Tobacco* about the time this was written (1604).

7. *brother*] brother-in-law.

discover] expose.

8–9. *prejudice . . . prejudice*] injure . . . injury.

10–11. *right . . . true . . . just*] A favourite trick of Marston's. Cf.
IV.i.556–7: 'Oh, I am an ass, true; I am a coxcomb, well; I am mad, good.
. . .' See also *DC.*, II.ii.2–3, and *Malc.*, IV.i.30–1. The pattern is so typical
of Marston and so rare elsewhere that it has been used to identify his hand
in the first two scenes of *Eastward Ho*, I.i.27–9 and I.ii.18–21. The first
occurrence is the closer to our passage: 'I am intertained among gallants,
true: They call me coozen *Franke*, right; I lend them monnies, good; they
spend it, well.'

Herc. And indeed, since the virtue of procreation growed
    hopeless in your husband, to whom should you rather
    commit your love and honour to, than him that is most   15
    like and near your husband, his brother ? But are you
    assured your friend and brother rests entirely constant
    solely to you ?

Gar. To me ? O, Fawn, let me sigh it with joy into thy
    bosom, my brother has been wooed by this and that and   20
    t'other lady to entertain them (for I ha' seen their
    letters), but his vow to me, O Fawn, is most immutable,
    unfeigning, peculiar, and indeed deserved.

Enter PUTTOTA *and a* Page, PUTTOTA *with a letter in her hand.*

Put. Never entreat me, never beseech me to have pity, for-
    sooth, on your master, Master Herod. Let him never be   25
    so daringly ambitious as to hope with all his vows and
    protestations to gain my affection, gods, my discretion!
    Has my sutlery, tapstry, laundry, made me be ta'en up

23.1. *her*] *Dilke;* his *Qq.*   25. Master] *TC;* M. *Qq.*   27. affection,
gods, my discretion !] *TC;* affection, gods, my discretiō ? *Q1;* affectiō, gods
my discretiō ? *Q2;* affection; gods, my discretion ! *Dilke;* affection ! God's
my discretion ! *AHB;* affection. Gods my discretion ! *Smith;* 'gainst my
discretion ! *conj. this ed.*

23. *peculiar*] particular, special.
    deserved] deserving. Cf. *Cor.*, III.i.290–4:

> Now the good gods forbid
> That our renowned Rome, whose gratitude
> Towards her deserved children is enroll'd
> In Jove's own book, like an unnatural dam
> Should now eat up her own !

27. *to gain my affection, gods, my discretion !*] I am strongly inclined to read
''gainst' for *gods*; Marston might be playing with gain/gainst as he did
with odd suit/old suit (I.ii.237); but I am not satisfied that the bibliographical evidence is strong enough. ''Gainst' would mean 'in spite of, in
contradiction of' (my powers of discernment).

28. *sutlery*] victualling (she 'diets' footmen: see 'Interlocutors', 20).
    tapstry] work as a tapstress, looking after drink. The only sense re-
corded by *O.E.D.* is 'tap-room'.
    ta'en up] advanced, promoted.

at the court—preferred me to a husband; and have I
advanced my husband, with the labour of mine own   30
body, from the black guard to be one of the duke's
drummers, to make him one of the court forkers ? Shall
I, that purify many lords and some ladies, can tell who
wears perfumes, who plasters, and for why, know who's
a gallant of a chaste shirt and who not; shall I become,   35
or dares your master think I will become, or if I would
become, presumes your master to hope I would become
one of his common feminines ? No, let Master Herod
brag of his brother's wife; I scorn his letters and her
leavings at my heel, i' faith, and so tell him.   40

32. forkers] *Q2;* gallants *Q1.*   32–3. Shall . . . ladies] *Q2; not in Q1.*
35. and who . . . shall] *Q2; not in Q1.*   36–7. if I would become] *Q2;* if I
become *Q1.*

---

31. *the black guard*] 'The lowest menials of a royal or noble household,
who had charge of pots and pans and other kitchen utensils, and rode in
the wagons conveying these during journeys from one residence to another; the scullions and kitchen-knaves' (*O.E.D.*).

32. *court forkers*] court cuckolds. The Q2 reading is probably only an
adjustment for the printed page. Q1's 'court gallants', perhaps with the
help of a gesture, served the purpose even better on the stage, since the
irony was added to the joke.

33. *purify*] i.e. do cleaning for; but probably with ironic overtones.

34. *who plasters*] i.e., who wears plasters; applications which might be
of either medicinal or cosmetic use. A passage in *Malc.* probably explains
it: 'Do you know Doctor Plaster-face ? by this curd, he is the most exquisite
in forging of veins, sprightening of eyes, dying of hair, sleeking of skins,
blushing of cheeks, surphling of breasts, blanching and bleaching of
teeth, that ever made an old lady gracious by torchlight . . .' (II.iii.29–34).
Marston may have been influenced by a passage in Jonson's *Cynthia's
Revels*, where Moria makes a similar declaration to Puttota's: 'I would
wish to be a wisewoman, and know all the secrets of court, citie, and
countrie. I would know what were done behind the arras, what vpon the
staires, what i' the garden, what i' the Nymphs chamber, what by barge,
& what by coach. I would tel you which courtier were scabbed, and which
not; which ladie had her owne face to lie with her a-nights, & which not;
who put off their teeth with their clothes in court, who their haire, who
their complexion; and in which boxe they put it' (IV.i.140–57).

38. *feminines*] women (usually used contemptuously). Marston used the
word in 'To Perfection. A Sonnet', which he contributed to Chester's
Love's Martyr in 1601: 'So haue I marueld to obserue of late, / Hard
fauour'd Feminines so scant of faire, . . .' (*Poems*, p. 178).

Page. Nay, costly, dear Puttota, Mistress Puttota, Madam
    Puttota, O be merciful to my languishing master. He
    may in time grow a great and well-graced courtier, for
    he wears yellow already. Mix therefore your loves. As
    for Madam Garbetza, his brother's wife, you see what   45
    he writes there.

Put. I must confess he says she is a spiny, green creature,
    of an unwholesome barren blood and cold embrace, a
    bony thing of most unequal hips, uneven eyes, ill-
    ranked teeth, and indeed one, but that she hires him, he   50

41. costly] *Qq; softly* Dilke.   43. a] *Q1; not in Q2.*   44. yellow] *Q2;*
green *Q1.*

---

41. *costly, dear Puttota*] Halliwell, Bullen and Smith all agree with
Dilke's change of *costly* to 'softly'. They miss a multiple pun. *Costly* is a
whimsical variant of dear; apart from the possible costliness of her court
clothing, the courting of such a 'handsome plum-cheeked wench' would
cost Herod dear. But above all there is the resemblance of her name
(spelled *Puttotto* twice in this passage in Q1) to the as yet rare and
expensive potato (probably the sweet potato here), then in demand for its
alleged aphrodisiac powers. See R. N. Salaman's scholarly and highly
readable *The History and Social Influence of the Potato* (1949), pp. 424–8.
Cf. also Dekker's *Satiromastix* (ed. Bowers), III.i.99: 'Wher's my most
costly and sumptuous Shorthose?' (Shorthose is the name of one of the
characters, but it also means 'sock, stocking'.)

44. *he wears yellow already*] Linthicum writes (p. 48): 'Yellow in hose
or footwear has three meanings in drama: love, marriage and jealousy
after marriage. Its connexion with love probably grew out of its association
with Hymen [traditionally dressed in a saffron robe]. . . . The many lovers
at Court possibly account for the fact that Marston's, Deloney's, and
Overbury's characters who go to Court assume yellow hose.' Linthicum
cites the present passage, among several others, in support of her statement, and though the Page does not mention stockings specifically, it
seems likely that he is referring to Herod's wearing the colours of a lover
(one immediately thinks of Malvolio in *Tw.N.*). See Linthicum, pp. 43–52,
for a detailed discussion of the symbolic values of the various shades of
yellow in the costume of Marston's day. Q1's *green* would carry much the
same connotation, since it 'symbolized youth and joy, and was therefore,
as Shakespeare said, "the colour of lovers"' (Linthicum, p. 31). Q1's
reading may have been changed in Q2 to avoid the repetition of the word
on l. 47; or it may well have originally been an error caused by the
compositor's eye picking up 'green' in the manuscript ahead of his copy.

47. *spiny*] thin and bony (perhaps, 'prickly' in character).

green] pale, ill-humoured.

49–50. *ill-ranked*] Cross notes that this is unrecorded in *O.E.D.*; *N&Q*,
CCVI (1961), 124.

endures not; yet for all this, does he hope to dishonest
me? I am for his betters, I would he should well know
it, for more by many than my husband know I am a
woman of a known, sound, and upright carriage, and so
he shall find if he deal with me, and so tell him, I pray   55
you. What, does he hope to make me one of his gills, his
punks, polecats, flirts, and feminines?

Exit. As PUTTOTA *goes out, she flings away the letter. The* Page
puts it up, and as he is talking, HERCULES *steals it out of his pocket.*

Page. Alas, my miserable master, what suds art thou washed
into! Thou art born to be scorned of every carted community. And yet he'll out-crack a German when he is   60
drunk, or a Spaniard after he hath eaten a fumatho, that

---

51. *dishonest*] defile (and hence defame).

54. *upright carriage*] *Upright*, of a person's carriage, means 'erect', and
of character, 'honourable'. It could also be used at this time in expressions
connoting lying on the back, 'supine'. Similarly, *carriage* means basically
'bodily deportment', but could also mean 'capacity for carrying'. For this
last sense (I.6), *O.E.D.* gives an example from *LLL.*, I.ii.74 ff.: 'Sampson
... was a man of good carriage, great carriage, for he carried the two gates
on his back like a porter.' Cf. also III.i.5, 'upright virtue'.

56. *gills*] = jills; lasses, wenches.

57. *punks, polecats*] Both are synonyms for whores.

flirts] hussies.

feminines] Cf. IV.i.38 n.

57.2. *puts it up*] puts it away (*into* a pocket, etc.). Cf. *The Three Parnassus
Plays*, ed. J. B. Leishman, p. 82: 'What, *Monsieur Kinsayder*, lifting vp
your legge and pissing against the world? Put vp man, put vp for shame ...'

58–9. *what suds art thou washed into*] What a mess you're in. Proverbial:
'To leave one (to like, to be) in the suds (sands)' (Tilley, S 953).

59–60. *every carted community*] '*Id est*, by every strumpet who has been
publicly whipped as such at the cart's tail!' (Dilke). 'Every community
of whores' (Wood). Dilke is right. *O.E.D.*'s sense †10 for *community* is
'A common prostitute'; its only example is from *Sir Giles Goosecap* (1606)
I.iv.137–8: 'one of these painted communities that are ravished with
coaches, and upper hands, and brave men of dirt. . . .' Cf. II.i.21.

60. *out-crack*] out-boast.

61. *fumatho*] 'If Cornish Pilchards, otherwise called *Fumadoes*, be so
saleable as they are in France, Spain and Italy . . .' Nashe, *The Prayse of
the Red Herring* (1599), *Works*, III, 192. 'Their pilchards . . . by the name
of *fumadoes*, with oil and a lemon, are meat for the mightiest Don in Spain'
(Fuller, *History of the Worthies of England*]1662], 1840 ed., I, 301).

he has lain with that and that and t'other lady, that he
lay last night in such a madonna's chamber, t'other
night he lay in such a countess's couch, tonight he lies
in such a lady's closet, when poor I know all this while   65
he only lied in his throat.   *Exit.*

Herc. [*reads*] 'Madam, let me sigh it in your bosom, how
immutable and unfainting and indeed—'

Gar. Fawn, I will undo that rascal. He shall starve for any
further maintenance.   70

Herc. You may make him come to the covering and recovering of his old doublets.

Gar. He was in fair hope of proving heir to his elder brother,
but he has gotten me with child.

---

62. lain] *Dilke;* lyen]*Qq;* lien *AHB.*   63. madonna's] *Q2;* maidens *Q1.*
64. lay] *Q2;* laide *Q1.*   countess's] *Q2;* Countesse *Q1.*   66. only] *Q2;*
not in Q1.   67. S.D.] *Smith.*   67–8. 'Madam . . . indeed—'] *so Smith;*
no inverted commas Qq.   68. unfainting] *Qq;* unfeigning *Dilke.*   69.
that] *Q2;* it, *Q1.*   74. me with] *Q2;* a *Q1.*

---

64. *such a countess's couch*] See IV.i.152. Marston deals with such 'false
braggarts of ladies' favours' (v.i.297–8) in *CS.*, 75–83:

> When as thou hear'st me aske spruce *Duceus*
> From whence he comes. And hee straight answers vs,
> From Lady Lilla. And is going straight
> To the Countesse of (   ) for she doth waite
> His comming. And will surely send her Coach,
> Vnlesse he make the speedier approch
> Art not thou ready for to breake thy spleene
> At laughing at the fondnes thou hast seene
> In this vaine-glorious foole ?

65. *closet*] private chamber, bower.

71–2. *covering and recovering*] patching and repairing.

73–4.] 'Persons expecting to become heirs fell into two classes: "heirs
apparent," and "heirs presumptive." The former's succession was
contingent only upon his outliving his ancestor—for example, an eldest
son. . . . On the other hand, an "heir presumptive" was one whose
succession might be defeated not only by his predeceasing the ancestor,
but also . . . by the birth of a child, either male or female, to the ancestor.
. . .' Clarkson and Warren, pp. 198–9. Though Herod is referred to as
'apparent heir' (v.i.303), he is actually 'presumptive heir', like the gallant
Marston wrote of in *SV.*, x, 27–32:

> And tell me *Ned*, what might that gallant be,

Herc. So, you withdrawing your favour, his present means   75
  fail him; and by getting you with child, his future means
  forever rest despairful to him.

Gar. O heaven, that I could curse him beneath damnation,
  impudent varlet. By my reputation, Fawn, I only loved
  him because I thought that I only did not love him; he   80
  vowed infinite beauties doted on him. Alas, I was a
  simple country lady, wore gold buttons, trunk sleeves,
  and flagon bracelets. In this state of innocency was I
  brought up to the court.

Herc. And now instead of country innocency have you got   85
  court honesty. Well, madam, leave your brother to my
  placing. He shall have a special cabin in the ship of fools.

Gar. Right, remember he got his elder brother's wife with
  child, and so deprived himself of th' inheritance.

---

80. him; he] *Q2;* him, but as hee *Q1.*

> Who to obtaine intemperate luxurie,
> Cuckolds his elder brother, gets an heire,
> By which his hope is turned to despaire?

In his note on this passage, Davenport points to a similar passage in
Donne (ed. Grierson, I, 42):

> In early and long scarcenesse may he rot,
> For land which had been his, if he had not
> Himselfe incestuously an heire begot.

Davenport suggests, 'It sounds as though there were some current piece
of scandal', but I have been no more successful than he was in locating it.

 75. *his present means*] See II.i.180–4, where it is clear that Garbetza
supports Herod.
 80. *I only did not love him*] I was the only one who did not love him.
 82. *gold buttons*] See Linthicum, pp. 278–9, on the popularity of buttons
during the reign of King James. The implication here is that Garbetza
took inordinate pride in being fashionable. However, see next note.
 trunk sleeves] 'Large sleeves, stuffed with wool, hair &c.' (Bullen). They
were by now apparently out of fashion, though popular during the closing
years of Elizabeth's reign, if *Shr.*, IV.iii.88–91, is an indication. See
Linthicum, pp. 174–5.
 83. *flagon bracelets*] This may simply mean 'huge, outsize' bracelets.
What they were is by no means certain, though *O.E.D.* suggests 'a chain-
bracelet to which a smelling bottle (F. *flacon*) could be attached'.

Herc. That will stow him under hatches, I warrant you.   90

Gar. And so deprived himself of inheritance. Dear Fawn,
    be my champion.

Herc. The very scourge of your most basely offending
    brother.

Gar. Ignoble villain, that I might but see thee wretched   95
    without pity and recovery! Well—   [*Exit* GARBETZA]

        Enter HEROD *and* NYMPHADORO.

Herc. Stand, Herod. You are full met, sir.

Herod. But not met full, sir. I am as gaunt as a hunting
    gelding after three trained scents. 'Fore Venus, Fawn, I
    have been shaling of peascods; upon four great   100
    madonnas have I this afternoon grafted the forked tree.

Herc. Is't possible?

Herod. Possible? Fie on this satiety, 'tis a dull, blunt, weary,

90. stow] *Q2;* follow *Q1.*   96. S.D.] *Dilke.*   99. 'Fore Venus, Fawn]
JOH; for Venus Fanne *Q1;* fore Venus fanne *Q2;* 'fore Venus's fan *Dilke.*
100–1. four great madonnas] *Q2;* faire *Madona Q1.*

---

90. *stow him under hatches*] Sailors were punished by being locked
under the deck, but there may be another joke here; cf. Mistress Page, in
Wiv., II.i.96: 'If he come under my hatches, I'll never to sea again.'

96. recovery] possibility or means of remedy (of your condition).

98–9. *as gaunt . . . gelding*] Cf. the proverb 'As gaunt as a greyhound'
(Tilley, G 444); but here referring to the horse that is made to follow the
greyhound.

99. *trained scents*] A *scent* is a trail indicated by an animal's odour.
Train (*O.E.D.* vb. II) has the sense of 'draw on' or sometimes 'lead
astray'. Perhaps 'a wild chase'.

100. *shaling of peascods*] shelling peas. But see Florio's Montaigne, I,
xliii, 369, 'Of Sumptuarie Lawes': 'Let Courtiers first begin to leave off
and loath these filthy and apish breeches, that so open shew our secret
parts: the bumbasting of long pease-cod-bellied doublets.'

101. *grafted the forked tree*] Crawford finds this in Montaigne's 'An
Apology of Raymond Sebond' (II, xii, 373): 'He would hardly have
perswaded *Calisthenes* to refuse his faire daughter *Agarista* to *Hippo-
clides,* because he had seen him graft the forked tree in her upon a table.'

103–4. *Fie . . . passion*] '. . . *Satiety begets distaste*: It is a dull, blunt,
weary, and drouzy passion.' Montaigne (Crawford), II, xv, 417.

103. *dull*] dulling, enervating.

blunt] blunting, stupefying; *O.E.D.*'s first example for this sense is
1656. *Weary* and *drowsy* have a similar function: making one weary,
drowsy.

and drowsy passion. Who would be a proper fellow to
be thus greedily devoured and swallowed among ladies?   105
Faith, 'tis my torment, my very rack.

Herc. Right, Herod, true, for imagine all a man possessed
were a perpetual pleasure, like that of generation, even
in the highest lusciousness, he straight sinks as unable
to bear so continual, so pure, so universal a sensuality.   110

Herod. By even truth, 'tis very right; and for my part,
would I were eunuched rather than thus sucked away
with kisses, enfeebling dalliance, and—oh, the falling
sickness on them all! Why did reasonable nature give so
strange, so rebellious, so tyrannous, so insatiate parts of   115
appetite to so weak a governess as woman?

107. Herod] *Q1 corr., Q2;* hered *Q1 uncorr.*   108. were] *Q1 corr.;* with
Q1 uncorr., Q2.   116. as] *Q1;* a *Q2.*

104–5. *to be*] if it means one has to be.

107. *all a man*] all of a man, 'al his severall members'. See next note.

107–10.] Cf. Montaigne (Crawford) II, xx, 500: 'When I imagine man
fraught with all the commodities may be wished, let us suppose, al his
severall members were for ever possessed with a pleasure like unto that of
generation, even in the highest point that may be: I find him to sincke
under the burthen of his ease, and perceive him altogether unable to
beare so pure, so constant, and so universall a sensuality.'

Smith indicates that 'were' is the uncorrected reading of Q1, 'with'
the corrected. Both words appear in the borrowed passage, and Marston
might have omitted one by inadvertence at first. But changes on sig. F2,
which would have been made at the same time as these on F4 (both pages
were on the inner forme), establish that the present reading is accurate
(and that the Q2 compositor was using uncorrected Q1 at this point).
In those copies of Q1 which read 'Herod' and 'were' on F4 (they are the
majority, by the way), on F2 (III.i.468–507) 'rake' is corrected to 'take', and
the 't' in 'canot' (494), tightly pushed against the margin, drops out as a
result of loosening of the formes to make the correction.

108. *generation*] the sex act.

109. *lusciousness*] pleasurableness.

111. *even*] exact, 'straight'.

112. *eunuched*] made a eunuch. Cross points out that this antedates
O.E.D.'s first example of the verb (1658). He ascribes the passage to *DC.*,
however. *N&Q*, CCII (1957), 65.

113–14. *the falling sickness*] epilepsy; but with *double entendre*; cf. *Rom.*,
I.ii.42.

115. *parts*] attributes; but also, organs.

Herc. Or why, O custom, didst thou oblige them to modesty,
  such cold temperance, that they must be wooed by
  men, courted by men? Why, all know they are more
  full of strong desires, those desires more impatient of   120
  delay or hindrance, they have more unruly passions
  than men, and weaker reason to temper those passions
  than men.
Nym. Why then hath not the discretion of nature thought it
  just that customary coyness, old fashions, terms of   125
  honour and of modesty, forsooth, all laid aside, they
  court not us, beseech not us, rather, for sweets of love,
  than we them, why? By Janus, women are but men
  turned the wrong side outward.

121. unruly] *Q2;* vnourely *Q1;* unhourely *TC.*   125. that] *Q2; not in*
Q1.   coyness] *Dilke;* coines (*perhaps merely an old spelling for coyness*)
Qq, TC.

119–20. *all know . . . desires*] a common enough accusation; but see
especially Montaigne, III, v, *passim.* Marston may have been thinking
particularly of this passage: 'without comparison they are much more
capable and violent in Loves-effects then we . . .' (III, v, 91).

125. *coyness*] Dilke was the first to interpret Qq's 'coines' as *coyness;*
Bullen and Smith follow him, and none of the three records the original
spelling. Sheares, Halliwell, Wood, and London simply reprint 'coines',
also without comment, although in glossing the word London spells it
'coins', and explains it as 'the compliments that custom demands men give
women'. Yet one would expect such figurative use to be set in a context
which makes the metaphor of 'payment' or 'dues' quite clear, as are all the
examples given by *O.E.D.* (none of which is persuasively similar to the
sense it would have here). Though *O.E.D.* gives no variant spellings for
coyness, it does list 'coie' as a variant for 'coy'; and the suffix '-ness' often
appears as '-nes' in the quartos (e.g. Qq's 'sicknes' for 'sickness' a few
lines earlier, on F4 recto). That coyness was considered 'customary' for
women is supported by *O.E.D.*'s first two examples, (i) 'The manner of
Ladies to salute Gentlemen with coynesse' (Lyly, *Euphues,* 1579); and (ii)
'This is but the coynesse of a bride' (Beaumont and Fletcher, *The Maid's
Tragedy,* 1611). Cf. also I.ii.170–3.

127. *court not us, beseech not us*] 'Omit *not* in both cases' (Deighton).
Deighton is thinking of 'hath not' on l. 124. But the double negative was
common at this time.

128–9. *women . . . outward*] Cf. *Tw.N.* (1600–1), III.i.13–15: 'A sentence
is but a cheveril glove to a good wit. How quickly the wrong side may be
turned outward!' Though Montaigne's essay 'Upon Some Verses of

Herc. O, sir, nature is a wise workman. She knows right well   130
    that if women should woo us to the act of love, we
    should all be utterly shamed: how often should they take
    us unprovided, when they are always ready?

Herod. Ay, sir, right, sir, to some few such unfortunate
    handsome fellows as myself am, to my grief I know it.   135

Herc. Why, here are two perfect creatures: the one,
    Nymphadoro, loves all, and my Herod here enjoys all.

Herod. Faith, some score or two ladies or so ravish me
    among them, divide my presence, and would indeed
    engross me were I indeed such an ass as to be made a   140
    monopoly of. Look, sirrah, what a vild hand one of
    them writes: who would ever take this for a 'd',
    'dearest', or read this for 'only', 'only dearest'?

Herc. Here's a 'lie' indeed.

Herod. True, but here's another much more legible, a good   145

139. presence] *Q1;* presents *Q2.*

Virgil' is the source of much of this dialogue, his own conclusion is more
complimentary to women. He closes the essay with this paragraph: '*I say,
that both male and female, are cast in one same moulde; instruction and
custome excepted, there is no great difference between them. Plato* calleth
them both indifferently to the society of all studies, exercises, charges and
functions of warre and peace, in his Commonwealth. And the Philosopher
Antisthenes took away al distinction betweene their vertue and ours. It is
much more easie to accuse the one sexe, then to excuse the other. It is that
which some say proverbially, *Ill may the Kill call the Oven burnt taile*'
(III, v, 154).

130–3.] Cf. Montaigne (Crawford) III, v, 136: 'Verily according to the
lawe which nature giveth them [women], it is not fit for them to will and
desire: their part is to beare, to obay and to consent. Therefore hath
nature bestowed a perpetuall capacity; on us a seld and uncertaine
ability. They have alwayes their houre, that they may ever be ready to let
us enter.'

140. *engross*] defined in the next line: 'made a monopoly of'. Cf.
II.i.149 n.

141. *vild*] See III.i.493 n.

143–4, 148. '*only*' . . . *a 'lie'* . . . '*one lie*'] Much of the humour is of
course lost because of changes, since Marston's time, in pronunciation
and spelling. Both were then flexible enough that an actor could adapt his
pronunciation to make 'only' and 'one lie' sound alike.

secretary: 'My most affected Herod, the utmost ambition of my hopes and only—'

Herc. There is 'one lie' better shaped by odds.

Herod. Right, but here's a lady's roman hand to me is
beyond all; look ye: 'To her most elected servant and   150
worthy friend, Herod Baldanzozo Esquire.' I believe
thou knowest what countess's hand this is. I'll show
thee another.

Herc. No, good Herod, I'll show thee one now: 'To his
most elected mistress and worthy laundress, divine   155
Mistress Puttotta, at her tent in the woodyard or elsewhere, give these—'

Herod. Prithee ha' silence—what's that?

Herc. 'If my tears or vows, my faithful'st protestations on
my knees—'   160

Herod. Good, hold.

Herc. 'Fair and only loved laundress—'

Herod. Forbear, I beseech thee.

Herc. '—might move thy stony heart to take pity on my
sighs—'   165

Herod. Do not shame me to the day of judgement.

---

151. Baldanzozo] *This ed.;* Baldonzozo *Qq.*   159. faithful'st] *Q2;* doubt-
lest *Q1.*

---

146. *secretary*] *O.E.D.* associates this hand with legal documents, but in
fact it was the 'workaday' English hand throughout the sixteenth and part
of the seventeenth century (G. E. Dawson and L. Kennedy-Skipton,
Elizabethan Handwriting 1500–1650 [1966], p. 8).

affected] beloved.

149. *roman*] i.e. italic; the more usual hand for women, it eventually
replaced secretary hand altogether (Dawson and Kennedy-Skipton, *ibid.*,
pp. 9–10). Malvolio says of 'Olivia's' letter: 'I think we do know the sweet
Roman hand' (*Tw.N.*, III.iv.31).

150. *elected*] See III.i.86–7 n.

151. *Baldanzozo*] See 'Interlocutors', 12 n.

152. *what countess's hand this is*] Cf. IV.i.64.

154 ff.] A similar exposure takes place in *AM.*, III.ii.90–104 (HHW, I,
37), where Feliche snatches the boasting Castillio's 'seeming letter' from
him, and reads aloud what turns out to be a tailor's bill.

161. *Good*] = good sir, good fellow.

164. *stony heart*] proverbial: 'A heart as hard as stone' (Tilley, H 311).

Herc. 'Alas, I write it in passion. Alas, thou knowest besides
    my loathed sister, thou art—'

Herod. For the Lord's sake.

Herc. 'The only hope of my pleasure, the only pleasure of 170
    my hopes. Be pleased therefore to—'

Herod. Cease, I beseech thee.

Herc. Pish, ne'er blush, man, 'tis an uncourtly quality. As
    for thy lying, as long as there's policy in't, it is very
    passable. Wherefore has heaven given man tongue but 175
    to speak to a man's own glory? He that cannot swell
    bigger than his natural skin, nor seem to be in more
    grace than he is, has not learned the very rudiments or
    A B C of courtship.

Herod. Upon my heart, Fawn, thou pleasest me to the soul. 180
    Why, look you, for my own part I must confess—

               Enter DONDOLO.

See, here's the duke's fool.

Don. Aboard, aboard, aboard, all manner of fools of court,
    city, or country, of what degree, sex, or nature!

Herod. Fool!   185

Don. Herod!

167–8. *besides my loathed sister*] The sentence is completed in l. 170,
but the sense of *besides* is not clear: (i) put side by side (in comparison)
with my sister-in-law [an odd sort of compliment]; (ii) together with my
sister-in-law (who, you know, supports me); (iii) in spite of my sister-in-
law; (iv) beyond even my sister-in-law. Perhaps a grotesque combination
of them all.

173–9.] A most 'Machiavellian' bit of advice. That Marston can bring
off such irony with so much ease speaks for his development since the
formal satires.

176. *swell*] boast; but also carrying through the physical image.

177–8. *to be in more grace than he is*] to be in more favour (with the
powers that be) than he really is; also, to be better off than he really is.

179. *courtship*] (i) courting; (ii) court-craft, flattery, etc. Both are
meant, especially the second.

183–4. *court, city, or country*] proverbial phrase: see Tilley, H 311.

185–6. *Fool!* / *Herod!*] not just greetings: Dondolo returns Herod's
half-contemptuous address by calling him a Herod, a silly ranter and
boaster; not much of a joke, but it was probably meant as one.

Herc. What, are ye full freighted ? Is your ship well fooled ?
Don. Oh, 'twas excellently thronged full: a justice of peace,
though he had been one of the most illiterate asses in a
country, could hardly ha' got a hanging cabin. Oh, we   190
had first some long fortunate great politicians, that
were so sottishly paradised as to think, when popular
hate seconded princes' displeasure to them, any unmerited violence could seem to the world injustice;
some purple fellows whom chance reared, and their own   195
deficiencies of spirit hurled down; we had some
courtiers that o'erbought their offices and yet durst fall
in love; priests that forsook their functions to avoid a
thwart stroke with a wet finger. But now, alas, Fawn,
now there's space and place.   200

187. freighted] *Q1;* fraughted *Q2.*   196. deficiencies] *TC;* deficiences
Qq.   200. space] *Q2;* place *Q1.*

---

187. *freighted*] Perhaps a pun on 'fretted' here (coming apart, or in distress), parallel to 'fooled' ('filled' with fools).

188. *justice of peace*] Country justices had short shrift from writers both before and after Shallow and Silence appeared at the Globe.

190. *country*] rural or country district.

hanging cabin] a hammock; probably with a pun on 'hanging'. Even though it was a ship specifically for fools, it was so crowded that the greatest fool of all could hardly find the smallest berth.

191–2. *that were so sottishly paradised*] that lived in such a fool's paradise.

193–4. *any unmerited violence*] i.e. any violence that might befall them. The foolishness was to expect the world to recognise an injustice was being done to (say) an imprisoned politician, when that injustice was sanctioned not only by the monarch's whim but by the people's dislike of the politician as well.

195. *purple*] clad in purple. In the sense 'of imperial or royal rank', *O.E.D.*'s first example is 1701. Here it may refer to churchmen, or more probably, men of wealth and importance, who can afford to wear purple robes.

reared] raised up, elevated.

196. *spirit*] = character.

197. *o'erbought their offices*] paid too high a price (as a bribe) to acquire their positions. The implication is that courting itself is an expensive enough occupation.

198–9. *priests . . . finger*] Obscure. *Avoid* may well have the sense it retains today, 'to escape'. But elsewhere in the play Marston uses it in the

Herc. Why, how gat all these forth? Was not the warrant
    strong?
Don. Yes, yes, but they got a supersedeas: all of them
    proved themselves either knaves or madmen and so
    were all let go. There's none left now in our ship but a   205
    few citizens that let their wives keep their shopbooks,
    some philosophers, and a few critics; one of which
    critics has lost his flesh with fishing at the measure of

204. or madmen] *Q1 corr.*, *Q2;* are made men *Q1 uncorr.*

---

sense 'to make void, of no effect; to remove' (cf. IV.i.628 and II.i.72). A
thwart stroke could mean an untoward blow (figurative or literal); *stroke*
had since the middle ages been applied to acts of divine chastisement, or
other acts causing injury or death, but usually with a conscious metaphor;
O.E.D.'s first example of the sense 'calamitous event' is dated 1700. *With
a wet finger* is proverbial for 'quickly', 'easily', or 'nimbly' (see Tilley,
f 234); it evidently applies here to *avoid* rather than to *stroke*. The point
is, why are the priests *foolish* to avoid their functions? And what would the
thwart stroke consist of? Priests had been fair game for satirists at least as
far back as Langland's *Piers Plowman* for leaving their parishes to seek
fortune elsewhere; perhaps Marston is referring to ministers with multiple
livings. Or he may be thinking back to the times in the previous century
when the ancestors of the Vicar of Bray changed their religious affiliations
to suit the political climate. In any case, one assumes the audience would
be happy to hear that priests were among the passengers on the ship of
fools. Smith suggests 'being rubbed off the preferred list'.

202. *strong*] of sufficient legal force.

203. *a supersedeas*] a stay. Wood brings attention to the definition in
Cowell's *Interpreter* (1607): 'a writ which lyeth in diuers, and sundry
cases, . . . it signifieth in them all a command, or request to stay or for-
beare the doing of that, which in apparence of laws were to bee done, were
it not for the cause, wherevpon the writ is graunted.'

204. *knaves or madmen*] i.e., unalleviated wickedness and hopeless
insanity are beyond the scope of this play, which deals with vice and folly
within the range normally observable in daily life.

206. *citizens*] i.e. 'flat-caps', bourgeois rather than gentlemen; shop-
keepers.

207–17.] Crawford finds the source in Montaigne, I, xxxviii, 304: 'This
man whom about mid-night, when others take their rest, thou seest come
out of his study meagre-looking, with eyes-trilling, flegmatike, squalide,
and spauling, doest thou thinke, that plodding on his books he doth seek
how he shall become an honester man; or more wise, or more content?
There is no such matter. He wil either die in his pursuit, or teach posteritie
the measure of *Plautus* verses, and the true Orthography of a Latine word.

208. *measure*] (correct) metre.

Plautus' verses; another has vowed to get the consumption of the lungs, or to leave to posterity the true   210
orthography and pronunciation of laughing; a third
hath melted a great deal o' suet, worn out his thumbs
with turning, read out his eyes, and studied his face out
of a sanguine into a meagre, spawling, fleamy loath-
someness, and all to find but why *mentula* should be the   215
feminine gender, since the rule is *Propria qua maribus
tribuuntur mascula dicas*. These philosophers, critics,
and all the maids we could find at sixteen, are all our
freight now.

Herc. Oh, then your ship of fools is full.   220
Nym. True, the maids at sixteen fill it.

221. sixteen] *This ed.; 17 Qq.*

210–11. *the true . . . laughing*] Bullen suggests that this is 'probably a
hit at Ben Jonson', who rhymed 'laughter' with 'slaughter' in *Volpone*
(1605), though Wood points out that *The Fawn* was probably earlier than
Volpone. See also *Works of Jonson*, IX, 694, where Simpson notes Jonson's
rhymes of 'laughter', 'daughter', and 'after'. But Dondolo is talking about
laughing, not 'laughter'; Marston may not be referring here to rhyme, but
to the transcription of the noise made in the act of laughing. Possibly we
have an example at IV.i.604: Q2 changes Q1's exclamation 'hah' to 'ha'.
It is one of only two variants between the quartos on page H1*v* (which is
printed in Q2 from Q1 standing type). Someone, not necessarily Marston,
evidently thought the true orthography of laughing important enough to
remove a letter from a finished page of type. Quy.: 'of Latin'?

214. *spawling*] spitting copiously.
fleamy] full of phlegm or mucus.

215. mentula] penis (Latin). Cross notes the use of the word in *DC.*
(IV.iii.4), though not for *Fawn*. He points out that it is not recorded in
O.E.D. and that he has not come across it in the contemporary drama.
The word is italicised in both plays, however, so that it would seem in-
correct to view it as English; *N&Q*, CC (1955), 427.

216–17. Propria . . . dicas] Things properly attributed to males should
be called masculine. This rule is in *Brevissima Institutio* (1549), by
William Lily, one of the basic grammar texts of the time.

218, 221. *maids . . . at sixteen*] Q2 follows Q1 in printing *16* the first
time and *17* the second. I doubt whether there is any significance in the
difference except that the Q1 compositor picked up the wrong number
from his fount box. Nymphadoro, the 'common lover', probably delivers
l. 221 with a sigh, since he is evidently not too successful in his 'trade'. But
Dondolo restores the proper cynical perspective.

Don. Fill it, quoth you ? Alas, we have very few, and these
    we were fain to take up in the country, too.

Herc. But what philosophers ha' ye ?

Don. Oh, very strange fellows. One knows nothing, dares   225
    not aver he lives, goes, sees, feels.

Nym. A most insensible philosopher.

Don. Another, that there is no present time, and that one
    man today and tomorrow is not the same man; so that
    he that yesterday owed money, today owes none,   230
    because he is not the same man.

Herod. Would that philosopher would hold good in law.

Herc. But why has the duke thus laboured to have all the
    fools shipped out of his dominions ?

Don. Marry, because he would play the fool himself alone,   235
    without any rival.

Herc. 'Ware your breech, fool.

Don. I warrant thee, old lad, 'tis the privilege of poor fools
    to talk before an intelligencer. Marry, if I could fool
    myself into a lordship, as I know some ha' fooled them-   240
    selves out of a lordship, were I grown some huge fellow
    and got the leer of the people upon me, if the fates had
    so decreed it, I should talk treason though I ne'er
    opened my lips.

---

232. philosopher] *Qq;* philosophy *TC.*   240. fooled] *TC;* foole *Qq.*

225–31.] Montaigne (Crawford) II, xii, 399–400: 'In few, *there is no
constant existence, neither of our being, nor of the objects.* And we, and our
judgement, and all mortall things else do uncessantly rowle, turne, and
passe away. Thus can nothing be certainly established, . . . The Stoicks
affirme, there is no present time, and that which we call present, is but
conjoyning and assembling of future time and past. *Heraclitus* averreth
that no man ever entered twise one same river. *Epicarmus* avoucheth, that
who ere while borrowed any mony, doth not now owe it; and that he who
yesternight was bidden to dinner this day, commeth to day unbidden;
since they are no more themselves, but are become others. . . .'

    241. *huge*] important, high-ranking.

    242. *leer*] i.e., ill will.

Herc. Indeed, *fatis agimur, cedite fatis.* But how runs　245
　　rumour ? What breath's strongest in the palace now ?
　　I think you know all.

Don. Yes, we fools think we know all. The prince hath
　　audience tonight, is feasted, and after supper is enter-
　　tained with no comedy, masque, or barriers, but with—　250

Nym. What, I prithee ?

Herod. What, I prithee ?

Don. With a most new and special shape of delight.

Nym. What, for Jove's sake ?

Don. Marry, gallants, a session, a general council of love　255
　　summoned in the name of Don Cupid, to which upon
　　pain of their mistress' displeasure shall appear all

---

245. *Herc.*] *all ed.; conj.* Herod, *this ed.*　　　Indeed] *Q2; In Q1.*　　246.
palace now ?] *TC;* Palace, now *Qq;* pallace ? Nowe, *JOH.*

---

245. *fatis agimur, cedite fatis*] 'By fate are we driven; yield ye to fate'
(Miller); Seneca, *Oedipus,* 980 (Loeb Library). (This begins the Chorus's
hymn on fate, following the messenger's account of Oedipus's plucking
out his eyes.)

246. *breath*] i.e. what is breathed, whispered, spoken; = rumour. This
is basically *O.E.D.*'s sense 9, but 'strongest' suggests a figurative use of
sense 4, a puff (of air or wind).

250. *barriers*] 'Tournament, or mock-contest with lists. This kind of
show frequently formed part of a Court entertainment on a great occasion,
the contestants being men of high rank, splendidly attired and mounted,
and the contest made the occasion of the most splendid possible display.
Ben Jonson wrote the poetical part of several Barriers and Tiltings, one of
the most splendid of which appears to have been *The Barriers* which
followed *The Masque of Hymen,* written for the infamous Somerset
wedding' (Wood).

253. *shape of delight*] i.e., kind of entertainment.

255. *session*] judicial sitting.

a general council of love] This is a comic descendent of the medieval
Courts of Love, with an admixture of the more recently popular masque.
Cf. the last scenes of Jonson's *Cynthia's Revels,* v.vii. and v.ix–xi. The
combination also appears in the Christmas Revels of the Inns of Court,
such as the *Prince d'Amour* Revels of 1597–8, which also included barriers.
See S. J. Finkelpearl's chapter on this event in his *John Marston of the
Middle Temple* (1969), 45–61.

favour-wearers, sonnet-mongers, health-drinkers, and
neat enrichers of barbers and perfumers; and to conclude, all that can wehee or wag the tail, are, upon   260
grievous pains of their back, summoned to be assistant
in that session of love.

Herc. Hold, hold, do not pall the delight before it come to
our palate. And what other rumour keeps air in men's
lungs?   265

Don. O, the egregiousness of folly! Ha' you not heard of
Don Zuccone?

Nym. What of him, good fool?

Don. He is separated.

Nym. Divorced?   270

Don. That salt, that criticism, that very all epigram of a

---

259. enrichers] *Q2;* in riches *Q1.*   264. in] *Q2;* on *Q1.*   266. O, the]
Q2 corr.; Other *Q1, Q2 uncorr.*

---

258. *favour-wearers*] i.e. displayers of love tokens. Unrecorded in
O.E.D. (See Cross, *N&Q* CCV (1960), 136.)

sonnet-mongers] Unrecorded in *O.E.D.* See Cross, *N&Q*, CCVIII (1963),
310.

health-drinkers] Unrecorded in *O.E.D.*

259. *neat*] elegant, smartly dressed; cf. IV.i.690, where it is implied that
this kind of 'neatness' was typical of lovers.

enrichers] Antedates *O.E.D.*'s first example. See Cross, *N&Q*, CCV
(1960), 136.

260. *wehee or wag the tail*] wehee = whinny; cf. *Every Man Out of his
Humour*, II.i.65. 'It is an ill horse than can neither whinny nor wag his
tail' (Tilley, H 671). Cf. also *Malc.*, III.ii.170–1. In this context a bawdy
sense is probably present.

260–1. *upon grievous pains of their back*] a parody of the legal phrase
'upon the pain of'; the sexual connotation of *back* is implied.

261–2. *assistant in*] present at.

263. *pall*] render stale or insipid (*O.E.D.* †8, *fig.*; first example 1700).

266. *egregiousness*] excellence (ironically); flagrancy. Antedates *O.E.D*'s
first example. See Cross, *N&Q*, CCV (1960), 136.

271. *salt*] piquancy, freshness (personified); perhaps 'wit' (though the
phrase 'Attic salt' is considerably later).

criticism] This is apparently the first appearance of the word in the
language. From the context it evidently means a 'critique', a summary (of
all that is best, here).

very all epigram] epitome (and) embodiment of wit. Crawford believed
Marston 'snapped up' the phrase from Montaigne, III, v, 119: 'They are
all epigram; not only taile, but head, stomacke and feet.'

woman, that analysis, that compendium of wittiness—

Nym. Now, Jesu, what words the fool has.

Don. We ha' still such words, but I will not unshale the jest
before it be ripe, and therefore kissing your worship's   275
fingers in most sweet terms without any sense, and with
most fair looks without any good meaning, I most courtlike take my leave, *basilus manus de vostro signioria.*

Herod. Stay, fool, we'll follow thee, for, 'fore heaven, we
must prepare ourselves for this session.   280

       Exeunt [DONDOLO, HEROD *and* NYMPHADORO.]

Enter ZUCCONE, *pursued by* ZOYA *on her knees, attended by* Ladies.

Zuc. I will have no mercy, I will not relent; justice' beard is
shaven, and it shall give thee no hold: I am separated,
and I will be separated.

Zoya. Dear my lord, husband.

Zuc. Hence, creature, I am none of thy husband, or father of   285
thy bastard. No, I will be tyrannous, and a most deep
revenger; the order shall stand. Ha, thou quean, I ha'
no wife now.

---

272. wittiness] *Q2;* witnes *Q1.*   274. unshale] *Q2;* vnshake *Q1.*
280.1. DONDOLO, HEROD *and* NYMPHADORO] *This ed.*

---

272. *analysis*] again, a table or summary of all the best. Cross points out
that this antedates *O.E.D.*'s first example of this sense (dated 1668);
N&Q, CXCIX (1954), 426. But see Nashe, *Works,* III, 318, where Nashe
uses the word as a synonym for 'compendium' in his Preface to Greene's
Menaphon (1589).

   compendium] an embodiment in miniature, an abstract.

   274. *unshale*] unshell, peel.

   277–8. *courtlike*] following the fashion of the court.

   278. basilus manus de vostro signioria] a corruption of old Spanish *beso
las manos de vostra signioria,* 'I kiss your worship's hands'. The phrase was
popular in the drama of the time, in various corrupt forms. Jonson provides
an Italian version in *Cynthia's Revels,* V.iii.246: 'Bascio le mane de vo'
signoria.' Montaigne criticises it as an affectation, in I, xliii, 369: 'Let
Courtiers first begin to leave off . . . That fond custome to kisse what we
present to others, and *Beso las manos* in saluting to our friends: (a
ceremonie heretofore only due unto Princes;) . . .'

   287. *quean*] whore.

Zoya. Sweet my lord.

Zuc. Hence, avaunt! I will marry a woman with no womb, a   290
creature with two noses, a wench with no hair, rather
than marry thee. Nay, I will first marry—mark me, I
will first marry—observe me, I will first marry a woman
that with thirst drinks the blood of man, nay, heed me,
a woman that will thrust in crowds, a lady that, being   295
with child, ventures the hope of her womb, nay, gives
two crowns for a room to behold a goodly man three parts
alive quartered, his privities hackled off, his belly
launched up. Nay, I'll rather marry a woman to whom
these smoking, hideous, bloodful, horrid, though most   300
just spectacles are very lust, rather than re-accept thee.
Was I not a handsome fellow, from my foot to my
feather ? Had I not wit, nay, which is more, was I not a

300. these] *TC;* this *Qq.*

---

296. *ventures the hope of her womb*] hazards, risks the life of her unborn
child.

297. *a room*] a place, a seat.

297–9. *a goodly man . . . launched up*] 'This is almost exactly taken from
the sentence pronounced on those who are convicted on high treason'
(Dilke). Bullen suggests there is an allusion to the execution of Sir Everard
Digby on January 30, 1606, but that would probably be too late for our
play. If a specific execution is meant, it may be one of the four answering
this description, between June of 1603 and June of 1605, described in
Stow's *Annals* (as continued and augmented by Edmund Howes [1631]).

298. *hackled*] = hacked.

299. *launched up*] = lanced, slit open.

300 *smoking*] steaming, reeking (usually associated with blood):
'. . . their steeds, / That stain'd their fetlocks in his smoking blood'
(*3H6*, II.iii.20–1).

bloodful] bloody. Cross notes that the word is unrecorded in *O.E.D.*;
N&Q, CXCIX (1954), 426. *O.E.D.* does record 'bloodiful' as a nonce-word
in Stanyhurst's *Aeneis* (1583), which Cross acknowledges in a later note on
Marston's use of *bloodful* in *Malc.* (HHW, I, 179). He points out, however,
that in *Malc.*, *bloodful* means 'full of blood', rather than 'bloody, covered
with blood'; *N&Q*, CC (1955) 481.

301. *very lust*] sheer delight.

re-accept] See Cross, *N&Q*, CCVIII (1963), 309 (antedates *O.E.D.*'s first
example).

    Don, and didst thou Acteon me? Did I not make thee
       a lady?   305

Herc. And did she not make you a more worshipful thing, a
       cuckold?

Zuc. I married thee in hope of children.

Herc. And has not she showed herself fruitful that was got
       with child without help of her husband?   310

Zuc. Ha, thou ungrateful, immodest, unwise, and one that,
       God's my witness, I ha' loved—but go thy ways, twist
       with whom thou wilt, for my part. Th'ast spun a fair
       thread: who'll kiss thee now? Who'll court thee now?
       Who'll ha' thee now?   315

Zoya. Pity the frailty of my sex, sweet lord.

Zuc. No, pity is a fool, and I will not wear his coxcomb. I
       have vowed to loathe thee. The Irishman shall hate *aqua*
       vitae, the Welshman cheese, the Dutchman shall loathe
       salt butter, before I re-love thee. Does the babe pule?   320

311. one] *Q2; not in Q1.*   317. his] *Q1;* hir *Q2.*   318–19. *aqua vitae*]
Dilke; aquauity *Qq.*

---

304. *Acteon*] cuckold. Cross notes that this antedates O.E.D.'s first
example of the verb (1615). Acteon's antlers (which sprouted when he was
turned into a stag after seeing Diana at her bath) evidently qualified as
'horns'. See *N&Q*, CXCIX (1954), 426.

306. *worshipful*] notable, honourable (ironically). Perhaps the line is an
aside.

312. *twist*] copulate. O.E.D. does not give this figurative sense, but the
intransitive senses 'to penetrate *into* something' and 'to coil or twine *about*
or *round*' are given dates later than this (the earliest is 1635).

313–14. *Th'ast spun a fair thread*] proverbial: see Tilley, T 252.

317. *coxcomb*] the jester's cap, in the shape and colour of a cock's comb.
O.E.D.'s *last* example for this literal use is dated 1605.

318–20. *The Irishman . . . salt butter*] All three associations were
proverbial. As Halliwell pointed out, they appear together in *Wiv.*
(c. 1597), II.ii.316–21: 'I will rather trust a Fleming with my butter,
Parson Hugh the Welshman with my cheese, an Irishman with my
aqua-vitae bottle, or a thief to walk my ambling gelding, than my wife
with herself.'

320. *pule*] whine, cry in a thin or weak voice. Marston uses *pule* several
times in *SV.*, e.g. VI, 18, and VIII, 9, 33, 52, usually in mockery of lovers'
sighs. He uses it with the present sense in *AM.*, III.ii.208–9: 'We wring
ourselves into this wretched world, / To pule, and weep, exclaim, to curse
and rail. . . .'

Thou shouldst ha' cried before, 'tis too late now. No,
the trees in autumn shall sooner call back the spring
with shedding of their leaves than thou reverse my just,
irrevocable hatred with thy tears. Away, go, vaunt!

Exeunt ZOYA *and the* Ladies.

Herc. Nay, but most of this is your fault, that for many   325
years, only upon mere mistrust, severed your body from
your lady, and in that time gave opportunity, turned a
jealous ass, and hired some to try and tempt your lady's
honour, whilst she, with all possible industry of deserv-
ing merit, diverting your unfortunate suspicion—   330

Zuc. I know't, I confess, all this I did, and I do glory in't.
Why, cannot a young lady for many months keep
honest? No, I misthought it. My wife had wit, beauty,
health, good birth, fair clothes, and a passing body; a
lady of rare discourse, quick eye, sweet language,   335
alluring behaviour, and exquisite entertainment. I misthought it, I feared, I doubted, and at the last I found it
out; I praise my wit, I knew I was a cuckold.

Herc. An excellent wit.

Zuc. True, Fawn, you shall read of few dons that have had   340

324.1. *Exeunt*] *AHB; Exit Qq.*   Ladies] *Dilke;* lady *Qq.*   328. ass,
and hired (hird) some to] *Q1 corr.;* asse, and heard some so *Q1 uncorr.;*
asse hired and some to *Q2.*   340. few dons] *Q2 corr. (Dons);* few dunces
Q1; some Lords *Q2 uncorr.*

324. *vaunt*] = avaunt, be off, begone.

326. *mistrust*] suspicion.

330. *diverting*] i.e. opposing, disproving.

333. *honest*] chaste, 'virtuous' (of a woman, usually).

misthought it] (strongly) doubted it.

334. *passing*] = surpassing, excellent.

336. *exquisite entertainment*] delightful charm (in company).

337. *doubted*] suspected.

338. *I praise . . . cuckold*] Cf. Master Ford: 'Heaven be praised for my
jealousy' (*Wiv.* II.ii.324).

340. *few dons*] The actor was probably expected to pronounce this
'dunce', and that is how it likely appeared in Marston's MS. The Q2
compositor logically thought it odd that Zuccone should refer to himself
and his fellow magnificoes as 'dunces', so changed the phrase to 'some

such a wit, I can tell you; and I found it out that I was a cuckold.

Herc. Which now you have found, you will not be such an ass as Caesar, great Pompey, Lucullus, Anthony, or Cato, and divers other Romans, cuckolds, who all knew   345 it, and yet were ne'er divorced upon't; or like that smith-god Vulcan who, having taken his wife taking, yet was presently appeased, and entreated to make an armour for a bastard of hers, Aeneas.

Zuc. No, the Romans were asses, and thought that a   350 woman might mix her thigh with a stranger wantonly, and yet still love her husband matrimonially.

341. that] *Q2; & Q1.*   347. taking] *Q2; not in Q1.*   349. Aeneas] *Q2; not in Q1.*   350. *Zuc.*] *Q1; Herc. Q2.*

lords'. Finally, someone, possibly Marston, indicated the change to 'dons' for the corrected Q2 reading.

343–9, 356–8.] more borrowing from Montaigne; III, v, 105–6 (Crawford): '*Lucullus, Caesar, Pompey, Anthony, Cato,* and divers other gallant men were Cuckolds, and knew it, though they made no stirre about it. . . . And the God of our Poet, when he surprised one of his companions napping with his wife, was contented but to shame them: . . . And which is more, she becomes a suitor to him in the behalfe of a bastard of hers. . . . Which is freely granted her: . . . In truth with an humanity, more then humane. And which excesse of goodnesse by my consent shall onely be left to the Gods: . . .' Marston splits the passage between two speakers. Hercules gives ironic reassurance to cuckolds; Zuccone is given Montaigne's comment that such complaisance is 'more than human'; the comedy of the exchange is therefore suspended somewhere between the two.

346–9.] This story is the episode in the *Aeneid* (VIII, 370–406) that supplied the 'certain verses of Virgil' which Montaigne took as his starting point for the fifth essay in Book III of the *Essays*—in turn a major source for this play.

347. *smith-god*] Unrecorded in *O.E.D.* See Cross, *N&Q*, CCVIII (1963), 310.

taking] *O.E.D.* sense VI.6.b. for take: 'Of a female animal: To admit (the male).'

348. *entreated*] persuaded by pleading.

351. *mix her thigh with*] *O.E.D.* records *mix* in the sense 'to have sexual intercourse with' only in the simple intransitive 'mix with' (for which the first example is dated 1615).

Herc. As indeed they say many married men lie sometime
with strange women, whom, but for the instant use, they
abhor.   355

Zuc. And as for Vulcan, 'twas humanity more than human;
such excess of goodness, for my part, shall only belong
to the gods.

Herc. Ass for you—

Zuc. As for me, my Fawn, I am a bachelor now.   360

Herc. But you are a cuckold still, and one that knows himself to be a cuckold.

Zuc. Right, that's it: and I knew it not, 'twere nothing, and
if I had not pursued it too, it had lain in oblivion, and
shadowed in doubt, but now I ha' blazed it.   365

Herc. The world shall know what you are.

Zuc. True, I'll pocket up no horns, but my revenge shall
speak in thunder.

Herc. Indeed, I must confess I know twenty are cuckolds,
honestly and decently enough; a worthy gallant spirit   370
(whose virtue suppresseth his mishap) is lamented but
not disesteemed by it. Yet the world shall know—

Zuc. I am none of those silent coxcombs: it shall out.

---

353. say many] *Q2;* say a many *Q1.*   357. shall] *Q1; not in Q2.*   364.
lain] *This ed.;* lyen *Qq;* laid *Dilke;* lien *Smith.*   370. honestly and de-
cently] *Q2;* and decently and stately *Q1.*   373. out] *Q2;* not *Q1.*

354. *the instant use*] the present moment's use; for *use,* see II.i.311 n.
Perhaps there is a pun here on abhor/whore as well.

359–60. *Ass for you . . . As for me*] another indication of the broad style
of acting for which this play seems intended. Cf. the 'many suchlike as-es
of great charge' in *Ham.* (*c.* 1601), v.ii.43.

363–5.] Montaigne (Crawford), III, v, 113–14: 'Wee flout him no lesse,
that toileth to prevent it, then laugh at him that is a Cuckold and knowes
it not. . . . It is a goodly sight, to draw our private misfortunes from out
the shadow of oblivion or dungeon of doubt, for to blazon and proclaime
them on Tragicall Stages: and misfortunes which pinch us not, but by
relation.'

365. *blazed*] made known, proclaimed.

367. *pocket up*] take (an affront) meekly.

369–72.] Montaigne (Crawford), III, v, 114: 'I know a hundred Cockolds,
which are so, honestly and little undecently. An honest man and a gallant
spirit, is moaned, but not disesteemed by it.'

Herc. And although it be no great part of injustice for him to
    be struck with the scabbard that has struck with the   375
    blade (for there is few of us but hath made someone
    cuckold or other)—

Zuc. True, I ha' done't myself.

Herc. Yet—

Zuc. Yet I hope a man of wit may prevent his own mishap,   380
    or if he cannot prevent it—

Herc. Yet—

Zuc. Yet make it known yet, and so known that the world
    may tremble with only thinking of it. Well, Fawn,
    whom shall I marry now ? O heaven, that God made for   385
    a man no other means of procreation and maintaining
    the world peopled but by women! O, that we could
    increase like roses by being slipped one from another,
    or like flies procreate with blowing, or any other way

381. cannot] *TC*; can *Qq*.   388. increase . . . another] *Q2;* get one an
other with child *Fawn Q1*.

374–6. *to be struck . . . blade*] proverbial: 'He that strikes with the sword
shall be beaten (stricken) with the scabbard' (Tilley, S 1047). The imagery
was specially suited to the subject. In *The Family of Love* (1602) a wronged
wife is advised: 'Faith, since he has strook with the sword, strike you with
the scabbard; in plain terms, cuckold him . . .' (v.i; Middleton, *Works* III,
95).

376–7. *there is few . . . other*] 'There is none of you all but hath made
one Cuckold or other'; Montaigne (Crawford), III, v, 115.

383–4. *that the world . . . it*] 'Cause your vertue to suppresse your
mishap; . . . that he which offends you, may tremble with onely thinking
of it'; Montaigne (Crawford), III, v, 114.

385 ff.] Bullen cites a similar passage in Sir Thomas Browne's *Religio
Medici* (c. 1635), in *Works*, I, 87: 'I could be content that we might procreate like trees, without conjunction, or that there were any way to
perpetuate the World without this trivial and vulgar way of coition: it is
the foolishest act a wise man commits in all his life.' Bullen also refers to
Euripides' *Hippolytus*, ll. 616–24, and to 'some reflections' of Montaigne,
which Wood locates in III, v, 126, where these sentiments are also found.
It is to Marston's credit that he puts such words into the mouth of a fool,
and has them thrown back at Zuccone at IV.i.551–2. We may observe as
well that Montaigne reconsiders his view a little later in the same essay
(III, v, 127): '*Are not we most brutish, to terme that worke beastly which
begets, and which maketh us ?*'

389. *blowing*] the term commonly used for the depositing of eggs by
insects, especially flies. Cf. I.ii.337 n.

than by a woman—by women, who have no reason in   390
their love, or mercy in their hate, no rule in their pity,
no pity in their revenge, no judgment to speak, and yet
no patience to hold their tongues:
Man's opposite, the more held down, they swell;
Above them naught but will, beneath them naught but
     hell.   395

Herc. Or that since heaven hath given us no other means to
allay our furious appetite, no other way of increasing
our progeny, since we must entreat and beg for
assuagement of our passions and entertainment of our
affections, why did not heaven make us a nobler   400
creature than women to sue unto? Some admirable
deity of an uncorruptible beauty, that might be worth
our knees, the expense of our heat, and the crinkling
of our hams.

394–5.] *so AHB; prose Qq.*   401. sue unto?] *TC;* shew vnto, *Q1, Q2 uncorr.;* shew vnto? *Q2 corr.;* shove into *conj. Brereton.*   402. might] *Q2; not in Q1.*   404. hams] *Q2; not in Q1*

390–5.] For a similar anti-feminist diatribe, see *Malc.*,I.ii.85 ff.

394. *the more held down, they swell*] a pun, of course, alluding to the pregnancy resulting from being 'held down'. 'Swell' also means 'to be arrogant'.

395. *Above them naught but will*] The following passage from Chapman's *All Fools* (1599), III.i.227–35, suggests what Marston is getting at: 'So (Nature in lieu of women's scarcity of wit, having indued them with a large portion of will) if they may (without impeach) enjoy their wills, no quieter creatures under heaven; but if the breath of their husbands' mouths once cross their wills, nothing more tempestuous. Why, then, sir, should you husbands cross your wives' wills thus, considering the law allows them no wills at all at their deaths, because it intended they should have their wills while they lived ?'

397. *furious*] fierce, extreme (without the modern connotation of anger). The phrase 'furious appetite' seems to be a sort of nonce semi-technical term for 'sexual needs'.

401. *sue unto*] The reading in TC is surely correct. Brereton defends his conjecture (*Elizabethan Drama* [1909], p. 99) as 'a reading which accords well with the bitterly cynical mood of the speaker.' He misses the fact that 'Faunus' is mocking Zuccone here by parodying him.

403. *the expense of our heat*] the expenditure of our (physical and sexual) energy.

403–4. *crinkling of our hams*] wrinkling of our thighs (through much

Zuc. But that we must court, sonnet, flatter, bribe, kneel,   405
    sue to so feeble and imperfect, inconstant, idle, vain,
    hollow bubble, as woman is! O, my Fawn!

Herc. O, my lord, look who here comes.

Enter ZOYA, *supported by a* gentleman usher, *followed by* HEROD
    and NYMPHADORO *with much state, soft music playing.*

Zuc. Death o' man, is she delivered?

Herc. Delivered? Yes, O my Don, delivered. Yes, Donna   410
    Zoya, the grace of society, the music of sweetly agreeing
    perfection, more clearly chaste than ice or frozen rain,
    that glory of her sex, that wonder of wit, that beauty
    more freshed than any cool and trembling wind, that
    now only wish of a man, is delivered, is delivered—   415

Zuc. How?

---

407. Fawn] *Q2;* face *Q1;* fate *TC.*   414. freshed] *Q2 corr.;* freshy *Q1,*
Q2 uncorr.

---

bending and bowing; also, perhaps, through the strain of the sex act). This
does not seem quite the same sense as that of *crinkling* in *WYW.* (III.iii.103–
5; HHW, II, 272), which, as Cross points out, corresponds to *O.E.D.*
sense 2 for *crinkle*: 'To bend shrinkingly or obsequiously with the body,
to cringe [1633]'. The passage in *WYW.* reads: 'There is a company of
unbraced, untruss'd rutters in the town, that crinkle in the hams, swearing
their flesh is their only living.' One may 'bend with the body obsequiously'
in the hams, but surely hams cannot themselves be described as doing this.
See *N&Q,* CCI (1956), 332.

    407. *bubble*] empty, worthless thing, Bertram is assured by one of the
lords that Parolles is a *bubble* in *All's W.* (1602) III.vi.5. Cf. II.i.579.

    411–12. *the music . . . perfection*] (alluding to the music or harmony of
the spheres in the old astronomy, symbolising perfection). Though the
concept was familiar to Elizabethans, the figurative use of *music* as 'essence'
is unrecorded in *O.E.D.*

    412. *more clearly chaste than ice*] proverbial: 'As chaste as ice (snow)'
(Tilley, I, I).

    414. *freshed*] continually refreshed (by her purity) and refreshing;
Marston evidently felt that Q1's 'freshy' (= fresh) sounded too archaic or
Spenserian.

    415. *delivered*] emancipated; a pun on Zuccone's use of *delivered*
(= given birth).

Herc. From Don Zuccone, that dry scaliness, that sarpego,
    that barren drought, and shame of all humanity.
Zoya. What fellow's that?
Nym. Don Zuccone, your sometime husband.   420

Enter PHILOCALIA.

Zoya. Alas, poor creature.
Phil. The princess prays your company.
Zoya. I wait upon her pleasure.

All but HERCULES, ZUCCONE, HEROD, *and* NYMPHADORO *depart.*

Zuc. Gentlemen, why hazard you your reputation in shame-
    ful company with such a branded creature?   425
Herod. Miserable man, whose fortune were beyond tears to
    be pitied, but that thou art the ridiculous author of
    thine own laughed-at mischief.
Zuc. Without paraphrase, your meaning?
Nym. Why, thou woman's fool—   430
Zuc. Good gentlemen, let one die but once.
Herod. Was not thou most curstfully mad to sever thyself
    from such an unequalled rarity?
Zuc. Is she not a strumpet? Is she not with child?
Nym. Yes, with feathers.   435

423.1.] *so TC; on ll. 422 and 423 Qq.*   432. curstfully] *Q1;* curs'dfully
Verulam Q2; curs dfully *or* curs 2 fully *other copies of Q2.*

---

417. *scaliness*] *O.E.D.*'s first example for this word is from 1611.
   sarpego] = serpigo, skin eruption. Cf. *DC.*, II.i.137; also *Meas.*, III.i.31,
and *Troil.*, II.iii.81.
   428. *laughed-at*] Unrecorded in *O.E.D.* See Cross, *N&Q*, CC (1955),
335.
   mischief] misfortune.
   431. *let one die but once*] a twist on the proverb: 'A man can die but once'
(Tilley, M 219).
   432. *curstfully*] savagely, viciously.
   435. *with feathers*] i.e. Zoya has been padded with cushions to counterfeit pregnancy.

Herc. Why, weakness of reason, couldst not perceive all was
    feigned to be rid of thee ?
Zuc. Of me ?
Nym. She with child ? Untrodden snow is not so spotless.
Herod. Chaste as the first voice of a newborn infant.   440
Herc. Know, she grew loathing of thy jealousy.
Nym. Thy most pernicious curiosity.
Herc. Whose suspicions made her unimitable graces motive
    of thy base jealousy.
Herod. Why, beast of man!   445
Nym. Wretched above expression, that snoredst over a
    beauty which thousands desired, neglectedst her bed,
    for whose enjoying a very saint would have sued.
Herc. Defamed her.
Herod. Suggested privily against her.   450
Nym. Gave foul language publicly of her.
Herc. And now lastly done that for her which she only
    prayed for, and wished as wholesome air for, namely,
    to be rid from such an unworthy—
Herod. Senseless—   455
Nym. Injurious—

436. *Herc.*] *Qq; Hero*[.] *London.*   447. neglectedst *TC*] neglecst *Qq*.
454. rid] *Q2; not in Q1.*

---

436. *weakness of reason*] There are two possible senses: (i) *weakness of
reason* is a quasi-oath, like 'death o' sense'; (ii) Zuccone is addressed as the
personification of stupidity. The second is more probable.

439. *Untrodden snow is not so spotless*] proverbial: 'As white as the driven
snow' (Tilley, S 591).

440. *voice*] i.e. 'utterance'.

441. *grew loathing of*] became revolted by. Perhaps this is elliptical for
'grew *to* loathing'.

442. *curiosity*] probably the modern sense of 'inquisitiveness' but
perhaps the older one of 'scrupulousness'.

443–4.] i.e. Zuccone based his jealousy on his wife's *good* qualities.

448. *for whose enjoying a very saint would have sued*] Cf. *The Metamorphosis of Pigmalion's Image*, stanza 37 (*Poems*, p. 61): 'When that he
found that warmth, and wished heate / Which might a Saint and coldest
spirit moue, . . .'

449. *Defamed*] dishonoured (by report).

450. *Suggested privily against*] secretly, privately maligned.

Herc. Malicious—
Herod. Suspicious—
Nym. Misshaped—
Herc. Ill-languaged—   460
Herod. Unworthy—
Nym. Ridiculous—
Herc. Jealous—
Herod. Arch coxcomb as thou art.

Exeunt NYMPHADORO *and* HEROD.

Zuc. Oh, I am sick, my blood has the cramp, my stomach   465
o'erturns. Oh, I am very sick.

Herc. Why, my sweet Don, you are no cuckold.

Zuc. That's the grief on't.

Herc. That's the grief on't?

Zuc. That I ha' wronged so sweet (and now, in my know-   470
ledge) so delicate a creature. Oh, methinks I embrace
her yet.

Herc. Alas, my lord, you have done her no wrong, no wrong
in the world; you have done her a pleasure, a great
pleasure. A thousand gentlemen, nay dukes, will be   475
proud to accept your leavings—your leavings. Now is
she courted: this heir sends her jewels, that lord
proffers her jointures, t'other knight proclaims
challenges to maintain her the only, not beautiful, but
very beauty of women.   480

Zuc. But I shall never embrace her more.

468–70. That's . . . That] *so HHW (conj.); Zuc.* thats the griefe on't *Herc.*
thats . the griefe ont that *Q1; Zuc.* thats the griefe on't *Herc.* thats . *Zuc.*
that I *(long space to margin) Q2.*

---

460. *ill-languaged*] foul-mouthed. Unrecorded in *O.E.D.*

468. *on't*] of it.

473. *Alas . . . wrong*] Could this be a quiet parody of the first line of
Greensleeves: 'Alas, my love, you do me wrong . . .'?

478. *jointures*] property held 'to the joint use of husband and wife for
life or in tail, as a provision for the latter during widowhood' (*O.E D.*). In
other words, 'that lord' is offering her marriage.

479–80. *the only . . . women*] not simply beautiful but the unique
personification of beauty in women. Cf. III.i.515, and n.

Herc. Nay, that's true, that's true. I would not afflict you,
only think how unrelentless you were to her but supposed fault.

Zuc. Oh, 'tis true, too true.   485

Herc. Think how you scorned her tears.

Zuc. Most right.

Herc. Tears that were only shed—I would not vex you—in
very grief to see you covet your own shame.

Zuc. Too true, too true.   490

Herc. For indeed she is the sweetest modest soul, the fullest
of pity,—

Zuc. O ay, O ay.

Herc. The softness and very courtesy of her sex, as one that
never loved any—   495

Zuc. But me.

Herc. So much that he might hope to dishonour her, nor any
so little that he might fear she disdained him. O, the
graces made her soul as soft as spotless down upon the
swan's fair breast that drew bright Cytherea's chariot. 500
Yet think—I would not vex you—yet think how cruel
you were to her.

Zuc. As a tiger, as a very tiger.

Herc. And never hope to be reconciled, never dream to be
reconciled, never.   505

Zuc. Never! Alas, good Fawn, what wouldst wish me to do
now?

Herc. Faith, go hang yourself, my Don. That's best, sure.

493. O ay, O ay (O I O I) *Q1;* O yes, O yes *Q2.*   498. disdained] *Q2;*
disclaim'd *Q1.*   501. cruel] *Q2;* ciuill *Q1.*

---

483. *unrelentless*] relentless, unrelenting.

494. *The softness . . . sex*] i.e. the personification or epitome of gentleness
and graceful considerateness in women.

500. *the swan's fair breast . . . Cytherea's chariot*] The sparrow and the
dove were more often associated with Aphrodite (called Cytherea after the
island of Cythera, where she came ashore after her birth in the sea).

508. *go hang yourself*] The lovelorn Alberto gets the same advice from
Feliche in *AM.*, v.i.55.

Zuc. Nay, that's too good, for I'll do worse than that, I'll
    marry again. Where canst pick out a morsel for me,   510
    Fawn?

Herc. There is a modest, matron-like creature—

Zuc. What years, Fawn?

Herc. Some fourscore wanting one.

Zuc. A good sober age. Is she wealthy?   515

Herc. Very wealthy.

Zuc. Excellent.

Herc. She has three hairs on her scalp and four teeth in her
    head, a brow wrinkled and puckered like old parch-
    ment half burnt. She has had eyes. No woman's jaw-   520
    bones are more apparent; her sometimes envious lips
    now shrink in, and give her nose and her chin leave to
    kiss each other, very moistly. As for her reverend
    mouth, it seldom opens, but the very breath that flies
    out of it infects the fowls of the air, and makes them   525
    drop down dead. Her breasts hang like cobwebs. Her
    flesh will never make you cuckold: her bones may.

Zuc. But is she wealthy?

Herc. Very wealthy.

Zuc. And will she ha' me, art sure?   530

Herc. No, sure, she will not have you. Why, do you think
    that a waiting-woman of three bastards, a strumpet
    nine times carted, or a hag whose eyes shoot poison,
    that has been an old witch, and is now turning into a

---

521. *apparent*] i.e., easily visible.
    sometimes] formerly.

523. *moistly*] a surreal variant, here, on the conventional description
of a kiss as 'moist', i.e. hearty, 'juicy'.

524. *it seldom opens, but*] I retain the comma from Qq for the subtle
double-take which is probably intended. The comma marks a pause but
not a division in the statement.

526–7. *Her flesh . . . bones may*] i.e. she *has* no flesh. But the sense may
also be similar to the passage in Marvell's 'To His Coy Mistress': 'Then
worms shall try / Thy long preserv'd virginity'.

532. *a waiting-woman of*] a female servant with.

533. *carted*] See IV.i.59–60 n.

gib-cat—what! will ha' you? Marry Don Zuccone, the 535
contempt of women and the shame of men, that has
afflicted, contemned so choice a perfection as Donna
Zoya's?

Zuc. Alas, Fawn, I confess; what wouldst thou ha' me do?

Herc. Hang yourself you shall not, marry you cannot. I'll 540
tell ye what you shall do. There's a ship of fools setting
forth: if you see good means and entreat hard, you may
obtain a passage, man, be master's mate, I warrant you.

Zuc. Fawn, thou art a scurvy bitter knave, and dost flout
Dons to their faces. 'Twas thou flatteredst me to this, 545
and now thou laughest at me, dost? Though indeed I
had a certain proclivity, but thou madest me resolute.
Dost grin and girn? O you comforters of life, helps in

---

535. gib-cat—what!] *AHB (after TC, Dilke)*; gib-cat what, *Q1 uncorr.*;
gib-cat, that, *Q1 corr.*; gib-cat [wil] *Q2*.   540. hang ... cannot] *Q2*;
selfe, ... not marrie ... cannot *Q1*; selfe, ... not marry, ... cannot *TC*.
542. see] *Q1*; make *Q2*; seek *TC*.   546. laughest (laughst)] *Q2*; laughtst
Q1.

---

535. *gib-cat*] Dilke has a long note on this word, concluding that 'the
term was originally applied to either sex [of cat], *deprived by an operation
from propagating their species*, and afterwards to *old* cats generally'. Bullen
(II, 203) cites this passage from Scot's *Discovery of Witchcraft*, v, i: 'Why
witches are turned into cats, he [Bodin] alledgeth no reason, and therefore
(to help him forth with that paraphrase) I say that witches are curst
queans, and many times scratch one another or their neighbours by the
faces; and therefore perchance are turned into cats. But I have put twenty
of these witchmongers to silence with one question: to wit—whether a
witch that can turn a woman into [a] ca[t] can also turn a cat into a woman.'
    536. *contempt*] = object of contempt. *O.E.D.*'s first example for this
sense (*O.E.D.* †3) is dated 1611 (the Bible). Cf. IV.i.581 n.
    542. *see good means*] find the right opportunity.
    544. *bitter*] harsh, cutting (in language) (*O.E.D.* 7); or, cruel (*O.E.D.*
†5).
    547. *proclivity*] propensity, tendency (that way). Cross notes that this
antedates *O.E.D.*'s first example for that sense (1649); *N&Q*, CCVI (1961),
390.
    548. *girn*] to show the teeth in laughing, to grin. Cf. *SV.*, xi, 75, and
AM., III.ii.128. Marston apparently does not use it in its surviving dialectal
sense of showing the teeth in rage, pain or disappointment (*O.E.D.*) or
simply making ugly faces. The Qq spelling is *gern*.

sickness, joys in death, and preservers of us in our
children after death, women, have mercy on me!   550

Herc. O, my Don, that God made no other means of procreation but by these women—I speak it not to vex you.

Zuc. O, Fawn, thou hast no mercy in thee—dost thou leer
on me? Well, I'll creep upon my knees to my wife—
dost laught at me?—dost girn at me?—dost smile?—   555
dost leer on me, dost thou? Oh, I am an ass, true; I am
a coxcomb, well; I am mad, good: a mischief on your
cogging tongue, your soothing throat, your oily jaws,
your supple hams, your dissembling smiles, and O the
grand devil on you all! When mischief favours our   560
fortunes, and we are miserably, though justly wretched,
More pity, comfort, and more help we have
In foes professed, than in a flattering knave.   *Exit*

Her. Thus few strike sail until they run on shelf;
The eye sees all things but his proper self.   565
In all things curiosity hath been vicious

556–7.] *So Dilke*; Asse true, . . . Coxcombe, wel, . . . mad, good: *Q1:* Asse,
Q2; . . . asse; true, . . . coxcomb; wel, . . . mad; good: *AHB* (*ad. JOH*); . . .
ass, true, . . . coxcomb. Well, . . . mad, good. *Smith.*   559. hams] *Q2;*
thumbes *Q1.*   561. miserably] *Q2;* miserable *Q1.*   566–7. been
vicious / At] *HHW;* been / Vitious at *Qq.*

551–2.] Cf. IV.i.385–7.

553. *leer*] See III.i.313 n. Cf. also *Troil.*, (*c.* 1602), V.i.97.

556–7.] For a discussion of this rhetorical device, see IV.i.10–11 n.

558. *cogging tongue*] cheating, wheedling flattery.

soothing throat] The verb still meant basically to flatter or humour a
person by assenting to or confirming the 'sooth' of his opinion or state of
mind; the modern sense, of assuagement, is considerably later. But
coupling it with *oily* shows the direction in which the word was moving.

559. *supple hams*] i.e., ready bows.

562–3.] proverbial: 'It is better to have an open foe than a dissembling
friend' (Tilley, F 410).

564. *shelf*] sandbank or submerged ledge of rock.

565.] proverbial: 'The eye that sees all things else sees not itself'
(Tilley, E 232).

566–70.] Cf. Montaigne (Crawford), III, v, 113: '*Curiosity is every where
vicious; but herein pernicious.* It is meere folly for one to seeke to be
resolved of a doubt, or search into a mischiefe; for which there is no
remedie, but makes it worse, but festereth the same: . . .'

At least, but herein most pernicious:
What madness is't to search and find a wound
For which there is no cure, and which unfound
Ne'er rankles, whose finding only wounds?   570
But he that upon vain surmise forsakes
His bed thus long, only to search his shame,
Gives to his wife youth, opportunity,
Keeps her in idle, full deliciousness,
Heats and inflames imagination,   575
Provokes her to revenge with churlish wrongs—
What should he hope but this? Why should it lie in
    women,
Or even in chastity itself (since chastity's a female),
T' avoid desires so ripened, such sweets so candied?
But she that hath out-borne such mass of wrongs,   580
Out-dured all persecutions, all contempts,
Suspects, disgrace, all wants, and all the mischief
The baseness of a cankered churl could cast upon her,
With constant virtue, best feigned chastity,
And in the end turns all his jealousies   585

---

574. idle, full (idle full)] *Q1;* idlefull *Q2.*   580. out-borne] *Q2;* not
borne *Q1.*   584. feigned] *Qq;* fined *conj. AHB;* restrain'd *conj. Brereton;*
famde *London.*

---

571. *upon vain surmise*] upon mere suspicion, on very slight evidence.
574. *deliciousness*] luxury.
578. *since chastity's a female*] Cf. Montaigne (Crawford), III, v, 108: 'It
lieth not in them [women] (nor perhaps in chastitie it selfe, seeing she is
female) to shield themselves from concupiscence and avoid desiring.'
579. *ripened*] i.e. tasty.
candied] Cf. II.i.151 n.
580. *out-borne*] endured.
581. *Out-dured*] out-lasted.
contempts] acts of contempt.
582. *Suspects*] suspicions.
wants] straits, hardships, circumstances of want.
583. *cankered*] ill-natured, spiteful.
584. *feigned*] formed, shaped, fashioned. Of the various emendations
proposed, London's ('famde') is the most attractive, but the Qq reading
makes sense, even though it is difficult to exclude the pejorative connotation usually attached to the word.

> To his own scorn, that lady, I implore,
> It may be lawful not to praise, but even adore.

Enter GONZAGO, GRANUFFO, *with full state. Enter the cornets sounding.*

Gon. Are our sports ready? Is the prince at hand?
Herc. The prince is now arrived at the court gate.
Gon. What means our daughter's breathless haste?   590

Enter DULCIMEL *in haste.*

Dul. O, my princely father, now or never let your princely
  wisdom appear.
Gon. Fear not, our daughter, if it rest within human
  reason, I warrant thee; no, I warrant thee, Granuffo, if
  it rest in man's capacity. Speak, dear daughter.   595
Dul. My lord, the prince—
Gon. The prince, what of him, dear daughter?
Dul. O Lord, what wisdom our good parents need
  To shield their chickens from deceits and wiles
  Of kite-like youth.   600
Gon. Her very phrase displays whose child she is.
Dul. Alas, had not your grace been provident,
  A very Nestor in advice and knowledge,
  Ha, where had your poor Dulcimel been now?
  What vainness had not I been drawn into!   605
Gon. 'Fore God, she speaks very passionately. Alas,

598–600.] *so HHW; prose Qq.*   602–5.] *so AHB; prose Qq.*   604. your]
TC; you *Qq.*   605. vainness] *Dilke;* vaines *Qq;* vaines (= veins ?) *TC.*

587.1. with full state] with full royal pomp.

588. *sports*] entertainment, revels.

594. *no, I warrant thee, Granuffo*] Perhaps there was some business here
that has been lost; or Gonzago is merely intensifying the rhetoric by
repetition.

599–600. *To shield . . . kite-like youth*] 'The Hen clocketh her Chickens,
feedeth them, and keepeth them from the Kite. Women must clocke their
Children, bring them vp well, and keepe them from euill happ.' Wilson,
p. 191.

603. *Nestor*] See III.i.355 n.

daughter, heaven gives every man his talent; indeed,
virtue and wisdom are not fortune's gifts, therefore
those that fortune cannot make virtuous, she commonly
makes rich. For our own part, we acknowledge heaven's   610
goodness, and if it were possible to be as wise again as
we are, we would ne'er impute it to ourselves; for as we
be flesh and blood, alas, we are fools, but as we are
princes, scholars, and have read Cicero *de Oratore*, I
must confess there is another matter in't. What of the   615
prince, dear daughter?

Dul. Father, do you see that tree that leans just on my
chamber window?

Gon. What of that tree?

Enter TIBERIO *with his train.*

Dul. O, sir, but note the policy of youth;   620
Mark but the stratagems of working love.
The prince salutes me, and thus greets my ear—

Gon. Speak softly, he is entered.

Dul. Although he knew I yet stood wavering what to elect

620–2.] *so AHB; prose Qq.*   624–8.] *so Qq; verse indicated:* wavering, /
what . . . affected, / yet . . . other, / . . . feares, / thus . . . *HHW.*

609–10. *those that fortune . . . rich*] Cf. Montaigne (Crawford), III, viii,
208: 'It is commonly perceived by the worlds actions, that fortune, to
teach us, how farre hir power extendeth unto all things; and who taketh
pleasure to abate our presumption, having not beene able to make silly
men wise, she hath made them fortunate, in envy of vertue: . . .' Marston
here stresses the *limits* of fortune's power (compared to that of heaven).
The rhythms of his prose here are fairly close to those of Celia's evaluation
of Fortune's gifts to women: 'for those that she makes fair she scarce
makes honest, and those that she makes honest she makes very ill-
favouredly' (*AYL.* [*c.* 1600], I.ii.40–2).

614. *Cicero* de Oratore] That Gonzago picks this author and this book
as the epitome of wisdom shows how thoroughly he (and a good many less
foolish men in the Renaissance) equated eloquence with profundity.

620. *policy*] cunning, craftiness. But *dukes'* policy is of course a different
matter. See also l. 638 below.

621. *working love*] scheming love (?); perhaps 'love at work'.

622. *salutes*] greets (generally).

greets my ear] addresses me, speaks to me.

624. *elect*] choose (to do).

because, though I affected, yet destitute of means to   625
enjoy each other, impossibility of having might kill our
hope, and with our hope desires to enjoy; therefore, to
avoid all faint excuses and vain fears, thus he devised:
To Dulcimel's chamber window
A well-grown plane tree spreads his happy arms.   630
By that, in depth of night one may ascend
(Despite all father's jealousies and fears)
Into her bed.

Gon. Speak low, the prince both marks and listens.

Dul. You shall provide a priest (quoth he). In truth I   635
promised, and so you well may tell him, for I temporised
and only held him off—

Gon. Politicly, our daughter to a hair.

Dul. With full intention to disclose it all to your preventing
wisdom.   640

Gon. Ay, let me alone for that. But when intends he this
invasion? When will this squirrel climb?

Dul. O, sir, in that is all: when but tonight?

Gon. This night?

Dul. This very night, when the court revels had o'erwaked   645
your spirits, and made them full of sleep, then—

627. with] *Q2;* which *Q1.*   630. plane tree] *Q2;* plantaine *Q1.*

---

625. *affected*] was fond of him.
destitute of] lacking.
628. *avoid*] put an end to.
632. *jealousies*] suspicions; see below, l. 659.
638. *politicly*] shrewdly. Bullen's silent emendation to 'politely' is unwarranted.
to a hair] Cf. III.i.25 and n.
639. *preventing*] perhaps a combination of 'anticipating' and 'forestalling'. But there is probably a parodic allusion to the theological use of *prevent*, said of God or of God's grace anticipating human action or need. Cf. the similar use of 'free grace', III.i.307.
645. *o'erwaked*] kept awake for too long. *O.E.D.*'s only example is from Greene's *Never Too Late* (1590): 'Thus watching thee, he ouerwaketh himselfe.'

Gon. Then *verbum sat sapienti*! Go, take your chamber,
   down upon your knees; thank God your father is no
   foolish sot, but one that can foresee and see.

                                      Exit DULCIMEL.

   My lord, we discharge your presence from our court.   650
Tib. What means the duke?
Gon. And if tomorrow past you rest in Urbin, the privilege
   of an ambassador is taken from you.
Tib. Good your grace, some reason?
Gon. What, twice admonished, twice again offending?   655
   And now grown blushless! You promised to get into
   Her chamber, she to get a priest—
   Indeed, she wished me tell you she confessed it—
   And there, despite all father's jealous fears,
   To consummate full joys. Know, sir, our daughter   660
   Is our daughter, and has wit at will
   To gull a thousand easy things like you.
   But sir, depart: the parliament prepared
   Shall on without you. All the court this night
   Shall triumph that our daughter has escaped   665
   Her honour's blowing up. Your end you see.
   We speak but short but full, *Socratice*.   *Exit.*

647–9.] *so Qq; verse London (ad. HHW).*   652–4.] *so Qq; verse AHB.*
666. honour's] *Q2; not in Q1.*

_____

   647. verbum sat sapienti] a word to the wise is enough. Proverbial
(Tilley, W 781), and here very ironic.
   649. *sot*] See III.i.284 n.
   650. *discharge your presence*] *Your presence* simply means 'you': 'we
dismiss you.'
   659. *jealous*] suspicious.
   666. *blowing up*] explosion, i.e. ruin. *O.E.D.*'s first example for the sense
'an explosion' is 1772. The image of explosion and undermining occurs
frequently in *Lust's Dominion* (*c*. 1600, first published as Marlowe's, 1657),
which Gustav Cross has argued was at least partly written by Marston (see
'The authorship of "Lust's Dominion"', *S.P.*, LV [1955], 1, 39–61). The
phrase *blowing up* or *blow up* appears at I.ii.282, II.v.1213 and II.vi.1331 of
Lust's Dominion in the edition of J. Le Gay Brereton (1931).
   667. Socratice] in the manner of Socrates; pithily. *O.E.D.*'s first
example of the adjective Socratic (from Latin *Socraticus*) is dated 1637.

Remaineth HERCULES *and* TIBERIO.

Tib. What should I think, what hope, what but imagine
         Of these enigmas ?
Herc.   Sure, sir, the lady loves you
         With violent passion, and this night prepares   670
         A priest with nuptial rites to entertain you
         In her most private chamber.
Tib.   This I know,
         With too much torture, since means are all unknown
         To come unto these ends. Where's this her chamber ?
         Then what means shall without suspicion   675
         Convey me to her chamber ? O, these doubts
         End in despair—

                Enter GONZAGO *hastily.*

Gon. Sir, sir, this plane tree was not planted here
         To get into my daughter's chamber—and so she
              prayed me tell you.
         What though the main arms spread into her window,   680
         And easy labour climbs it ? Sir, know
         She has a voice to speak, and bid you welcome,
         With so full breast that both your ears shall hear on't—
         And so she prayed me tell you. Ha' we no brain ?
         Youth thinks that age, age knows that youth is vain.

                                        [*Exit.*]   685

668–9.] *so AHB;* prose *Qq.*   669. enigmas] *Q2;* engines *Q1.*   678.
plane tree] *Q2;* Plantine *Q1.*   681. Sir] *Qq;* yet Sir *TC.*   685. S.D.]
Dilke.

---

669. *enigmas*] one of the figures Puttenham discusses as 'abuses or rather
trespasses in speach'; he defines enigma as 'speaking obscurely and in
riddle'. In the same sentence he lists the 'merry skoffe called *Ironia*',
which Dondolo refers to at v.i.459 (Puttenham, p. 154).

     683. *so full breast*] such strength, loudness.

     685.] proverbial: 'Young men think old men fools but old men know
that young men be fools' (Tilley, M 610). Cf. III.i.334–5. Cf. also Chapman's *All Fools* (1599), v.ii.205–6, and Parrott's note.

     go neatly] Cf. IV.i.259 n.

Tib. Why, now I have it, Fawn, the way, the means, and
     meaning. Good duke, and 'twere not for pity, I could
     laugh at thee. Dulcimel, I am thine most miraculously.
     I will now begin to sigh, read poets, look pale, go
     neatly, and be most apparently in love. As for—   690
Herc. As for your father—
Tib. Alas, he and all know, this an old saw hath been:
     Faith's breach for love and kingdoms is no sin.   *Exit.*
Herc. Where are we now ? Cyllenian Mercury,
     And thou quick issue of Jove's broken pate,   695
     Aid and direct us. You better stars to knowledge,
     Sweet constellations, that affect pure oil

688. am] *Q2;* come, *Q1.*   691. your] *TC;* you *Qq.*   694. now ? . . .
Mercury,] *TC;* now . . . Mercurie ? *Q1;* now, . . . Mercurie ? *Q2.*   695.
issue] *Q2;* messenger *Q1.*   697. affect] *Q2;* effect *Q1.*

690. *apparently*] manifestly. Cf. II.i.253 n.
693.] Cf. Tilley, K 90: 'For a kingdom any law may be broken.' Also
cf. III.i.502–3 and n.
694. *Cyllenian Mercury*] *Cyllenian* is from Cyllene, 'An hill of Archadie,
where they say Mercurius was nourished' (Cooper) See Cross, *N&Q*,
CCI (1956), 332. *O.E.D.*'s only example, dated 1738, pertains to thievery.
The phrase appears also in *Malc.*, v.iii.98, but there Mercury is the 'god
of ghosts' in a grim masque. Mercury's 'Cyllenian rod' is mentioned in the
Ashby Entertainment, l. 310, but in *CS.*, II, 142, 'Cyllenian' probably
refers to Venus (see Davenport's note, *Poems*, p. 237). In *SV.*, II, 27–30,
Mercury is described as "Ioues lust pander", and perhaps this is partly his
function here; his famed eloquence is invoked to persuade 'most cold'
Tiberio (who has done considerable warming up since the play began) to
carry out Dulcimel's plan. The change from Q1's 'messenger' to Q2's
'issue' on l. 695 makes it fairly certain that 'and thou' refers to Athene,
rather than (again) to Mercury. Hercules prays for wisdom as well as for
eloquence. Cf. a similar invocation in Jonson's *Cynthia's Revels*, v.v.64:
'And thou, the other sonne of mighty IOVE, / *Cyllenian* MERCVRY (sweet
MAIAS ioy) . . .'
697. *constellations*] the astrological term referred to by 'Faunus' at
II.i.86. 'The configuration or position of "stars" (i.e. planets) in regard to
one another, as supposed to have "influence" on terrestrial things'
(*O.E.D.* †1). Marston's use of 'stars' in the previous line is different,
however. There the reference is to lodestars, or guides (to knowledge).
697–8. *that affect pure oil . . . muses*] In these lines Hercules is obviously
speaking for the author. *Pure oil* refers to the burning lamps of dedicated
scholar-poets, as does *holy vigil*, the traditional image of poets and
scholars working late into the night in service of the muses.

And holy vigil of the pale-cheeked muses,
Give your best influence, that with able spright
We may correct and please, giving full light   700
To every angle of this various sense:
Works of strong birth end better than commence.   *Exit.*

701. sense] *Q2;* fence *Q1.*   702. *Exit.*] *Most eds.; Exit. | Finis Actus quarti. Qq.*

---

699. *spright*] spirit.

701. *this various sense*] This is a very odd and difficult phrase. It evidently refers to the implications and significances of the play's characters, events, and ideas at the point we have now reached; all this is summed up by the word *sense*. As for *various*, *O.E.D.* has no record of the sense 'characterised by variety of attributes' before 1633; the only meanings recorded are associated with changefulness, variableness. I can only suggest that Marston's use of *various* antedates *O.E.D.*'s examples for the sense 'varied', that *sense* means more or less 'subject matter', and that Marston is vaguely paraphrasing the lines from Juvenal which he quoted in his address to the reader (ll. 27–8):

> Quicquid agunt homines, votum, timor, ira, voluptas,
> Gaudia, discursus, nostri farrago libelli est.

702. *Works of strong birth*] i.e. what has been produced from a solid foundation. I do not think that this is much more than a spoken hope that the author's play may be of some value. It is very doubtful that it refers to Hercules' original impulses as expressed in his soliloquies at the end of the first and second scenes of Act I.

Act V

Whilst the act is a-playing, HERCULES *and* TIBERIO *enter;*
TIBERIO *climbs the tree, and is received above by* DULCIMEL,
PHILOCALIA, *and a* Priest. HERCULES *stays beneath.*

Herc. Thou mother of chaste dew, night's modest lamp,

Act V] ACTVS QVINTVS. *Qq.*　　0.1. *enter*] *TC; enters Qq.*

0.1–3] For the development of the dumbshow in English drama, see
F. L. Lucas, *Works of Webster*, I, 223, F. A. Foster's article 'The dumb
show in Elizabethan drama before 1620', *Englische Studien*, XLIV (1912),
8–17, and Dieter Mehl's *The Elizabethan Dumbshow* (1965); the last has
a chapter on Marston.

0.1 Whilst the act is a-playing] Only Marston uses *act* to mean 'the
music announcing the end of the act'. Possibly this amounted to an
interlude, but it is clear from the SDs in *Soph.* that he was primarily
interested in the way music could mark out act division, change the mood,
and provide theatrical flow through overlapping dumbshow. The first act
of *Soph.* ends with 'the Cornets and Organs playing loud full Musicke for
the Act'. 'Whil'st the Musicke for the first Act soundes', more characters
enter to mime the beginning of Act II (HHW, II, 18–19). He specifies
'Organ mixt with Recorders for this Act' after Act II (HHW, II, 32);
between III and IV 'Organs Violls and Voices play for this Act' (HHW,
II, 43) and between IV and V 'A Base Lute and a Treble Violl play for this
Act' (HHW, II, 51). Similarly, dumbshow begins Act II of *Malc.* 'whilst
the act is playing'. *O.E.D.*, which does not record this sense, gives 1613
(*H8*) for the first use of *act* as part of a play, overlooking Shakespeare's
earlier use in *AYL.* (II.vii.142–3) '. . . one man in his time plays many
parts, / His acts being seven ages'. Richard Hosley cites the present passage
as evidence of a regular practice of inserting music between acts at the
second Blackfriars. Since he also argues that the 'upper station' was used
both as a musicians' gallery and a discovery space, the presence of four
actors 'above' during a musical interlude might have caused traffic
problems. See *The Revels History of Drama in English*, III (1975), 197–235.
Hosley suggests that the 'tree' Tiberio climbs is 'either a property tree set
up against the tiring-house façade or one of the columns of the tiring-
house façade', *ibid.*, p. 223. Since so much is made of it in the play the first
alternative seems more likely.

1. *mother . . . lamp*] the moon. Hercules is addressing Artemis, or

Thou by whose faint shine the blushing lovers
Join glowing cheeks, and mix their trembling lips
In vows well kissed, rise all as full of splendour
As my breast is of joy! You genital,   5
You fruitful well-mixed heats, O, bless the sheets
Of yonder chamber, that Ferrara's dukedom,
The race of princely issue, be not cursed,
And ended in abhorrèd barrenness.
At length kill all my fears, nor let it rest—   10
Once more my tremblings—that my too cold son
(That ever scorner of humaner loves)
Will still contemn the sweets of marriage,
Still kill our hope of name in his dull coldness.
Let it be lawful to make use, ye powers,   15
Of human weakness, that pursueth still

---

5. genital] *Qq;* genial *Dilke.*   10–11. rest— . . . tremblings—] *This ed.;*
rest, . . . tremblinges, *Qq;* rest . . . tremblings, *TC;* rest . . . tremblings
AHB.   12. humaner] *Q2;* humaine *Q1.*   14. kill] *Q2;* till *Q1.*   15.
powers] *Q2;* sowers *Q1.*

Diana, protectress not only of virginity but of all chastity, and goddess of
the moon. She is also the presiding goddess of childbirth, and the rest of
Hercules' prothalamion is quite evidently more concerned with the
production of an heir to the dukedom of Ferrara than with the happiness
of the two lovers.

   5. *genital*] = fruitful (l. 6), life-generating. Dilke emends to 'genial' and
writes: 'By the omission of a letter I have slightly changed a very ex-
ceptionable word, and still preserved the meaning: if the present reading
be not correct.' 'Genial' would indeed preserve the meaning; the sense of
'nuptial' or 'generative' is the earliest recorded use of the word (1566).
Spenser, in his *Epithalamion*, refers to 'The bridale bowre and geniall bed'
(l. 399); Jonson uses the same phrase, 'genial bed', in *Hymenaei* (1606),
l. 169. The only *O.E.D.* example of this sense of genital is dated 1652.
   11. *Once more my tremblings*] The punctuation provided here makes
sense, I believe, of a phrase either ignored or puzzled over by previous
editors. Hercules realistically breaks off in mid-sentence, taken by his
recurrent fears (tremblings) about the fate of the succession.
   12. *humaner loves*] more human (as opposed to bookish) kinds of love.
But it may simply be a case of lazy use of the comparative. Cf. Prologus,
14 and n.
   16. *still*] always, continually.

What is inhibited, and most affects
What is most difficult to be obtained.
So we may learn that nicer love's a shade—
It follows fled, pursued flies as afraid—   20
And in the end close all the various errors
Of passages most truly comical
In moral learning, with like confidence
Of him that vowed good fortune of the scene
Shall neither make him fat, or bad make lean.   25

Enter DONDOLO *laughing.*

Don. Ha, ha, ha!
Herc. Why dost laugh, fool? Here's nobody with thee.
Don. Why, therefore do I laugh, because there's nobody

---

17. *inhibited*] prohibited. Cf. *Oth.* (1604), I.ii.78–9: 'a practiser / Of arts inhibited and out of warrant'.

19–20.] proverbial: 'Love (Woman, Honor), like a shadow (crocodile, death), flies one following and pursues one fleeing' (Tilley, L 518); 'Follow love (pleasure, glory) and it will flee, flee love (pleasure, glory) and it will follow' (Tilley, L 479). Master Ford, as 'Brook', has learned that 'Love like a shadow flies when substance love pursues; / Pursuing that that flies, and flying what pursues', *Wiv.*, II.ii.216–17.

19. *nicer*] shy, coy.

21–3. *And in the end close . . . learning*] To *close* can mean to end, conclude; and *passages* can mean events, transactions, proceedings; in both cases, the senses mentioned are present in this passage. But the overriding image is that of a maze (cf. II.575–6). He hopes that 'we' (l. 19) may enclose (*close*, *O.E.D.* I.3) all the turns and windings (*errors*, *O.E.D.*, 1) of the comic paths or byways (*passages*, *O.E.D.*, II.a.) we have been following, within a moral lesson. These lines are an elaborate reworking of the already expressed hope that 'we may correct and please' (IV.i.700).

23–5. *with like confidence . . . lean*] with the same spirit of confidence as his who swore that the success of his play would not make him fat nor its failure make him lean. We have here the old opposition of moral and aesthetic success to popular or commercial success. Cf. Horace, *Epistles*, II, i, *valeat res ludicra, si me / palma negata macrum, donata reducit opimum.* 'Farewell the comic stage, if denial of the palm sends me home lean, its bestowal plump!' (H. R. Fairclough, Loeb Library). Jonson alludes to this at the end of *Every Man Out* (1599), V.xi.84–7.

27–9. *Why dost laugh . . . fool alone*] Cf. Montaigne (Crawford), III, viii, 201: '*Miso*, one of the seaven sages (a man of Timonian disposition and Democraticall humour) being demanded, where-at he laughed alone; he answered, because I laugh alone.'

with me; would I were a fool alone. I' faith, I am come
to attend—let me go—I am sent to the princess, to   30
come and attend her father to the end of Cupid's
Parliament.

Herc. Why, ha' they sat already upon any statutes?

Don. Sat? Ay, all's agreed in the nether house.

Herc. Why, are they divided?   35

Don. O ay, in Cupid's parliament all the young gallants
are o' the nether house, and all the old signiors that can
but only kiss are of the upper house. Is the princess
above?

Herc. No, sure, I think the princess is beneath, man. Ha'   40
they supped, fool?

Don. O yes, the confusion of tongues at the large table is
broke up, for see, the presence fills. A fool, a fool, a fool,
my coxcomb for a fool!

Enter SIR AMOROUS, HEROD, NYMPHADORO, GARBETZA,
DONETTA, *and* POVEIA.

Herod. Stop, ass. What's matter, idiot?   45

Don. O, gallants, my fools that were appointed to wait on
Don Cupid have launched out their ship to purge their

44.1. *Nymphadoro*] *TC; Nymphadon Qq.*   44.2. *Donetta*] *Dilke; Donella
Qq.*   45. What's matter] *Qq;* what's the matter *TC.*

---

31. *to the end of*] for the purpose of; or, less likely, 'until the end of'.

33. *sat . . . upon*] discussed, passed.

34. *the nether house*] the lower house, the Commons; perhaps punning
on 'sat' (l. 33) and certainly preparing for the puns in the following lines.

35. *are they divided?*] have they voted? Dondolo takes the sense
'separated'.

39–40. *above . . . beneath*] One trusts that this is Faunus's taste in
humour rather than Hercules'.

42. *the confusion of tongues*] i.e. the 'Babel'.

43. *presence*] presence-chamber; cf. I.ii.68.

43–4.] Cf. *R3*, v.iv.7, 13. Marston either borrows or parodies Shakespeare's line in *SV.*, VII, I, *WYW.*, II.i.126, and *Eastward Ho*, III,iv.5.

47–8. *launched . . . water*] Cf. *Wint.*, IV.iv.788–90: 'he is gone abroad a new
ship to purge melancholy and air himself. . . .'

stomachs on the water, and before Jupiter, I fear they
will prove defective in their attendance.

Herod. Pish, fool, they'll float in with the next tide.   50

Don. Ay, but when's that? Let's see mine almanac or
prognostication.

Sir Amor. What, is it for this year?

Don. In true wisdom, sir, it is. Let me see the moon: 'fore
pity, 'tis in the wane. What grief is this, that so great a   55
planet should ever decline or lose splendour! [*Reads.*]
'Full sea at—'

Sir Amor. Where's the sign now, fool?

Don. In Capricorn, Sir Amoroso.

Gar. What strange thing does this almanac speak of, fool?   60

Don. Is this your lady, Sir Amorous?

Sir Amor. It is. Kiss her, fool.

Herod. You may kiss her now, she is married.

Sir Amor. So he might ha' done before.

Don. In sober modesty, sir, I do not use to do it behind.   65

Herod. Good fool, be acquainted with this lady too. She's of
a very honest nature, I assure thee.

Don. I easily believe you, sir, for she hath a very vile face, I
assure ye.

56–7. S.D. *and inverted commas*] *This ed.*   68. vile] *Q2;* good *Q1.*
69. ye] *Q1;* you *Q2.*

---

49. *defective*] at fault, missing.

51–2. *almanac or prognostication*] For a discussion of the popularity of,
and satire on, almanacs, see F. P. Wilson, 'Some English mock-prognos-
tications', *The Library*, XIX (1938), 6–43. See *Prince d'Amour*, pp. 33–6,
for similar mock prognostications.

56. *decline*] here = diminish in brightness. In astrology, this would
mean to deviate from the equator or the ecliptic.

59. *Capricorn*] This is for Sir Amoroso's benefit; the goat represents
both lechery and (because of its horns) cuckoldry.

64–5.] *WYW.,* IV.i.337–9, where Albano and Quadratus have a similar
exchange.

68–9.] Cf. IV.i.609–10 n., and III.i.109. Q1's 'good' was probably in the
stage version, where the irony would be apparent. Marston evidently felt
that readers needed more guidance, hence the unsubtle use of *vile* in Q2.

Gar. But what strange things does thy almanac speak of,   70
    good fool?

Don. That this year no child shall be begotten but shall
    have a true father.

Sir Amor. That's good news, i' faith, I am glad I got my
    wife with child this year.   75

Herc. Why, Sir Amorous, this may be, and yet you not the
    true father; may it not, Herod?

Gar. But what more says it, good Fawn?

Herc. Faith, lady, very strange things. It says that some
    ladies, of your hair, shall have feeble hams, short   80
    memories, and very weak eyesight, so that they shall
    mistake their own page, or even brother-in-law, some-
    times for their husbands.

Sir Amor. Is that all, Fawn?

Herc. No, Sir Amorous, here's likewise prophesied a great   85
    scarcity of gentry to ensue, and that some boors shall be
    dubbed Sir Amoroso. A great scarcity of lawyers is like-
    wise this year to ensue, so that some one of them shall
    be entreated to take fees o' both sides.

Enter DON ZUCCONE, *following* DONNA ZOYA *on his knees.*

Zuc. Most dear, dear lady! Wife, lady, wife! O do not but   90
    look on me, and ha' some mercy!

Zoya. I will ha' no mercy, I will not relent.

Zuc. Sweet lady!

Zoya. The order shall stand. I am separated, and I will be
    separated.   95

87. boors] *Dilke;* Bores [= boors] *Qq;* bores *AHB.*

---

80. *of your hair*] with hair of the same colour as yours, i.e., that look like
you.

    feeble hams] i.e. so that they find it necessary to lie down.

    86. *boors*] peasants, clowns. Bullen's reading, 'bores', which is followed
by Smith, is grossly anachronistic. Hercules is punning on 'boars', whose
tusks qualified them as horned beasts; i.e., 'some cuckolds shall be called
Sir Amoroso'. Cf. Chapman's *The Gentleman Usher,* I.i.60: 'boars yield fit
game for boors'.

    91 ff.] Note how Zoya's words echo Zuccone's, IV.i.281–324.

Zuc. Dear! My love! Wife!

Zoya. Hence, fellow, I am none of thy wife. No, I will be tyrannous and a most deep revenger; the order shall stand. I will marry a fellow that keeps a fox in his bosom, a goat under his armholes, and a polecat in his   100 mouth, rather than re-accept thee.

Zuc. Alas, by the Lord, lady, what should I say? As heaven shall bless me—what should I say?

Herod. Kneel and cry, man.

Zoya. Was I not handsome, generous, honest enough from   105 my foot to my feather, for such a fellow as thou art?

Zuc. Alas, I confess, I confess.

Zoya. But go thy ways, and wive with whom thou wilt, for my part. Thou hast spun a fair thread: who'll kiss thee now? Who'll court thee now? Who'll ha' thee now?   110

Zuc. Yet be a woman, and for God's sake help me.

Herod. And do not stand too stiffly.

Zuc. And do not stand too stiffly—! Do you make an ass of me? But let these rascals laugh at me. Alas, what could I do withal? 'Twas my destiny that I should abuse you.   115

Zoya. So it is your destiny that I should thus revenge your abuse. No, the Irishman shall hate *aqua vitae*, the Welshman cheese, and the Dutchman salt butter, before I'll love or receive thee. Does he cry? Does the

---

117. hate] *Q2;* eate *Q1.*   *aqua vitae*] *TC;* Aquauitę *Qq.*

99–101. *that keeps . . . his mouth*] All this is to be taken half-literally, as comic grotesquerie; but the fox was traditionally a figure of malice, and both the goat and the polecat (weasel) were proverbially smelly; perhaps the fox is here for its smell as well: 'I'd marry a man that stinks all over before I'd remarry you.' Marston may be remembering Tucca's words to Crispinus (Marston) in *Poetaster* (1601), III.iv.367–78: 'Hang him, fustie *satyre*, he smells all goate; hee carries a ram, vnder his arme-holes, the slaue: . . .'

112. *And do not stand too stiffly*] Herod has been prompting Zuccone (see l. 104) and perhaps he has quietly 'fed' Zuccone this line, the irony (and obscenity) of which Zuccone catches only after he has spoken it. The sense of the line is much the same, however, if Herod is only offering it as a recommendation to Zuccone.

114–15. *what . . . withal?*] what else could I do?

babe pule? 'Tis too late now, thou shouldst ha' cried   120
before. 'Tis too late now: go bury thy head in silence,
and let oblivion be thy utmost hope.

The courtiers address themselves to dancing, whilst the DUKE *enters*
with GRANUFFO, *and takes his state.*

Herc. Gallants, to dancing. Loud music, the duke's upon
entrance.
Gon. Are the sports ready?   125
Herc. Ready.
Gon. 'Tis enough. Of whose invention is this parliament?
Herc. Ours.
Gon. 'Tis enough:
This night we will exult. O let this night   130
Be ever memorised with prouder triumphs.
Let it be writ in lasting character
That this night our great wisdom did discover
So close a practice—that this night, I say,

---

122. *let oblivion . . . hope*] Phrases similar to this are associated with
Marston throughout his adult life. Back in 1598, he closed *SV.* with a
poem 'To euerlasting Obliuion': 'But as for mee, hungry *Obliuion* /
Deuoure me quick, . . .' (ll. 5–6). And the stone marking his burial-place
in the Temple church was inscribed 'OBLIVIONI SACRVM'. Cf. the conclusion of *Prince d'Amour* (p. 90): 'This Prince raigned not full forty
years. He dyed of a common infectious disease, called Opinion, . . . and
may be buried in Oblivion with his Ancestors, if tongues dig him not up.'
    122.1. *address themselves to dancing*] apply themselves to dancing,
begin to dance.
    122.2. *state*] throne. Cf. *1H4* (1597), II.iv.415–17: 'This chair shall be
my state, this dagger my sceptre, and this cushion my crown.'
    125. *sports*] See IV.i.588 n.
    127. *invention*] devising.
    128. *Ours*] i.e. mine and Dondolo's. It is not clear from IV.i.248–64
whether Hercules has had previous knowledge of the court of Cupid when
Dondolo describes it to him and his companions. In the meantime,
however, he has evidently collaborated with Dondolo in gearing the
entertainment to his own purposes, and the two of them share the official
duties of the court, under the presiding figure of Cupid.
    131. *Be ever memorised*] be always remembered (or) be made memorable.
triumphs] festivities.
    132. *character*] writing, printing.
    134. *close a practice*] secret an intrigue. Cf. I.ii.152.

Our policy found out, nay, dashed the drifts   135
Of the young prince, and put him to his shifts—
Nay, past his shifts ('fore Jove, we could make a good
    poet).
Delight us, on. We deign our princely ear:
We are well pleased to grace you; then scorn fear.

Cornets playing. DRUNKENNESS, SLOTH, PRIDE, *and* PLENTY
lead CUPID *to his state, who is followed by* FOLLY, WAR, BEGGARY,
                        and LAUGHTER.

Stand. 'Tis wisdom to acknowledge ignorance   140
Of what we know not; we would not now prove foolish.
Expound the meaning of your show.

138. deign] *Q2;* dare *Q1.*   139. you] *Q 2;* him *Q1.*   139.3. LAUGHTER]
Q2; Slaughter *Q1.*

---

135. *drifts*] schemes, plots.
136. *put him to his shifts*] forced him to extremities. *O.E.D.*'s first
example for this sense of *shift*, 'an expedient necessitated by stress of
circumstances', is dated 1647, but it appears much earlier, e.g. *Tit.*
(*c.* 1592), IV.ii.176: 'For it is you that puts us to our shifts.' There might
be a pun in 'past his shifts' on the sense of *shift* as chemise, shirt or
nightdress. I am uncertain whether it is this paranomasia or the drifts/
shifts rhyme, or something else, which persuades Gonzago that he 'could
make a good poet'.
138. *We deign our princely ear*] We condescend to give you hearing.
139.1–3.] This short pageant has aspects of the masque about it, and
particularly foreshadows what Jonson was later to call the anti-masque (in
his introduction to *The Masque of Queens* [1609]), a group of grotesque
anarchic figures which are dispelled by powers of reason or beauty. The
odd array of personifications in the present 'masque' seems to be introduced solely to show that Cupid rules over them; it is not clear whether
his rule limits their activities or on the contrary initiates them. Though
they are introduced helter-skelter, their significance may be clarified by
arranging them in couples: Drunkenness (leading to) Folly; Sloth (leading
to) Beggary; Pride (leading to) War; Plenty (leading to) Laughter.
Other orders may of course be at least equally valid. John Peter has
pointed out the similarity between the cyclical pattern in Marston's *Hist.*
(1599) and a medieval tag involving some of the same abstractions as in the
present masque:

> Pees maketh plente.
> Plente maketh pryde.
> Pryde maketh plee.
> Plee maketh pouert.
> Pouert makethe pees.

Herc. Triumphant Cupid, that sleeps on the soft cheek
         Of rarest beauty, whose throne's in ladies' eyes,
         Whose force writhed lightning from Jove's shaking
             hand,   145
         Forced strong Alcides to resign his club,
         Plucked Neptune's trident from his mighty arm,
         Unhelmèd Mars, he (with those trophies borne),
         Led in by Sloth, Pride, Plenty, Drunkenness,
         Followed by Folly, War, Laughter, Beggary,   150
         Takes his fair throne. Sit pleased, for now we move
         And speak not for our glory but for love.

               HERCULES *takes a bowl of wine.*

Gon. A pretty figure. What, begins this session with cere-
        mony?
Herc. With a full health to our great mistress, Venus,   155
         Let every state of Cupid's parliament
         Begin the session, *et quod bonum faustumque sit precor.*

---

148. those] *Q2;* these *Q1.*   150. Laughter] *Qq;* Slaughter *TC.*   157.
et] *Q1;* not in *Q2.*

The 'rhyme' appears in *Secular Lyrics of the XIVth and XVth Centuries,*
ed. R. H. Robbins (1952), p. 81. Peter observes that 'the term Litigation
("plee") is suppressed, and Envy and War substituted for it' in *Hist.;*
Complaint and Satire in Early English Literature (1956), p. 220. The
probable connection between this scene and Inns of Court Revels has been
dealt with in the Introduction. See Philip J. Finkelpearl's book and article
cited there. The mixture of mythological with allegorical figures was
characteristic as well of Royal entries and Lord Mayor's shows. See David
M. Bergeron's *English Civic Pageantry 1558–1642* (1971), esp. pp. 71–89.

  145. *force writhed*] power wrenched.
  146. *Alcides*] = Heracles, Hercules.
  153. *a pretty figure*] i.e. Gonzago is complimenting Hercules's rather
pompous rhetoric.
  156. *state*] estate, = rank (within parliament).
  157. et quod bonum faustumque sit precor] and I pray that whatever
is good and auspicious may follow. 'This was an usual form of address in
meetings on important occasions' (Dilke). Dilke points out that Jonson has
Cicero use the expression in *Catiline,* IV, 64–5: 'What may be happy, and
auspicious still / To Rome, and hers.' Jonson uses it also in *Sejanus,* V, 523–4.

HERCULES *drinks a health.*

Gon. Give't us, we'll pledge; nor shall a man that lives,
  In charity refuse it. I will not be so old
  As not be graced to honour Cupid. Give't us full.   160
  When we were young we could ha' trolled it off,
  Drunk down a Dutchman.
Herc. 'Tis lamentable pity your grace has forgot it. Drunkenness! O, 'tis a most fluent and swelling virtue, sure
  the most just of all virtues, 'tis justice itself, for if it   165
  chance to oppress and take too much, it presently
  restores it again. It makes the king and the peasant
  equal, for if they are both drunk alike, they are both
  beasts alike. As for the most precious light of heaven,
  Truth, if Time be the father of her, I am sure Drunken-   170
  ness is oftentimes the mother of her, and brings her
  forth. Drunkenness brings all out, for it brings all the

157.1. *so TC; in right margin opposite ll.* 156–8 *Qq.*

---

158. *pledge*] drink to the health proposed.

158–9. *that lives,* / *In charity refuse it.*] The phrase may have been 'that
lives in charity', i.e. under love's (or Cupid's) dispensation. But the Qq
have a comma after *lives* and the present reading makes good enough sense.

161. *trolled it off*] 'To *troll*, or *troll the bowl*, appears . . . to have been a
common phrase in drinking for passing the vessel about' (Dilke). This is
substantially *O.E.D.*'s definition for *troll* (III, †6), the *last* example for
which is dated 1600. But here the word is applied to the drinking itself:
'gulped it down'.

162. *Drunk down a Dutchman*] Sugden writes, 'The D[utch] (and the
Germans also) were heavy drinkers', and gives many examples, including
several from Marston. He ascribes the present one to *Insatiate C.*

163–74] Another of Marston's mock encomiums. This one is very much
like Valerio's praise of the horn in Chapman's *All Fools*, v.i.230–326.

164. *fluent and swelling virtue*] *Virtue* here combines the senses 'gift' and
'power'. *Swelling* suggests superabundance; the whole phrase suggests
generosity, munificence.

165–7. *'tis justice . . . again*] Like ideal justice, when drunkenness takes
too much (drink), it is fair and returns it (through spewing).

167–8. *It makes the king and the peasant equal*] 'He that is drunk is as
great as a king' (Tilley, K 57). Tilley's first example is dated 1672.

170. *Truth, if Time be the father of her*] Cf. Tilley, T 580: 'Truth is
time's daughter.'

170–2.] The proverbial connotation between truth and drink is at least
as old as Pliny (*Historia Naturalis*, II, xiv, 141).

drink out of the pot, all the wit out of the pate, and all
the money out of the purse.

Gon. My lord Granuffo, this Fawn is an excellent fellow.   175

Don. Silence.

Gon. I warrant you for my lord here.

Cupid. Since multitude of laws are signs either of much
tyranny in the prince or much rebellious disobedience
in the subject, we rather think it fit to study how to   180
have our old laws thoroughly executed, than to have new
statutes cumbrously invented.

Gon. Afore Jove, he speaks very well.

Herc. O, sir, love is very eloquent, makes all men good
orators; himself then must needs be eloquent.   185

Cupid. Let it therefore be the main of our assembly to
survey our old laws, and punish their transgressions, for
that continually the complaints of lovers ascend up to
our deity that love is abused, and basely bought and
sold, beauty corrupted, affection feigned, and pleasure   190

---

184. love] *Q1;* oue *Q2.*

---

177. *I warrant . . . here*] Gonzago is being funny: 'I guarantee you
silence on behalf of Granuffo (*my lord here*).' Dondolo had called for
silence before Granuffo could 'reply'.

180–2. *fit to study . . . invented*] Cf. James's first speech to Parliament
(*The Kings Maiesties Speech* [1604], C3*v*): '. . . the execution of good
Lawes is farre more profitable in a Commonwealth, then to burden mens
memories with the making of too many of them.' Marston may or may not
have had this speech in mind (the idea is common in Renaissance writings
on politics), but what is more important is that Cupid is signalling the
pièce de résistance of the play, a series of witty parodies of 'our old laws',
aimed directly at the Inns of Court men in the audience. Marston couches
the various offences against Cupid in terms normally applied to land holding, hoarding, uttering and forging, and so on, with frequently ingenious
matching. It is a comic valediction to the law books willed him by his
father. I shall point out the parallels as they occur.

184–5. *love . . . orators*] proverbial: 'Love makes all men orators'
(Tilley, L 522).

186. *main*] end, purpose. Note that Cupid again emphasises 'our old
laws'. Rather than invent laws especially for this session, Marston will
adapt already existing ones, recognisable to the audience.

herself sophisticated; that young gallants are proud in
appetite and weak in performance; that young ladies
are phantastically inconstant, old ladies impudently
unsatiate. Wives complain of unmarried women, that
they steal the dues belonging to their sheets; and maids   195
make exclaim upon wives, that they unjustly engross all
into their own hands, as not content with their own
husbands, but also purloining that which should be
their comfort. Let us therefore be severe in our justice;
and if any of what degree soever have approvedly   200
offended, let him be instantly unpartially arrested and
punished. Read our statutes.

Herc. 'A statute made in the five thousand and four hundred

196. make] *Q1; not in Q2.*   203–8. 'A . . . love.'] *Smith;* A . . . loue. *Qq;
italics Dilke. So for the other statutes.*

---

191. *sophisticated*] adulterated, corrupted. Cf. *Lr.,* III.iv.110–12: 'Ha!
here's three on's are sophisticated! Thou art the thing itself.'

proud] vigorous, valiant (but with a pun on the sense 'lascivious').

193. *phantastically*] capriciously. Cf. *AYL.,* III.ii.431: 'fantastical,
apish, shallow, inconstant', and *H5,* II.iv.26–8: 'she is so idly king'd, / Her
sceptre so fantastically borne / By a vain, giddy, shallow, humorous
youth . . .'.

193–4. *impudently unsatiate*] shamelessly insatiable.

196. *make exclaim*] make outcry (with the semi-legal force of making a
complaint or claim). Cf. *R2,* I.ii.1–2: 'Alas, the part I had in Woodstock's
blood / Doth more solicit me than your exclaims'.

engross] monopolise; but in this context, there is probably also a pun on
the sense 'to make gross, bulky'.

200. *degree*] station, rank.

200–1. *have approvedly offended*] are proven to have offended.

203–7.] '*A statute . . . lord of Hymen . . .*'] This follows closely the form
introducing statutes of the realm, for example those for the year 1547:
'Statutes made in the Parliament begun at Westminster the fourth Day of
November in the first Year of the Reign of our most dread Sovereign Lord
Edward the Sixth, by the Grace of God King of England, France and
Ireland, Defender of the Faith, and of the Church of England, and also of
Ireland, in Earth the Supreme Head: . . .' For other comic parodies of this
formula, see *LLL.* (*c.* 1593), III.i.183–8; and Marston's own *WYW.,*
III.iii.6–8, where it appears as part of a similar trial scene, in which
schoolboys try their masters: '*Honorificacuminos Bidet, Emperor of Cracks,
Prince of Pages, Marquess of Mumchance, and sole Regent over a Bale of
False Dice: . . .*' Halliwell first pointed out the similarity of the present
passage to that in *LLL.,* where the monarch described is again Cupid:

threescore and three year of the easeful reign of the
mighty potent Don Cupid, emperor of sighs and   205
protestations, great king of kisses, archduke of dalliance,
and sole lord of Hymen, for the maintaining and reliev-
ing of his old soldiers, maimed or dismembered in love.'
Don. Those that are lightly hurt shame to complain; those
that are deeply struck are past recovery.   210
Cupid. On to the next.
Herc. 'An act against the plurality of mistresses.'
Cupid. Read.
Herc. 'Whereas some over-amorous and unconscionable

207. lord of Hymen] *Deighton;* lou'de of *Her Q1;* lou'de of him *Q2.*

> Regent of love-rhymes, lord of folded arms,
> Th' anointed sovereign of sighs and groans,
> Liege of all loiterers and malcontents,
> Dread prince of plackets, king of codpieces,
> Sole imperator, and great general
> Of trotting paritors.

207. *sole lord of Hymen*] See Introduction, p. 50, for discussion of the
bibliographical aspects of this reading. As Deighton (whose emendation
this is) points out, the *lord/lov'd* confusion is found, though in reverse, in
Fletcher's *The Elder Brother* (*c.* 1625), V.ii.15. I am inclined to agree with
Wood when he writes of Deighton's reading: 'This is that rare thing—a
perfect unchallengeable emendation.'

207–8. *for the maintaining . . . love*] Cf. *H5*, IV.i.140–7: 'But if the cause
be not good, the king himself hath a heavy reckoning to make, when all
those legs and arms and heads, chopped off in a battle, shall join together
at the latter day and cry all 'We died at such a place'; some swearing, some
crying for a surgeon, some upon their wives left poor behind them, some
upon the debts they owe, some upon their children rawly left.' England's
many wars were the source of a number of statutes aimed at providing
some relief and support for veterans, many of whom became beggars on
returning home. The statutes 39 Eliz. (1597) c.21 and 43 Eliz. (1601) c.3
closely resemble this one. Again the context (the wars of love) provides an
extra meaning for *dismembered*; see II.i.349 n. Cf. *Prince d'Amour*, p. 45,
for the same pun.

212. '*An act against the plurality of mistresses.*'] This is chiefly a parody
of Acts passed against enclosure (cf. especially 25 Henry VIII c.13 [1533–
34]). Plurality apparently did not acquire its ecclesiastical sense of holding
more than one benefice till later in the century. For a discussion of
enclosure and its interest for the dramatists, see Clarkson and Warren,
pp. 89–92, and R. H. Tawney, *The Agrarian Problem in the Sixteenth
Century* (1912), to which they refer as their chief source. Cf. *Prince
d'Amour*, p. 58, for a similar parodic statute.

214. *unconscionable*] inordinately.

covetous young gallants, without all grace of Venus, or   215
the fear of Cupid in their minds, have at one time en-
grossed the care or cures of divers mistresses, with the
charge of ladies, into their own tenure or occupation,
whereby their mistresses must of necessity be very ill
and unsufficiently served, and likewise many able   220
portly gallants live unfurnished of competent entertainment, to the merit of their bodies; and whereas
likewise some other greedy strangers have taken in the
purlieus, outset land, and the ancient commons of our

224. outset] *Q1 corr.*, *Q2;* a sette *Q1 uncorr.*

---

217. *cures*] charges, offices, cares; not necessarily ecclesiastic. Perhaps
there is a pun on the medical sense of *cures*.

218. *charge*] (i) title, rank, 'mistresses known as ladies'; (ii) custody,
'cares or cures'. Perhaps a pun, but the syntax seems to require a choice
between one sense and the other; the first sense seems more likely.

occupation] = occupancy. But the word had become strongly associated
with the keeping of women and pandering. Cf. Pompey's explanation of
his 'mystery' in *Meas.*, IV.ii.38–42: 'Painting, sir, I have heard say, is a
mystery; and your whores, sir, being members of my occupation, using
painting, do prove my occupation a mystery. . . .' Middleton's use of the
term in *A Trick to Catch the Old One* (1604–7), IV.iv.258–60, is even closer
to Marston's: 'The said widow, late in the occupation of the said Anthony
Medler, and now in the occupation of Walkodine Hoard.' This is probably
what Doll Tearsheet refers to in *2H4* (1598), II.iv.159–62: 'A captain!
God's light, these villains will make the word as odious as the word
"occupy"; which was an excellent good word before it was ill sorted.'
See also A. R. Humphreys's note in the Arden edition of *2H4*, II.iv.145.

221. *portly*] stately, imposing.

221–2. *unfurnished . . . bodies*] unprovided with activity sufficient to
satisfy their bodies' standards.

224. *purlieus*] 'Purlue is all that ground neere any Forest' (Cowell's
Interpreter [1607]).

outset land] 'an enclosure from the outlying moorland, pasture, or
common' (*O.E.D.*); from Scottish law.

commons] the undivided land held in common by the whole community.
There is a pun, of course, on *common* as an adjective for prostitutes, e.g.
Jonson's Doll Common in *The Alchemist*. As Clarkson and Warren point
out (p. 91), the joke was a favourite of Dekker's, e.g. in *The Honest Whore 2*,
IV.i.288–90 (ed. Bowers):

> Thus (for sport sake) speake I, as to a woman,
> Whom (as the worst ground) I would turne to common:
> But you I would enclose for mine owne bed.

sovereign liege Don Cupid, taking in his very highways,   225
and enclosing them, and annexing them to their own
lordships, to the much impoverishing and putting of
divers of Cupid's true hearts and loyal subjects to base
and abominable shifts: Be it therefore enacted, by the
sovereign authority and erected ensign of Don Cupid,   230
with the assent of some of the lords, most of the ladies,
and all the commons, that what person or persons soever shall, in the trade of honour, presume to wear at
one time two ladies' favours, or at one time shall
earnestly court two women in the way of marriage, or if   235
any under the degree of a duke shall keep above twenty
women of pleasure, a duke's brother fifteen, a lord ten,
a knight or a pensioner or both four, a gentleman two,
shall *ipso facto* be arrested by folly's mace, and instantly
committed to the ship of fools, without either bail or   240

Clarkson and Warren quote most of *Fawn*, v.i.214–21, to illustrate their
section on enclosure.

231–2. *some of the lords. . . . commons*] Another instance of a favourite
Marston formula (cf. II.i.12–13), and another variant to the pun on
commons, here referring to the House of Commons.

233. *the trade of honour*] If the rest of the passage had not already
indicated who the accused would be, this would. Cf. Nymphadoro's
phrase 'the trade of marriage', III.i.130.

234. *favours*] See III.i.94 n.

235–8. *or if any . . . a gentleman two*] The idea of quotas may have
originated in the statute on which the whole passage is based (25 Henry
VIII, c.13), where tenant farmers were limited to keeping two thousand
sheep, but the owner of an estate of inheritance in the land was permitted
more. But more immediate is the budgeting of retainers in the proclama-
tion for James's coronation: 'Earls may bring sixteen servants to our
Coronation; Bishops and Barons, ten; Knights, six; and Gentlemen,
four' (Robert Steele, ed., *A Bibliography of Royal Proclamations* [1910],
I, 110).

238. *pensioner*] = gentleman-pensioner, one of forty gentlemen who
acted as guards or attendants to the sovereign on state occasions; instituted
by Henry VIII in 1509 (*O.E.D.*).

240–1. *bail or mainprize*] Both are legal terms for actions procuring the
release of a prisoner pending his appearance in court; with *bail* the surety
is the payment of a specifically named sum, while with *mainprize* the
surety is his own or another person's cognisance.

mainprize, *Millesimo centesimo, quingentesimo quadra-
gesimo nono. Cupidinis semper unius.*'
Nymphadoro, to the bar.

Nym. Shame o' folly, will Fawn now turn an informer? Does
    he laugh at me?   245

Herc. Domina Garbetza, did he not ever protest you were
    his most only elected mistress?

Gar. He did.

Herc. Domina Donetta, did he not ever protest you were his
    most only elected mistress?   250

Don. He did.

Herc. Domina Poveia, did he not ever protest that you were
    his most only elected mistress?

Pov. He did.

Nym. Mercy!   255

Cupid. Our mercy is nothing, unless some lady will beg thee.

Ladies. Out upon him, dissembling, perfidious liar!

Herc. Indeed 'tis no reason ladies should beg liars.

Nym. Thus he that loveth many, if once known,
    Is justly plagued to be beloved of none.   *Exit.* 260

Herc. 'An act against counterfeiting of Cupid's royal coin,
    and abusing his subjects with false money.' To the bar,

---

241. *quingentesimo*] *Q1; quigintesimo Q2.*   249. Donetta] *London; Donella
Qq.*   260. beloved] *Q2;* beleeu'de *Q1.*

241–2. Millesimo . . . nono] a hybrid Latin-Italian 'date' which makes
about the same sense as the dating of the first statute of the session
(ll. 203–4).

242. Cupidinis semper unius] Cupid ever One. Since *Cupid* is in the
genitive, it probably modifies the preceding numbers: 'The thousandth
hundredth five hundredth fortieth ninth (or forty-ninth) [year of the
reign] of Cupid, ever One.'

256. *Our mercy is nothing*] our mercy is non-existent, there is no mercy.
beg thee] petition to take you into her custody. This was usually
applied to a minor, an heiress or an idiot (*O.E.D.*).

261–2. '*An act against counterfeiting . . . false money.*'] There were many
Tudor laws against counterfeiting: cf. 4 Henry VII, c.18; 1 Mary (second
session), c.6 (1553); 5–6 Edward VI (1552), c.4; 1–2 Philip and Mary,
c.11 (1554); 5 Eliz., c.11; 14 Eliz., c.3; 18 Eliz., c.1 (1576). The second
last of these, concerned with the counterfeiting of *foreign* coins, may
provide the basis of the pun on 'stranger parts' (l. 267).

Sir Amorous. 'In most lamentable form complaineth to
your blind celsitude your distressed orators, the
women of the world, that in respect that many spend-   265
thrifts, who having exhausted and wasted their substance, and in stranger parts have with empty shows
treasonably purchased ladies' affections, without being
of ability to pay them for it with current money, and
therefore have deceitfully sought to satisfy them with   270
counterfeit metal, to the great displeasure and no small
loss of your humblest subjects: May it therefore with
your pitiful assent be enacted, that what lord, knight, or
gentleman soever, knowing himself insufficient, bankrout, exhausted, and wasted, shall traitorously dare to   275
entertain any lady as wife or mistress, *ipso facto* to be
severed from all commercement with women, his wife
or mistress in that state offending to be forgiven with a
pardon of course, and himself instantly to be pressed to
to sail in the ship of fools, without either bail or main- 280
prize.'

Don.   Sir Amorous is arrested.

282. *Don.*] *London; Herc. Qq.*

---

264. *celsitude*] = 'Highness'. Marston uses it with the same comic tone
in *WYW.*, III.iii.38.

orators] petitioners, suppliants.

266–7. *substance*] goods, means, wealth. The figurative meaning is, of
course, virility; the metaphor is continued throughout the passage. The
reader may determine the details of this ingeniously elaborated obscenity
for himself.

267. *empty shows*] Cf. the quotation from Montaigne in IV.i.100 n.

274–5. *bankrout*] bankrupt.

275. *traitorously*] This is no comic exaggeration: 'every such Offence
[i.e. of counterfeiting] shall be deemed and adjudged Misprision of High
Treason' (14 Eliz., c.3).

277. *severed from all commercement*] removed from, forbidden all dealings.

278. *in that state offending*] i.e., involved in this crime.

279. *of course*] in ordinary or due course.

pressed] = impressed, forced (into military service).

282. *Don.*] London's emendation is surely correct. The Qq make a
point of beginning a new speech with this line, and Dondolo makes or
announces the other arrests during the session.

arrested] = apprehended (as guilty); convicted.

Sir Amor. [*Points at* GARBETZA] Judgement of the court.

Herc. I take my oath upon thy brother's body, 'tis none of
    thine.   285

Sir Amor. By the heart of dissemblance, this Fawn has
    wrought with us as strange tailors work in corporate
    cities, where they are not free: all inward, inward, he
    lurked in the bosom of us, and yet we know not his
    profession. Sir, let me have counsel?   290

Herc. 'Tis in great Cupid's case; you may have no counsel.

---

283. *Sir Amor.* (*Sir Amar.*)] *Q2; Don, Amar. Q1.*   S.D.] *This ed.*   Judgement of the court] *Q2;* Sir iudgement of the countrie *Q1.*   291. Cupid's]
Q2; not in Q1.

283.] The stage direction is based on Dilke's note: 'From the reply of
Hercules it is evident that Sir Amoroso appeals to the pregnancy of his
wife, as a proof of his innocence; he must here, therefore, be supposed to
point to her.' The Q1 reading *countrie* is a correct term for jury (see
O.E.D.'s article for *country,* sb. I.7). Marston may be simplifying for a
reading public less specialised than the Blackfriars audience.

284–5. *'tis none of thine*] i.e., the child is not yours.

286–8. *this Fawn has wrought . . . free*] The meaning is not certain:
Fawn has worked with us as do tailors who are foreigners (strange) in
incorporated cities in which they have not been admitted to the privileges
of the corporation (i.e. are not *'free* of the corporation'). The key word is
inward (l. 288). I suggest this means that these 'non-union' tailors must
work secretly, in the back room as it were (*inward*). Tailors were always
targets for satirists, at least as far back as Dunbar.

288–9. *he lurked in the bosom of us*] i.e. like the snake in Aesop's fable
who bit the man who befriended him. Cf. Tilley, B 546: 'He will creep
into your bosom'.

289–90. *and yet . . . profession*] but we do not know what *he* really does
for a living. Perhaps Sir Amoroso is suggesting that Faunus is a common
informer.

291.] '"It is a settled rule at common law," says Sir W. Blackstone,
"that *no counsel* shall be allowed a prisoner upon his trial in *any capital
crime,* unless some point of law shall arise proper to be debated, which,"
as he justly observes, "seems not of a piece with the rest of humane treatment of the prisoners by the English law"' (Dilke, who abridges slightly
from *Blackstone's Commentaries* [1769 ed., IV, 349] and adds italics).
Blackstone's concluding observation is apparently espoused by Sir
Amoroso (l. 292), whose reference to Normandy may simply be the
normal reaction of an 'Italian' Englishman to the lack of British justice.
Wood tentatively offers: 'Are we subject to arbitrary justice, lynch law,
like that of the Norman courts ?'

Sir Amor. Death o' justice! Are we in Normandy? What is
 my lady's doom then?

Cupid. Acquitted by the express parol of the statute.
 Hence, and in thy ignorance be quietly happy. Away 295
 with him—on.   [*Exit* AMOROSO.]

Herc. 'An act against forgers of love letters, false braggarts
 of ladies' favours, and vain boasters of counterfeit
 tokens.'

Herod. 'Tis I, 'tis I, I confess guilty, guilty.   300

Herc. I will be most humane and right courteously lan-
 guaged in thy correction, and only say, thy vice, from
 apparent heir, has made thee an apparent beggar, and
 now of a false knave hath made thee a true fool. Folly, to
 the ship with him, and twice a day let him be ducked at 305
 the main-yard.   [*Exit* HEROD.]

Cupid. Proceed.

Herc. 'An act against slanderers of Cupid's liege ladies'
 names, and lewd defamers of their honours.'

---

292. *Sir Amor.* Death] *Q2; Don. Amor.* Sir death *Q1.* 294. express
parol] *Q2;* right penaltie *Q1.* 296. S.D.] *This ed.* 302–3. vice, from
apparent heir,] *Smith (ad. London);* vice apparent here *Q1;* vice frō apparāt
here, *Q2.* 306. S.D.] *This ed.* 308. liege ladies'] *Qq;* liege, ladies'
Smith.

---

294. *express parol*] explicit statement (see v.i.277–9); legal jargon. Q1's
'right penaltie' means much the same.

295. *ignorance*] either (i) lack of self-knowledge (which protects you
from pain), or (ii) obscurity, being unknown—a sense unrecorded in
O.E.D. Cf. v.i.122 n.

297–8. *forgers . . . braggarts . . . boasters*] *Braggarts* and *boasters* are
comic variants of 'utterers'. Cf. the statute against forging and uttering,
33 Henry VIII, c.1.

302. *correction*] rebuke, reproof.

302–4. *thy vice . . . true fool*] For the legal aspects of inheritance involved
here, see IV.i.73–4 n. In Hercules' account of Herod's progress from vice
to folly, Marston makes explicit the moral (and comic) pattern of the play.

308–9.] There were a number of acts against slander, especially against
slander of royalty, in the middle of the sixteenth century, two in 1554
alone (1–2 Philip and Mary, c.3 and c.10).

309. *lewd*] wicked, base; but the word was already being used in its
surviving sense of 'lascivious'.

honours] a pun: (i) titles, ranks; (iii) reputations (of chastity).

Zuc. 'Tis I, 'tis I, I weep and cry out, I have been a most   310
    contumelious offender. My only cry is *miserere.*

Cupid. If your relenting lady will have pity on you, the fault
    against our deity be pardoned.

Zuc. Madam, if ever I have found favour in your eyes, if
    ever you have thought me a reasonable handsome   315
    fellow, as I am sure before I had a beard you might, O
    be merciful!

Zoya. Well, upon your apparent repentance, that all
    modest spectators may witness I have for a short time
    only thus feignedly hated you that you might ever after   320
    truly love me, upon these cautions I re-accept you: first
    you shall vow—

Zuc. I do vow, as heaven bless me, I will do—

Zoya. What?

Zuc. Whate'er it be. Say on, I beseech you.   325

Zoya. You shall vow—

Zuc. Yes.

Zoya. That you shall never—

Zuc. Never—

Zoya. Feign love to my waiting-woman or chambermaid.   330

Zuc. No.

Zoya. Never promise them such a farm to their marriage—

Zuc. No.

Zoya. If she'll discover but whom I affect.

Zuc. Never.   335

---

311. miserere] have mercy.

318. *apparent*] evident.

319. *modest*] fair, honest (as judges). Cf. *Per.*, v.i.121–3: 'Falseness
cannot come from thee; for thou lookest / Modest as Justice, and thou
seem'st a palace / For the crown'd Truth to dwell in.'

321. *cautions*] provisos, conditions. The scene anticipates in some ways
the 'proviso' scene in Congreve's *The Way of the World* (1700).

332. *promise them . . . marriage*] bribe them with the promise of a fixed
yearly income as a dowry gift.

334.] if she'll only reveal whom I love.

Zoya. Or if they know none, that they'll but take a false oath
    I do, only to be rid of me.

Zuc. I swear I will not. I will not only not counterfeitly love
    your women, but I will truly hate them, an't be possible;
    so far from maintaining them, that I will beggar them.   340
    I will never pick their trunks for letters, search their
    pockets, ruffle their bosoms, or tear their foul smocks—
    never, never.

Zoya. That if I chance to have a humour to be in a masque,
    you shall not grow jealous.   345

Zuc. Never.

Zoya. Or grudge at the expense.

Zuc. Never, I will eat mine own arms first.

339. them, . . . possible;] *This ed. (ad. Dilke);* them . . . possible, *Qq;*
them;. . . possible, *AHB.*

---

336. *if they know none*] if they know I love no one (have no lover); i.e.,
rather than 'if they know of none'; there is no question of there being a
lover, as the rest of the sentence shows.

341. *trunks*] coffers, chests.

342. *ruffle their bosoms*] i.e. in search of notes that might be kept in that
time-honoured hiding place. According to *O.E.D. ruffle* is the spelling of
two quite distinct verbs, one meaning 'to put into disarray', the other 'to
handle roughly' or 'to handle (a woman) with rude familiarity'. It is quite
probable that the present use is a mixing of the two words.

foul smocks] Cf. II.i.313 n.

344. *be in a masque*] The spellings *mask* and *masque* were interchangeable, so although *Qq* print *maske*, there was ample reason for Bullen to
believe that Zoya was thinking of the fashionable entertainment rather
than the covering mentioned in Prologus, 16. Zoya's phrase *to be in* a
[mask/masque] could mean simply 'to wear', though it seems more likely
that it would apply to participating in the entertainment, as we know
members of the nobility did in England. Finally, the mention of expense
(l. 347) argues in favour of *masque*; participation in one would involve
considerable expenditure on lavish costume. The only expense involved
in the face mask was the cost of the silk or satin covering and skin or silk
lining (see Linthicum, p. 272).

348. *eat mine own arms*] i.e. sell my own coat of arms to finance your
participation in the masque. Marston used the expression in *CS.,* I, 98
('Eates vp his armes'), but there it referred to a soldier's expedient of
selling his uniform and weapons to pay for food and women. See Davenport's note, *Poems,* p. 226, where a similar passage is quoted from Jonson's
Every Man in his Humour: 'Hard is the choise when the valiant must eate
their armes, or clem [= starve]' (III.vi.79–80).

Zoya. That you shall not search if my chamber door hinges
    be oiled to avoid creaking.   350

Zuc. As I am a sensible creature—

Zoya. Nor ever suspect the reason why my bedchamber
    floor is double-matted.

Zuc. Not as I have blood in me.

Zoya. You shall vow to wear clean linen, and feed whole-   355
    somely.

Zuc. Ay, and highly. I will take no more tobacco, or come to
    your sheets drunk, or get wenches. I will ever feed on
    fried frogs, broiled snails, and boiled lambstones. I will
    adore thee more than a mortal, observe and serve you   360
    as more than a mistress, do all duties of a husband, all
    offices of a man, all services of thy creature, and ever
    live in thy pleasure, or die in thy service.

Zoya. Then here my quarrel ends: thus cease all strife.

Zuc. Until they lose, men know not what's a wife.   365
    We slight and dully view the lamp of heaven,
    Because we daily see't, which but bereaved
    And held one little week from darkened eyes,
    With greedy wonder we should all admire.

---

355. linen] *Q2;* lining *Q1.*   359. broiled] *Q2;* wild *Q1.*

349. *search if*] check to see whether.

351. *a sensible creature*] a creature with senses, capable of feeling.

355. *clean linen*] Cf. II.i.57 and n.

357. *highly*] i.e. richly (to increase virility).

358. *or get wenches*] or beget only girls (i.e. as a result of smoking and drinking).

359. *fried frogs, broiled snails, and boiled lambstones*] aphrodisiacs, again; cf. II.i.149–52.

360. *observe*] honour, worship, treat with ceremonious respect. Cf. Donne 'The Canonisation', ll. 5–6: 'Take you a course, get you a place, / Observe his honour, or his grace . . .', and *Caes.*, IV.iii.45–6: 'Must I observe you ? must I stand and crouch / Under your testy humour ?'

362. *offices*] functions, duties.

creature] See I.ii.291 n.

363. *in thy pleasure*] with the purpose of satisfying your will.

364. *thus cease all strife*] thus let all our strife cease.

367. *bereaved*] taken away, removed.

369. *admire*] gaze at it with wonder and reverence.

Opinion of command puts out love's fire.   370

Herc. 'An act against mummers, false seemers, that abuse
　　ladies with counterfeit faces, courting only by signs, and
　　seeming wise only by silence.'

Cupid. The penalty:

Herc. To be urged to speak, and then if inward ability   375
　　answer not outward seeming, to be committed instantly
　　to the ship of fools during great Cupid's pleasure. My
　　Lord Granuffo, to the bar. Speak, speak, is not this law
　　just?

Gra. Just, sure; for in good truth or in good sooth,   380
　　When wise men speak, they still must open their mouth.

Herc. The brazen head has spoken.

Don. Thou art arrested.

Gra. Me?

Herc. And judged. Away.   *Exit* GRANUFFO. 385

---

370. Opinion] *Q2;* And provvde hayht *Q1.*   374. penalty:] *This ed.;*
penalty. *Qq;* penalty? *Dilke.*   380–1.] *so Dilke; prose Qq.*

---

370. *Opinion . . . fire*] Lines 366–70 suggested that we have a false,
undervaluing opinion of the sun because we take it for granted. In this
line Zuccone says that the lamp (*fire*) of love, like that of heaven, can also
be put out, precisely by our taking our right to it for granted. Q1's *And
provvde hayht* [height] *of command* stresses the husband's overweening
confidence in his right to the wife's affection simply because of the power
a husband legally has over her (= command). Q2's *Opinion of command,*
more elliptical because of the jargonistic weight carried by *Opinion,* means
much the same except that it stresses the basic falsity of the arrogant
husband's view. *Opinion* in Marston almost always means invalid, foolish
opinion; cf. I.i.59 and n.

371–3.] a parody of the numerous laws against itinerant actors and other
such 'vagabonds', passed throughout the sixteenth century. For Granuffo's
special case, 25 Henry VIII (1533), c.3 is of interest because it singles out
'standing mute' as an offence, and 3 Henry VIII (1511), c.9 mentions
both 'mummers' and the use of 'visors' (i.e. *counterfeit faces*). It seems to
be straining things to include Granuffo in a court of Cupid, since we have
seen him only in conjunction with Gonzago, but we are probably to
assume that when he 'keeps his lust privately' (III.i.299) he proceeds in a
manner similar to what he uses in the Court of Urbin. A statute in *Prince
d'Amour* (p. 61) suggests that silent courting is pursued by men who trust
to money rather than wit to win women's favours.

382. *The brazen head has spoken*] another allusion to the story of Friar
Bacon and the brazen head; cf. I.ii. 122–5 n.

Gon. Thus silence and grave looks, with hums and haws,
Makes many worshipped, when if tried th' are daws.
That's the morality or *l'envoy* of it, *l'envoy* of it. On.

Herc. 'An act against privy conspiracies, by which if any
with ambitious wisdom shall hope and strive to outstrip   390
Love, to cross his words, and make frustrate his sweet
pleasures, if such a presumptuous wisdom fall to nothing, and die in laughter, the wizard so transgressing is
ipso facto adjudged to offend in most deep treason, to
forfeit all his wit at the will of the lord, and be instantly   395
committed to the ship of fools for ever.'

Gon. Ay, marry, sir. O, might Oedipus riddle me out such a
fellow! Of all creatures breathing, I do hate those

386. and grave] *Q2;* can enuie *Q1.*   387. th' are (the'are)] *Q2;* were *Q1.*
388. morality] *Q2;* mortality *Q1.*

---

386. *silence and grave looks*] Cf. *Ashby Entertainment,* 339–44:

> From Ladies yᵗ are rudly coy,
> barring theire loues from modest joy,
> from ignorant scilence & proude Lookes;
> from those that aunswer out of bookes,
> from those who hate oʳ chast delight,
> I bless the fortune of each starry Knight . . .

387. *daws*] = jackdaws, proverbially stupid.

388. *l'envoy*] 'a term borrowed from the old French poetry: it appeared
always at the head of a few concluding verses to each piece, which either
served to convey the moral, or to address the poem to some particular
person' (Dilke).

389. '*An act against privy conspiracies . . .*'] There are similarities here
to 3 Henry VII (1486), c.14, 14 Eliz. (1570), c.2 and especially 3 James
(1605), c.5, where the secrecy of the conspiracy is emphasised (privy =
secret). But the resemblances are only general, and the 1605 statute is
probably too late for our play.

390. *ambitious wisdom*] (unwarranted) pretentions to wisdom. The
connotations of *ambitious* were almost always bad ones in the plays of
Shakespeare and his contemporaries; this is especially so in Shakespeare's
history plays and, of course, III.ii. in *Caes.* (ll. 28, 83, 91, 95, and 118).
Cf. also *Fawn,* I.ii.10, and IV.i.26.

391. *cross his words*] thwart his commandments.

393. *wizard*] sage (often used contemptuously).

397–8. *might Oedipus riddle me out such a fellow*] probably means no
more than 'might Oedipus find me such a fellow'. The allusion is to
Oedipus's solving the riddle of the Sphinx.

things that struggle to seem wise, and yet are indeed
fools. I remember when I was a young man in my   400
father's days, there were four gallant spirits for resolution, as proper for body, as witty in discourse as any
were in Europe, nay Europe had not such; I was one of
them; we four did all love one lady, a modest, chaste
virgin she was; we all enjoyed her, I well remember,   405
and so enjoyed her, that despite the strictest guard was
set upon her, we had her at our pleasure—I speak it for
her honour and my credit. Where shall you find such
witty fellows nowadays? Alas, how easy it is in these
weaker times to cross love-tricks—ha, ha, ha! Alas,   410
alas, I smile to think—I must confess with some glory
to mine own wisdom—to think how I found out, and
crossed, and curbed, and jerked, and firked, and in the
end made desperate Tiberio's hope. Alas, good silly
youth, that dares to cope with age and such a beard—I   415
speak it without glory.

Herc. But what yet might your well-known wisdom think
    If such a one, as being most severe,
    A most protested opposite to the match
    Of two young lovers, who having barred them speech,   420
    All interviews, all messages, all means
    To plot their wished ends, even he himself

    401–2. *four gallant spirits for resolution*] four gallant lads of resolute
spirit. 'Read, "four *as* gallant spirits for resolution, as," etc., omitting the
comma after "spirits"' (Deighton, p. 11). The emendation is probably
unnecessary. For an interesting parallel (and, perhaps, source) cf. *2H4*,
III.ii.21–7.
    411. *glory*] honour, praise. The word had several senses bordering on
'boast, boasting', but it does not quite mean that here. It does a few lines
later, though.
    413. *jerked, and firked*] the two words were virtually synonymous, used
figuratively for 'beat, whip, drub', and often paired as here.
    416. *glory*] boasting.
    418. *as*] (used as an expletive here only).
    419. *most protested opposite*] strongly declared opponent. For *protested*,
see Cross, *N&Q*, CCVI (1961), 390–1. (*O.E.D.*'s first example is from *DC.*,
but Marston already used it in *AR.*)

Was by their cunning made the go-between,
The only messenger, the token-carrier,
Told them the times when they might fitly meet,   425
Nay, showed the way to one another's bed?

Gon. May one have the sight of such a fellow for nothing?
Doth there breathe such an egregious ass?
Is there such a foolish animal in *rerum natura*?
How is it possible such a simplicity can exist? Let us   430
not lose our laughing at him, for God's sake! Let
Folly's sceptre light upon him, and to the ship of fools
with him instantly.

Don. Of all these follies I arrest your grace.

Gon. Me? Ha, me? Me, varlet? Me, fool? Ha! To th' jail   435
with him! What, varlet, call me ass, me?

Herc. What, grave Urbin's duke?
Dares Folly's sceptre touch his prudent shoulders?
Is he a coxcomb? No, my lord is wise,
For we all know that Urbin's duke has eyes.   440

Gon. God a-mercy, Fawn, hold fast, varlet, hold thee, good
Fawn, railing reprobate!

Herc. Indeed, I must confess your grace did tell
And first did intimate your daughter's love
To otherwise most cold Tiberio;   445
After conveyed her private favour to him,
A curious scarf, wherein her needle wrought
Her private love to him.

Gon.   What, I do this? Ha!

437–40.] *so AHB; prose Qq.*   441. fast] *Q1; not in Q2.*   448. love]
Q2; fauour *Q1.*

---

429. *foolish animal*] Cf. III.i.382 and n.

rerum natura] i.e., the universe.

430. *simplicity*] ignorance. Gonzago may mean 'simpleton', however;
O.E.D.'s first example for that sense is dated 1633.

440.] an ironic echo of II.i.557.

442. *railing reprobate*] The phrase *could* mean 'haranguing villain'; but
Gonzago has already caught a glimpse of the truth and is trying to soften
Faunus ('good Fawn'), calling him 'joking scamp"

447. *curious*] carefully, beautifully made.

Herc. And last, by her persuasion, showed the youth
    The very way and best-elected time   450
    To come unto her chamber.
Gon.   Thus did I, sir?
Herc. Thus did you, sir; but I must confess
    You meant not to do this, but were rankly gulled,
    Made a plain natural. This sure, sir, you did.
    And in assurance, Prince Tiberio,   455
    Renownèd, witted Dulcimel, appear!
    The acts of constant honour cannot fear.

                         HERCULES *Exit.*

TIBERIO *and* DULCIMEL *above are discovered, hand in hand.*

Dul. Royally wise, and wisely royal father—
Don. That's sententious now, a figure called in art *Ironia.*
Dul. I humbly thank your worthy piety,   460
    That through your only means I have obtained
    So fit, loving, and desired a husband.
Gon. Death o' discretion! If I should prove a fool now, am

456. Renownèd] *TC;* Renowmed *Qq.*   459. a figure called in] *Q2; not in*
Q1.   460–2.] *so AHB; prose Qq.*   462. loving] *Qq;* [so] loving *AHB.*
463. now,] *London;* now *Qq;* now! *Dilke;* now. *JOH.*

---

450. *best-elected*] best chosen, most appropriate.
453. *rankly gulled*] completely fooled. For *rank* as an adverb, see Cross,
N&Q, CCVIII (1963), 308.
454. *plain natural*] perfect simpleton.
457. *The acts . . . fear*] i.e. those whose actions are done in the spirit of
constancy and honour can have nothing to fear. Hercules is addressing
these words to the young couple, whom he has invited to appear before
the 'most protested opposite to [their] match'.
459. Ironia] Puttenham writes (p. 189): 'Ye doe likewise dissemble,
when ye speake in derision or mockerie, & that may be many waies: as
sometime in sport, sometime in earnest; and priuily, and apertly, and
pleasantly, and bitterly: but first by the figure Ironia, which we call the
drye mock: as he that said to a bragging Ruffian, that threatened he would
skill and slay, no doubt you are a good man of your hands: . . .' Cf. also
IV.i.669 n.
460. *your worthy piety*] (used as a nonce address of respect, like Your
Grace). Gonzago had made a point of lecturing Tiberio on the 'piety of a
man', III.i.399; cf. III.i.475.
463. *discretion*] i.e. wisdom; another not altogether irrelevant exclamation.

not I an ass, think you, ha? I will have them both
bound together, and sent to the Duke of Ferrara   465
presently.

Tib. I am sure, good father, we are both bound together as
fast as the priest can make us already. I thank you for it,
kind father, I thank you only for 't.

HERCULES *enters in his own shape.*

Herc. And as for sending them to the Duke of Ferrara, see,   470
my good lord, Ferrara's o'erjoyed prince meets them in
fullest wish.

Gon. By the Lord, I am ashamed of myself, that's the plain
troth. But I know now wherefore this parliament was.
What a slumber have I been in!   475

Herc. Never grieve or wonder: all things sweetly fit.

Gon. There is no folly to protested wit.

Herc. What still in wond'ring ignorance doth rest,
In private conference your dear-loved breast
Shall fully take. But now we change our face: 480

469.1.] *so JOH* (*ad. Dilke*); *in left margin opposite ll. 478–80 Q1; in left
margin opposite ll. 471–5 Q2.*   474. parliament] *Q2; not in Q1.*   476.
fit] *Q2;* still *Q1.*   477. wit] *Q2;* will *Q1.*

---

466. *presently*] immediately.

469.1. *in his own shape*] i.e., as Hercules, Duke of Ferrara, rather than
Faunus.

471–2. *in fullest wish*] in fulfilment of your wish; perhaps also, wholeheartedly.

474. *troth*] truth.

477.] There is no folly to compare with (self-) proclaimed wisdom.
Cf. *DC.*, I.ii.160–1: Of all the fools that would all man out-thrust, / He
that 'gainst Nature would seem wise is worst.'

480. *But now we change our face*] Hercules has already changed his face
from parasitaster to duke (469.1). It is doubtful that he becomes Faunus
again for the epilogue. Rather, the phrase simply indicates that the actor is
about to address the audience directly, as the author's spokesman.

Epilogus

And thus in bold yet modest phrase we end.
He whose Thalia with swiftest hand hath penned
This lighter subject, and hath boldly torn
Fresh bays from Daphne's arm, doth only scorn
Malicious censures of some envious few,   485
Who think they lose if others have their due.
But let such adders hiss; know, all the sting,
All the vain foam of all those snakes that ring
Minerva's glassful shield, can never taint,
Poison, or pierce; firm art disdains to faint.   490
But yet of you that with impartial faces,
With no preparèd malice, but with graces
Of sober knowledge have surveyed the frame

488. ring] *TC;* ringes *Qq.*

---

482. *Thalia*] muse of comedy and idyllic poetry; used here and in the epilogue of *Malc.*, 14, in the sense 'talent as comic dramatist'. *O.E.D.*'s first example is dated 1656.

483–4. *torn | Fresh bays from Daphne's arm*] i.e. has made this new effort for poetic laurels. The allusion is to the nymph who was pursued by Apollo and turned into a tree, the laurel.

485. *censures*] judgements, opinions (*O.E.D.* 3); cf. III.i.39 and Prologus, 26. But Marston's use here is very close to *O.E.D.* 4, unfavourable opinion, hostile criticism.

487. *adders*] Cf. the first Prologue to Jonson's *Poetaster* (1601), in the guise of Envy, who invites the audience to 'take my snakes among you' (44). As Dilke says of Marston's passage, 'This is another allusion to some of his contemporaries: but it is not just perhaps to fix these things at random.'

488. *foam*] i.e. of venom.

489. *Minerva's glassful shield*] the aegis, in whose mirror surface Perseus was able to see Medusa when he killed her. Minerva (Athena) afterward attached the snake-covered head to the shield.

Of his slight scene, if you shall judge his flame
Distemperately weak, as faulty much   495
In style, in plot, in spirit, lo, if such,
He deigns, in self-accusing phrase, to crave
For praise but pardon, which he hopes to have;
 Since he protests he ever hath aspired
 To be belovèd, rather than admired.   500

498. For] *Qq;* Not *AHB.* 500. admired.] admirde. / FINIS. *Qq.*

---

494. *flame*] brightness of fancy, power of thought (*O.E.D.*, 6†c). Cross points out that this antedates *O.E.D.*'s first example (1642). *N&Q*, CCII (1957), 66.

495. *Distemperately weak*] i.e. if the readers judge that the 'flame' informing the play is a weak one because it proceeds from a badly balanced temperament (a bad balance of the humours).

498. *For praise but pardon*] Bullen's emendation, which is followed by London and Smith, is surely unnecessary. But = only, merely.

499–500.] a return to the sentiment with which he opened the address 'To My Equal Reader', 1–3.

Index to Annotations

The following is a list of words whose sense or usage antedates the earliest example in the *Oxford English Dictionary*.